A Beginner's Year of Watercolor

LOU RIPOLL

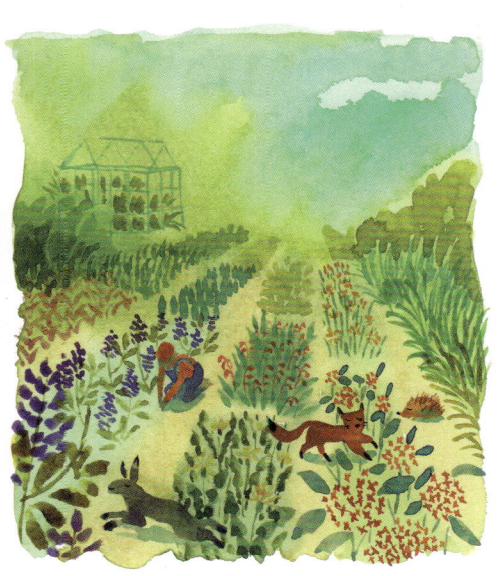
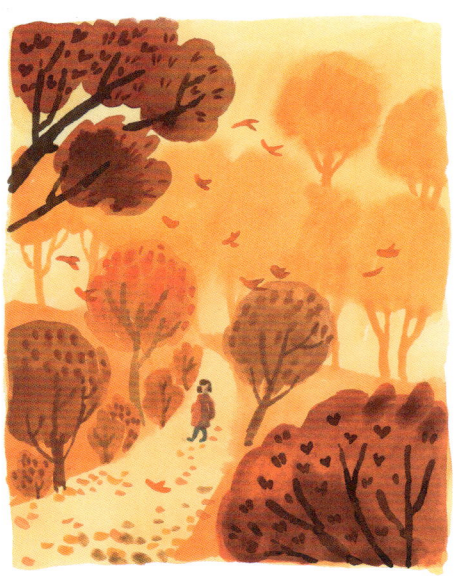
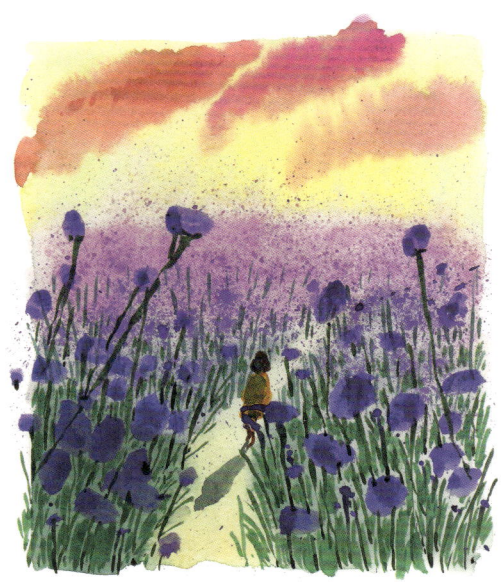

DOVER PUBLICATIONS
Garden City, New York

This Dover edition, first published in 2025, is a new English translation of
Une année d'aquarelle by Lou Ripoll, published by Mango, Paris, France, in 2022.
The original French work has been translated into English by Janet Ross Snyder.

Library of Congress Cataloging-in-Publication Data

Names: Ripoll, Lou author | Ripoll, Lou. Année d'aquarelle par Bleu tango
Title: A beginner's year of watercolor / Lou Ripoll.
Other titles: Année d'aquarelle par Bleu tango. English
Description: Garden City, New York : Dover Publications, 2025. | Summary:
    "Every week, beginners will learn new watercolor techniques with easy-to-
    follow, step-by-step exercises while creating beautiful art inspired by different
    landscapes, environments, animals, people, and plants"—Provided by publisher.
Identifiers: LCCN 2025016236 | ISBN 9780486854892 trade paperback
Subjects: LCSH: Watercolor painting—Technique
Classification: LCC ND2420 .R5713 2025 | DDC 751.42/2—dc23/eng/20250625
LC record available at https://lccn.loc.gov/2025016236

Printed in India
85489201   2025
www.doverpublications.com

I dedicate this book to my father, who taught me how to look at the world, and to my mother, who taught me how to draw it.

And also, some thoughts for my aunt Anne when she paints my year of watercolor between two bursts of laughter, as only she knows how to do.

Contents

Before Starting ... 6

Week 1
Dark Strokes on Light Strokes ... 8

Week 2
Overlapping Pale Strokes ... 10

Week 3
Strokes of Color on Wet Paper ... 12

Week 4
Wash on Wet Paper ... 16

Week 5
Quick Wash on Dry Paper ... 18

Week 6
Painting on Wet Paper ... 22

Week 7
Strokes on Wet Watercolor ... 24

Week 8
Making Heavily Loaded Pigment
Bloom in Wet Watercolor ... 28

Week 9
Blooms of Pigments Between
Two Wet Strokes ... 30

Week 10
Pushing Back the Wet Pigments
by Adding Pure Water ... 34

Week 11
Pushing Back the Wet Pigments
with Wet Pigments ... 36

Week 12
Creating Gradations by Wetting
the Paper ... 40

Week 13
Gradation by Colored Wet Strokes ... 42

Week 14
Gradation on Dry Paper, Part 1 ... 46

Week 15
Gradation on Dry Paper, Part 2 ... 48

Week 16
Creating Depth with Blurriness
and Sharpness ... 52

Week 17
Creating Depth with Contrasting
Harmonies ... 54

Week 18
Creating a Luminous Atmosphere
on Wet Paper, Part 1 ... 58

Week 19
Creating a Luminous Atmosphere
on Wet Paper, Part 2 ... 60

Week 20
Defining Depth by Light and Dark ... 64

Week 21
Atmospheric Perspective ... 66

Week 22
Shadows with Blue ... 70

Week 23
Splashes of Light and Shadow ... 72

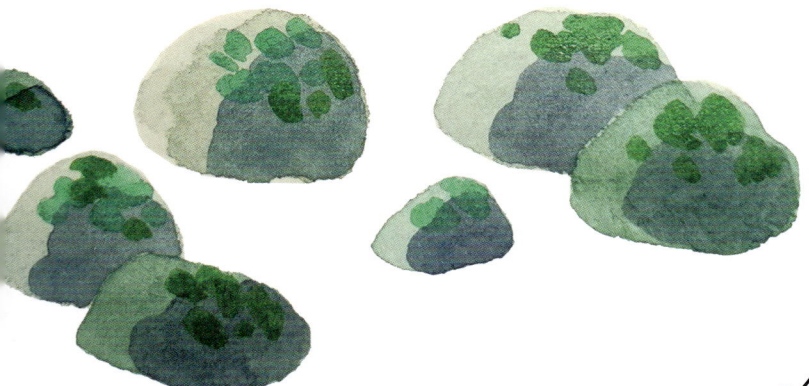

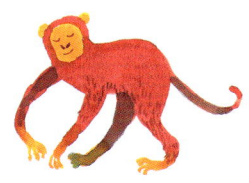

Week 24
Where Is the Light Coming From?   76

Week 25
Shaping the Volumes with Blue   78

Week 26
Lightening a Color   82

Week 27
Warm and Cool Colors   84

Week 28
Camaïeux: Painting with Monochromes or
  Adjacent Colors   88

Week 29
Complementary Colors   90

Week 30
Desaturating a Color with Its
  Complement   94

Week 31
Shading a Volume with Its Complement   96

Week 32
The Colorful Grays   100

Week 33
The Colorful Blacks   102

Week 34
Shaping the Line with the Brush   106

Week 35
Drawing Animals by Shaping the Line   108

Week 36
The Expressivity of Movement   112

Week 37
The Virtues of the Flat Brush   114

Week 38
Using a Dry Brush   118

Week 39
Spattering and Splashes   120

Week 40
Painting with Salt   124

Week 41
Liquid Gum Resist   126

Week 42
Interpreting the Textures   130

Week 43
Animating with Patterns   132

Week 44
Masses and Textures   136

Week 45
Foliage, Trees, and Forests   138

Week 46
Painting a Crowd   142

Week 47
People and Their Ways of Moving   144

Week 48
A Little Anatomy   148

Week 49
The Lines of Force   150

Week 50
Playing with Scale   152

Week 51
Occupy the Space   156

Week 52
It's Your Turn to Play!   158

Before Starting

The Minimum Colors to Get Started

Everyone has their own color preferences. If you are a complete beginner and you need to buy your first pans or tubes of paint, here is my advice for a "minimal palette."

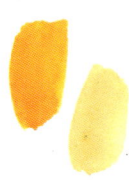

Yellows: a golden or primary yellow, a lemon yellow, a Naples yellow (practical, because it's impossible to obtain by mixing).

Reds: a red that tends toward orange, a tomato red, very vermilion, a pink that leans toward magenta, a madder pink. And why not a violet?

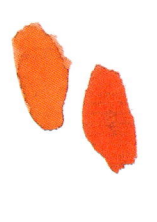
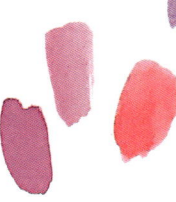

Blues: A Prussian blue, nice and dark, a cobalt blue (or ultramarine), a clear and luminous cyan blue.

Greens: a sap green, a yellow green (anise, for example), an apple green, and a pale or dark emerald green.

Browns: a nice, dark burnt earth (to be able to mix it with Prussian blue to get a pretty, colorful black), a burnt sienna that borders on red, an ocher.

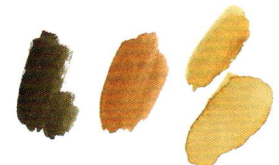

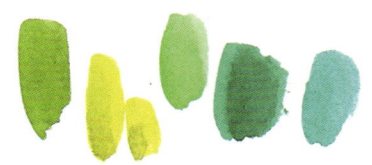

Possibly a white gouache, which makes it possible to give the colors a milky tone. This effect is different from colors diluted with water.

It is better to set up your watercolor box yourself, rather than buy one that's already made, because the ready-made sets are filled with soft colors—for example, too many browns—rather than vibrant colors. It is possible to tone down a bright color, but you can never brighten a dull color.

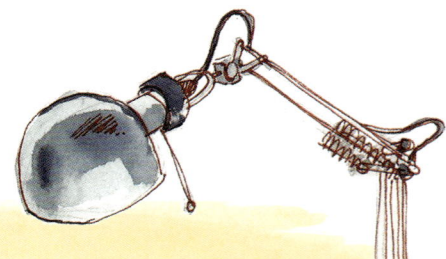

Tip

What is a good way to set up an area for painting with watercolor? Set up in the daylight! Not with your back to the window, though. And when the sky is too gray or night has fallen? A lamp with a daylight light bulb (cool white) is perfect.

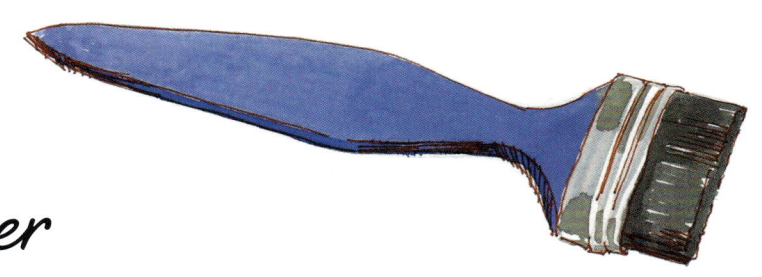

Brushes and Paper

The quality of your paper makes a big difference! There are different types of paper, and the effects they produce vary tremendously.

Textured, rough, or rag papers (very rough): They present a rough surface and give character to watercolor washes.

Satiny pressed papers: They are smooth and can withstand a lot of water without crinkling. They are very pleasant to use. The brush glides, the paper absorbs the water, and the color pops.

Laid papers, with fine lines: Like their textured cousins, they give character to the washes, but they are not my favorite papers.

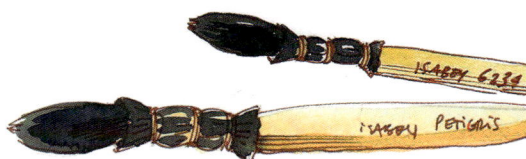

The best brands of paper are Fabriano, Arches, and Dalbe. My brushes are made of natural material. Marten-hair brushes are my preference but also the most expensive. Effective and soft, their bristles retain a lot of water and color. They allow one to be generous with the application.

Take care of your brushes; they are precious. Rinse them well after each use, store them in their protective tube, and do not let them soak in a glass of water; they could lose their shape.

Tip

Watercolor paper is very expensive, especially in a block of ten sheets. To save money, buy a very large sheet (19 x 25 inches or larger) of a good brand and cut it yourself. This is much less expensive than a block of twelve or sixteen letter-sized sheets.

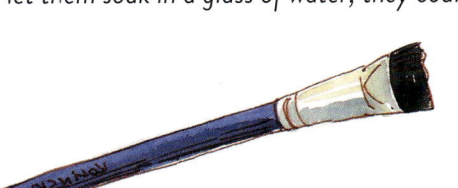

The Essentials

The pans: I like the watercolor pans that contain dry color. When a pan is too soft, you get too much color at a time. I prefer to rub it to obtain pigments.

The palette: Any paper will do, except paper that peels and leaves crumbs of paper on the brush.

The rag: Any scrap of salvaged cloth will do. Grab your rags!

The water jar: Any container will do. Certain watercolor pigments are toxic; clean the jar well after use. When I start, I put out five or six jars of clean water so that I'm not constantly changing the water. I use one for dark colors, another for pale colors, one for yellow, another for blues and greens, etc.

Week 1
Dark Strokes on Light Strokes

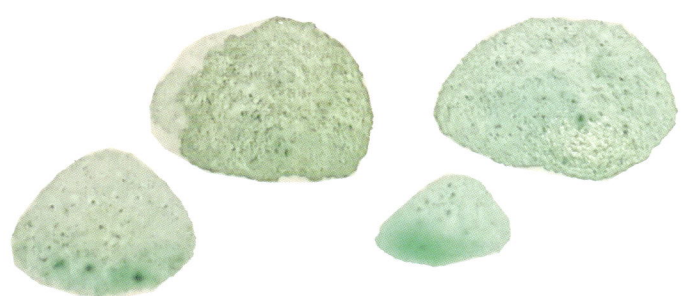

We are going to start slowly . . . with rocks! With the brush, apply strokes of verdigris paint mix to the paper to create these little rocks.

A paint mix is a color that is more or less diluted. Always prepare the colored paint mix in a little well in your watercolor box, in a large enough quantity so that you don't have to remix the color.

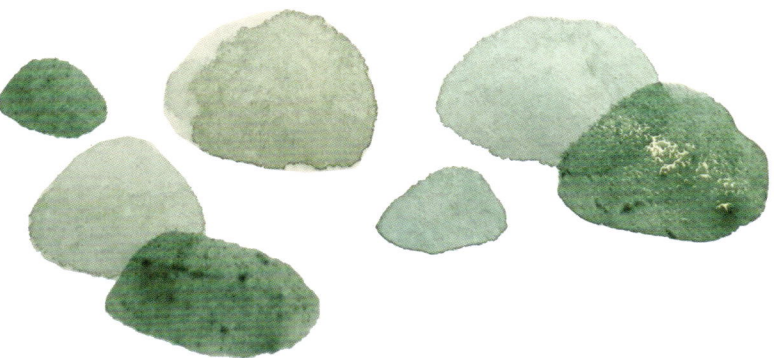

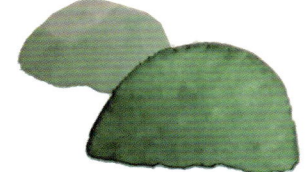

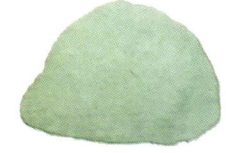

When some rocks are dry, draw darker strokes on top of them, overlapping the colors.

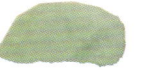

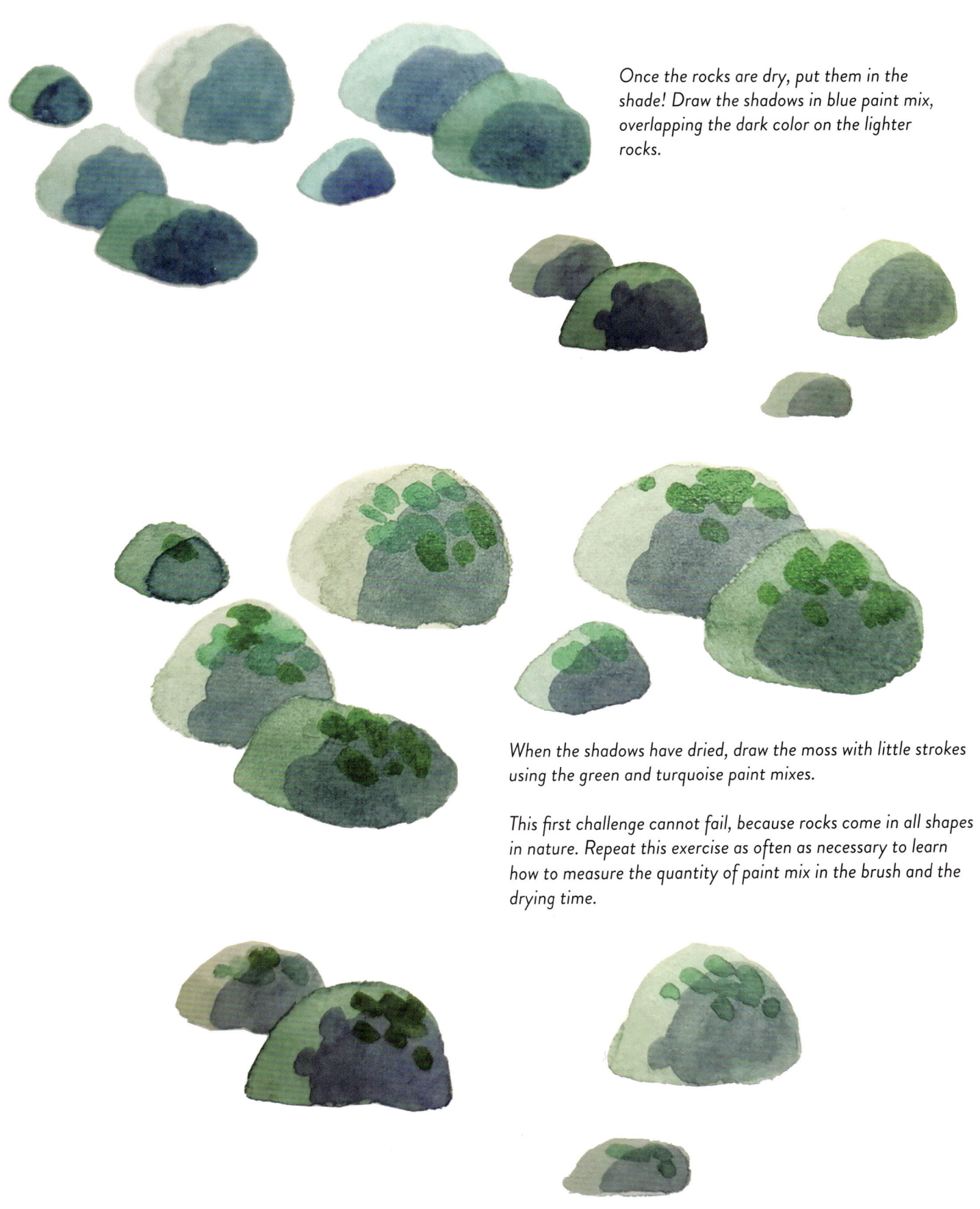

Once the rocks are dry, put them in the shade! Draw the shadows in blue paint mix, overlapping the dark color on the lighter rocks.

When the shadows have dried, draw the moss with little strokes using the green and turquoise paint mixes.

This first challenge cannot fail, because rocks come in all shapes in nature. Repeat this exercise as often as necessary to learn how to measure the quantity of paint mix in the brush and the drying time.

Week 2
Overlapping Pale Strokes

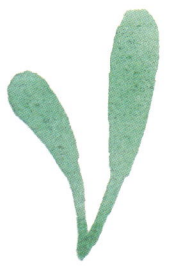

Draw aquatic plants—the ones that grow at the edges of ponds. Prepare sufficient quantities of colored paint mixes—green, turquoise, celadon blue green, and blue—in the little wells in your watercolor box.

Paint plants in different shades. Draw the stem with the point of a brush. Without raising your hand, press on the brush to widen its shape. Then let it dry. Don't worry about the exactness of the forms. A stroke of color on paper is bound to be lovely!

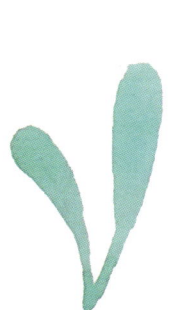
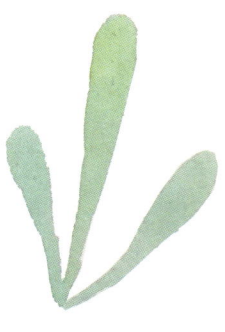

Overlap other plants by varying the shapes and the shades. Wait for the watercolor to dry between the layers.

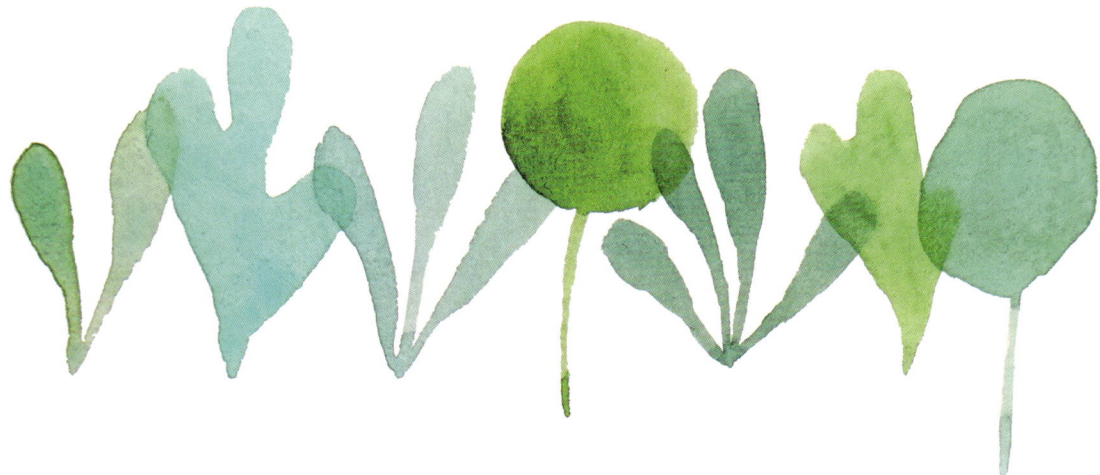

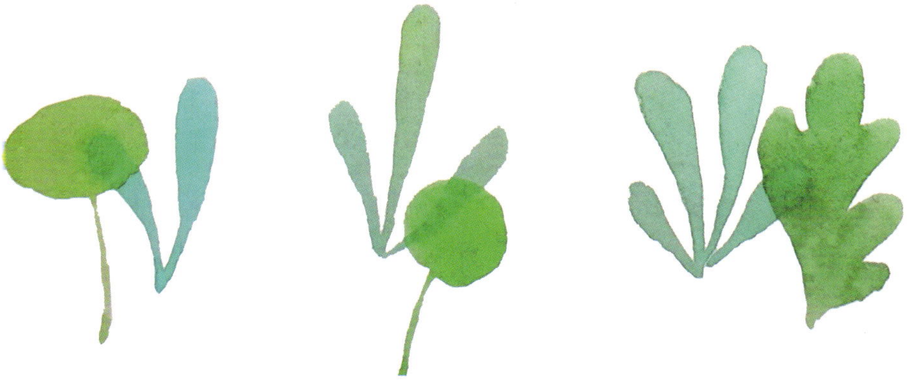

*Play around with the shades of the colors!
The variations are infinite.*

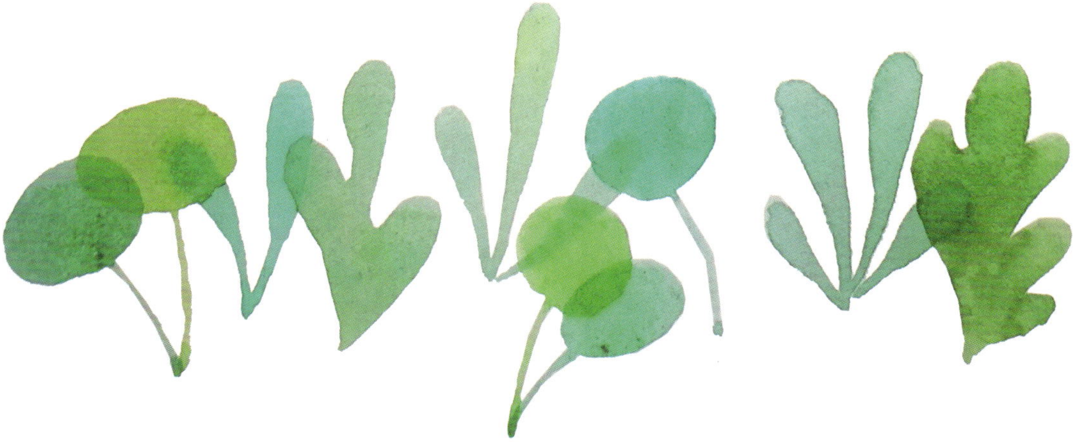

*For the reflections of the water, use the same method. Overlap some strokes of color,
always starting with the lightest colors.*

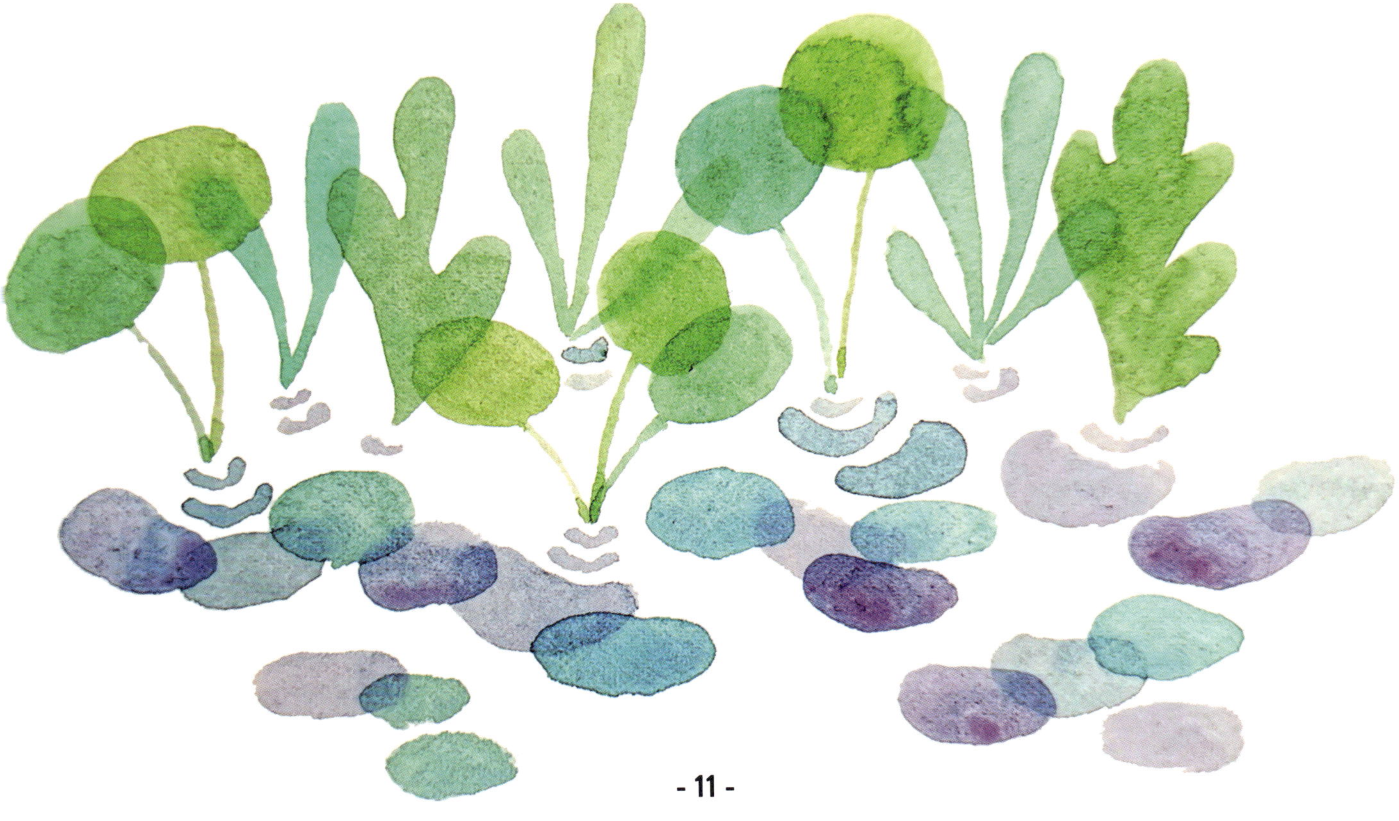

Week 3

Strokes of Color on Wet Paper

Let's tackle the great question of watercolor: the water!
Watercolor painting means playing with wetness.

Draw some plants and rocks, playing with the overlaps
learned in the past two weeks.

Paint the shadows of the rocks in blue.
Place a little moss at the top of each one.

Once everything is dry, carefully rinse your
brush. Dampen the paper with pure water, only
where you will draw the reflections;
avoid the plants and rocks.

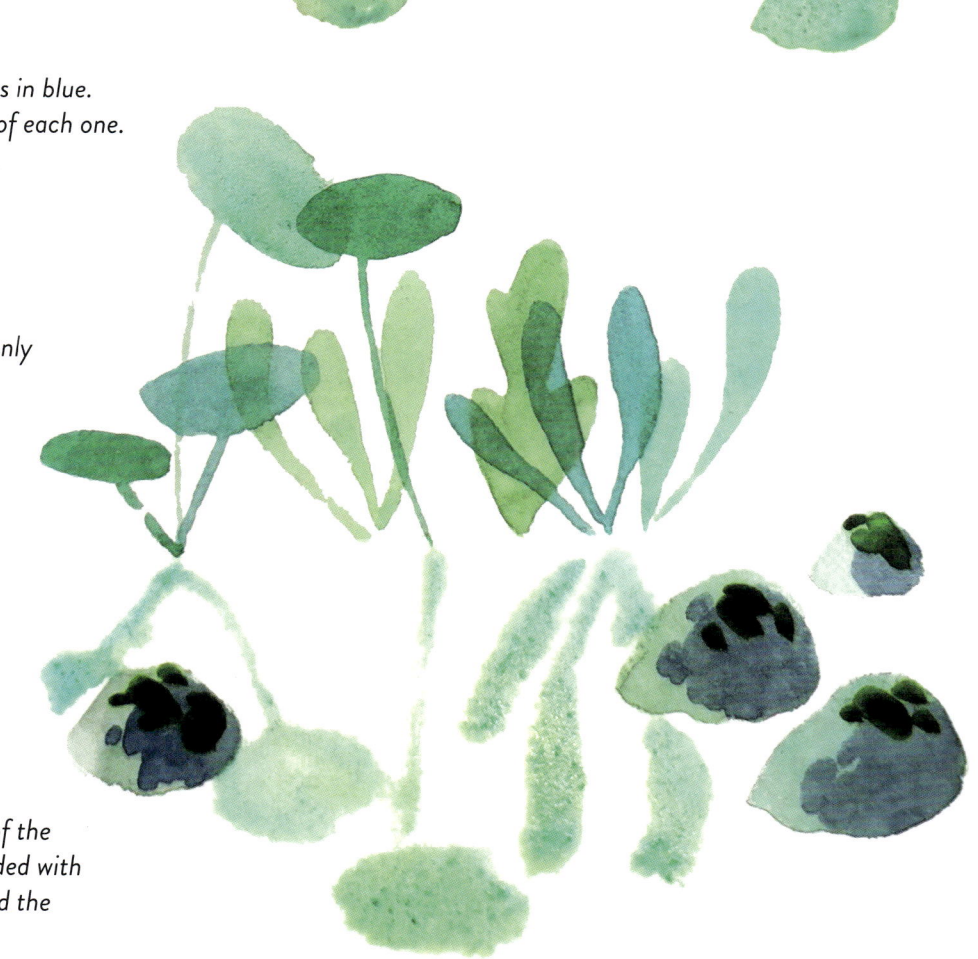

Without waiting, draw the reflections of the
plants in the wet zone with a brush loaded with
colored paint mix. Everything blurs, and the
pigments diffuse in this wet zone.

For the reflections of the rocks, wait for the paper to be just moist—it has almost returned to a matte finish—so that these reflections are sharper than those of the plants.

This exercise is more difficult. You will start over several times before finding the right touch, the right amount of water, and the right timing to paint on wet paper. Each trial will be different. That's one of the charms of watercolor: It's impossible to get the same result twice!

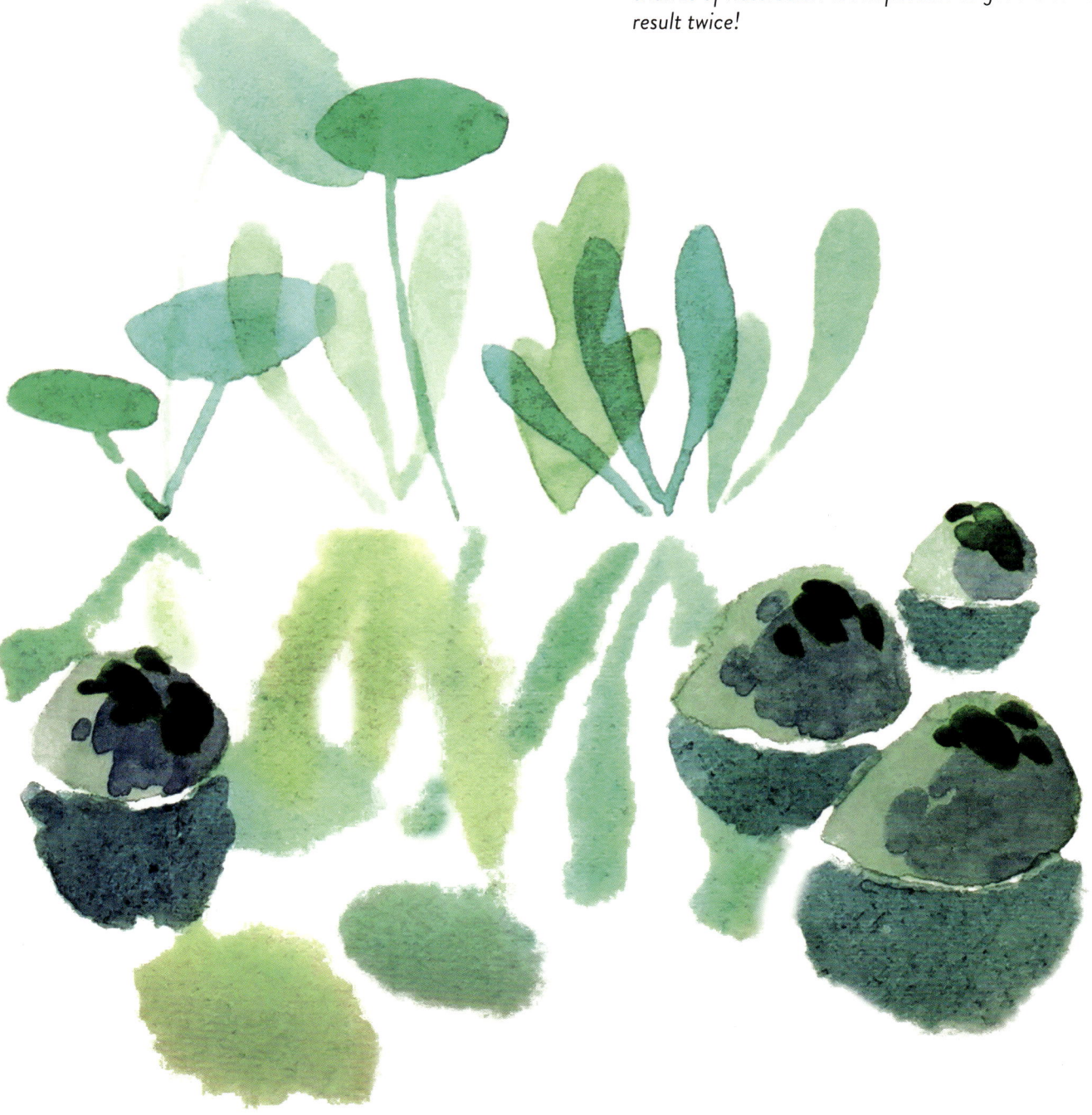

For More Practice

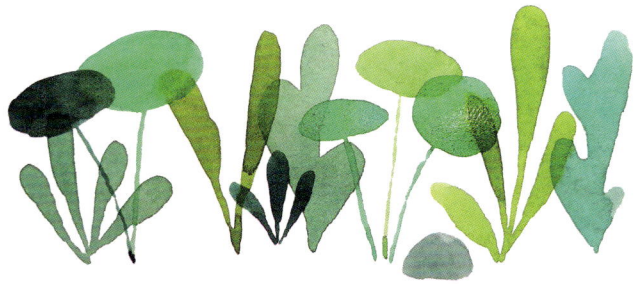

What do you think about this little pond, which has plants and mossy rocks on the edge?

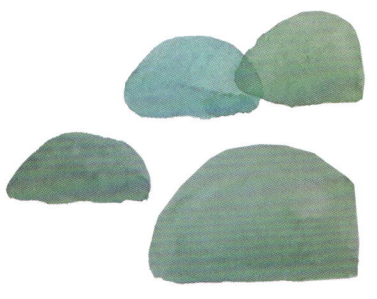

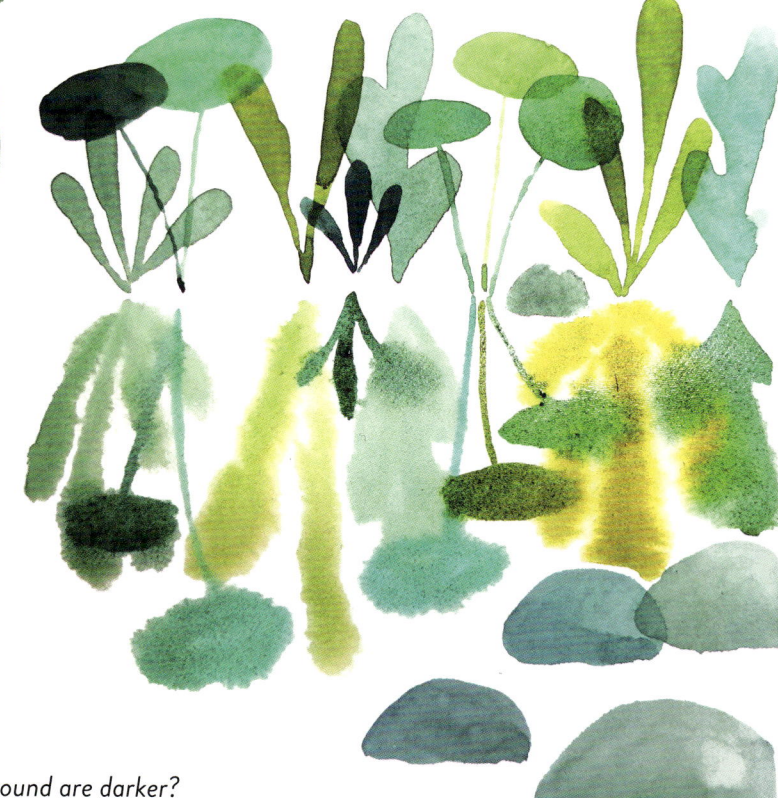

For the reflections of the plants, place the color on paper when it's quite wet. For the reflections of the rocks, wait until the paper is almost dry.

Have you noticed that the rocks in the foreground are darker? That way, they seem closer and give depth to your composition.

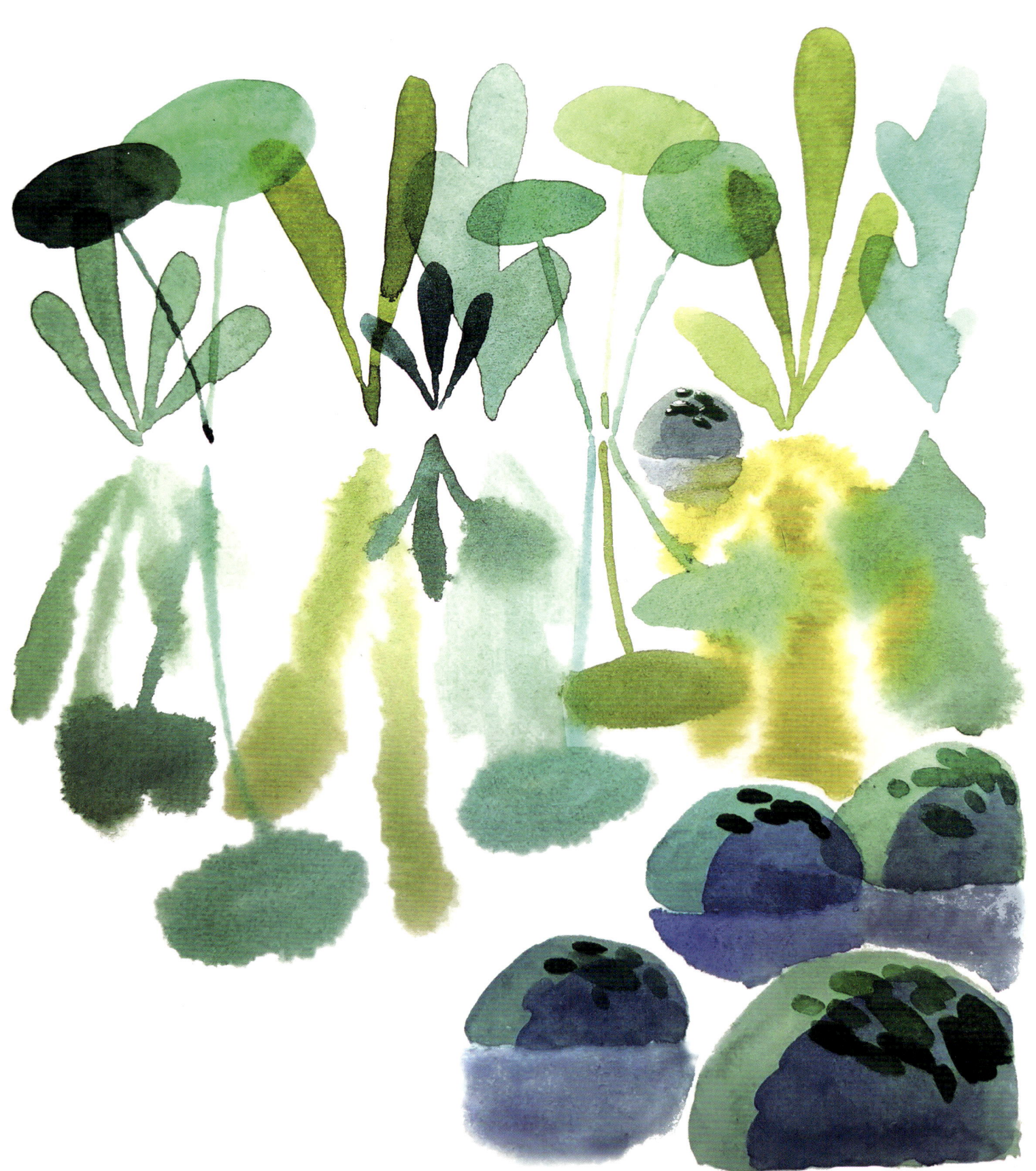

Week 4
Wash on Wet Paper

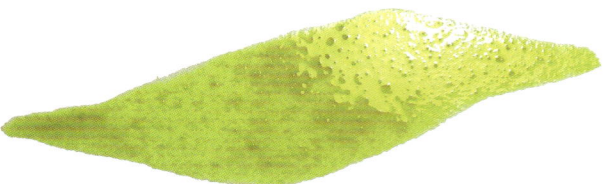

Paint the desired shape with a clear, well-diluted paint mix, in a wash. Then prepare a sufficient quantity of colored paint mix in a little well in your watercolor box.

With a brush, apply this colored paint mix on the wet surface of the wash. Magically, the pigments are distributed uniformly! The final color will be lighter than the paint mix, because it will have been diluted by the clear starting wash.

Continue with a second field in a wash, leaving a white space between the two washes. This separation keeps the colors from mixing.

Continue the washes, making the fields smaller and more fragmented. The farther away they are, the smaller they are.

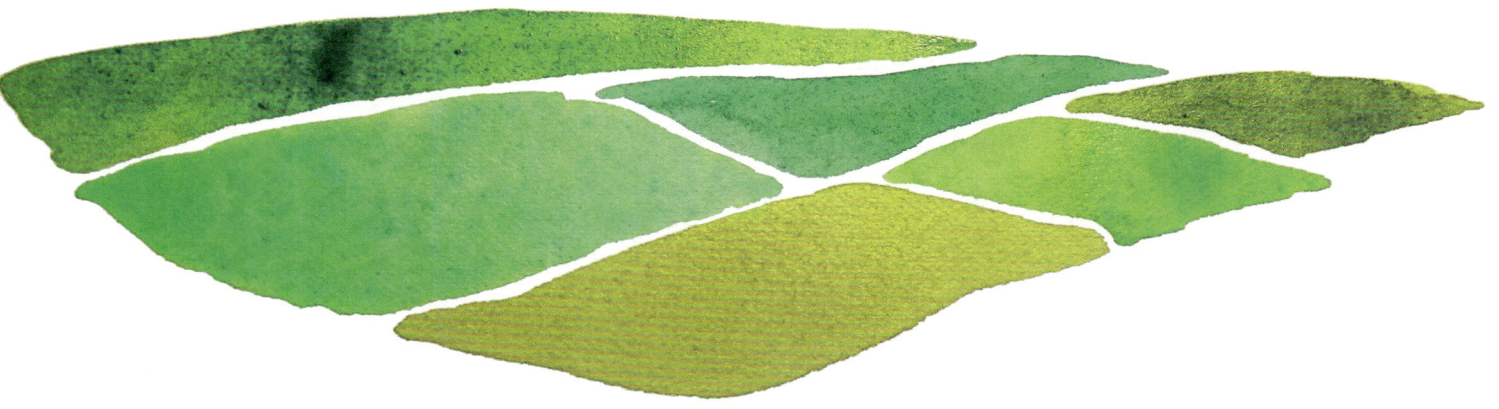

Once the fields are dry, add some trees. Draw silhouettes of trees in greens or dark browns, barely sketched. There it is! A green countryside is laid out before your eyes.

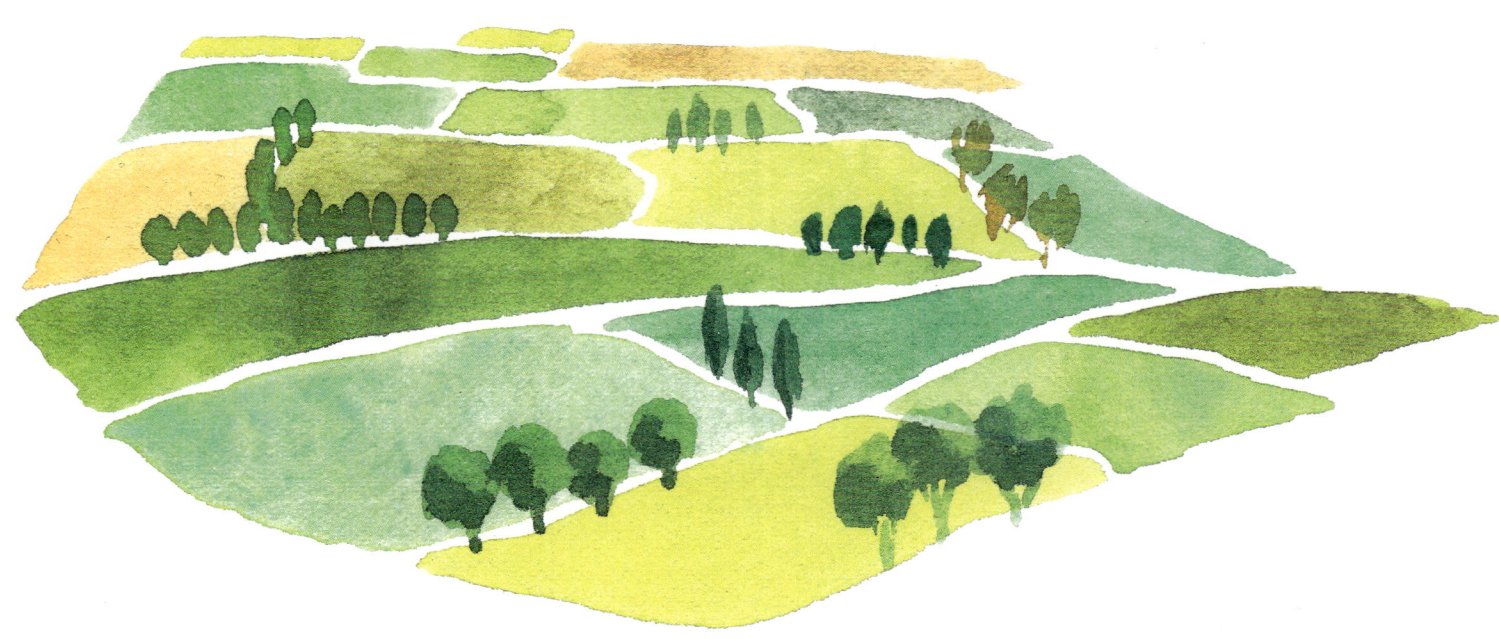

Repeat the exercise by multiplying the fields endlessly. Cover your paper with meadows by varying the colors: a little brown, all the shades of green and yellow . . . you're the one planting these fields in watercolor!

Week 5

Quick Wash on Dry Paper

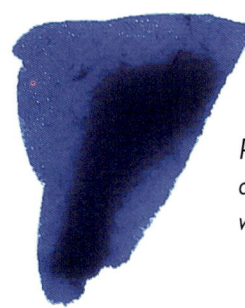

Prepare a large enough quantity of a paint puddle in a little well in your watercolor box.

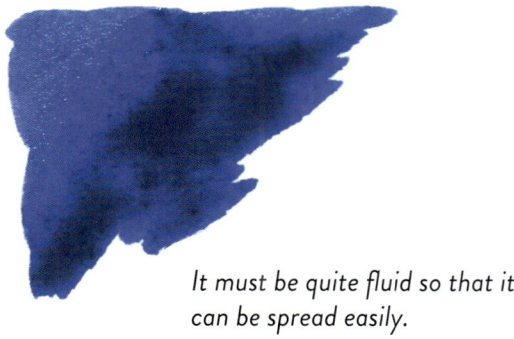

It must be quite fluid so that it can be spread easily.

Spread this paint on the paper rapidly. No zone should dry until you have filled the entire surface.

By being quick, you can avoid blotches and tide lines that can form when the watercolor dries too fast. This requires a little practice!

This technique is very useful:
Practice as many times as necessary to master the quickness of the movement. Covering the paper is a race against the clock before the watercolor dries.

This technique is very useful for drawing a cloudy sky. Trace the outline of the clouds with a light paint mix. Then spread the paint quickly.

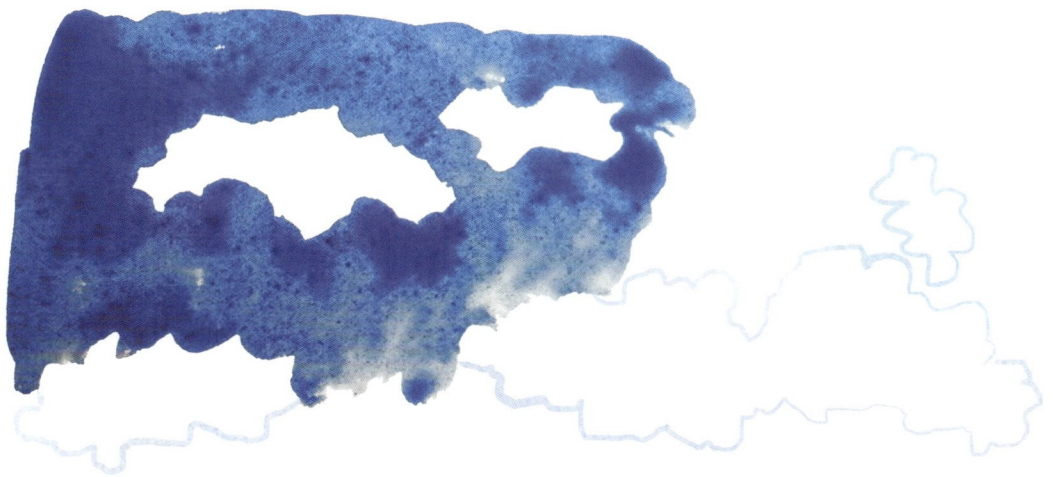

A wash of watercolor is never uniform, unlike a stroke of colored ink. That is not a problem. That's what makes it pretty!

For More Practice

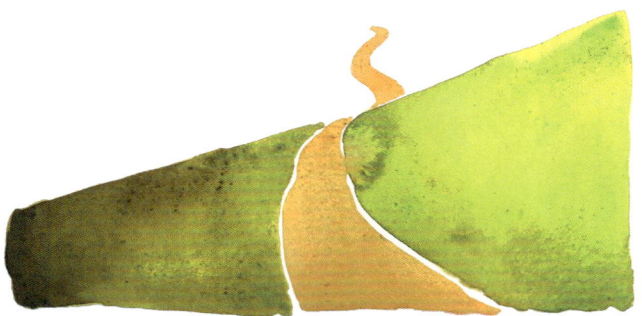

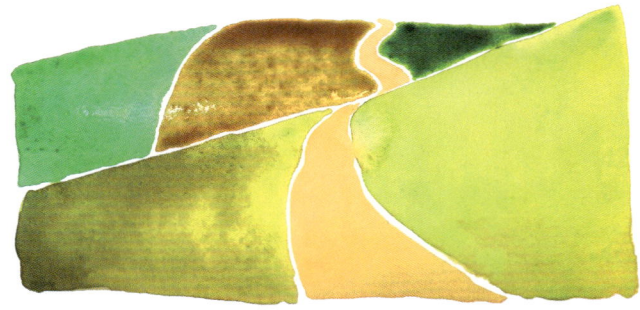

What a land of plenty! Fields as far as the eye can see, and a sky so blue that you're happy to have a few clouds to draw. And a road that's perfect for walking along with your sweetheart.

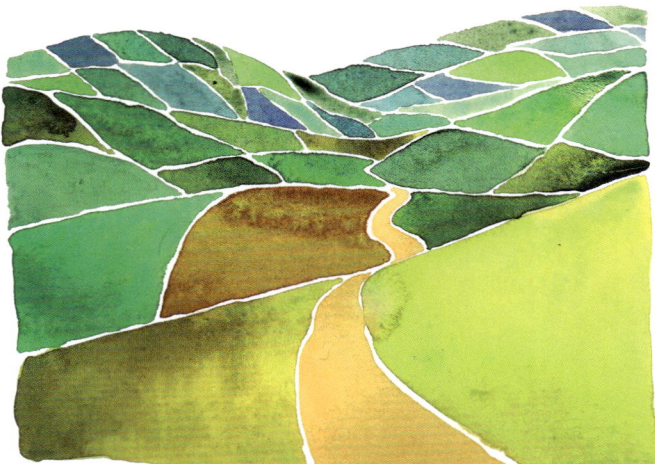

What is important? The farther away the fields, the smaller they are, the more fragmented they are, and the bluer they are. Therefore, they seem more distant. And the trees in the foreground are darker, of course.

At the very end, add two silhouettes in blue and a fence that borders the road. There's no need to fuss about details. They are so small that a light brushstroke suggests them easily.

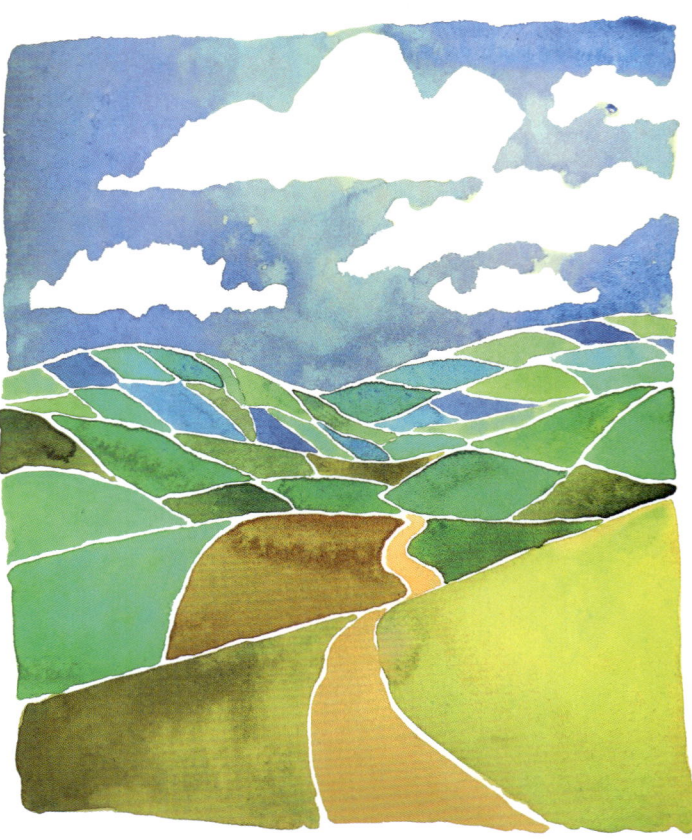

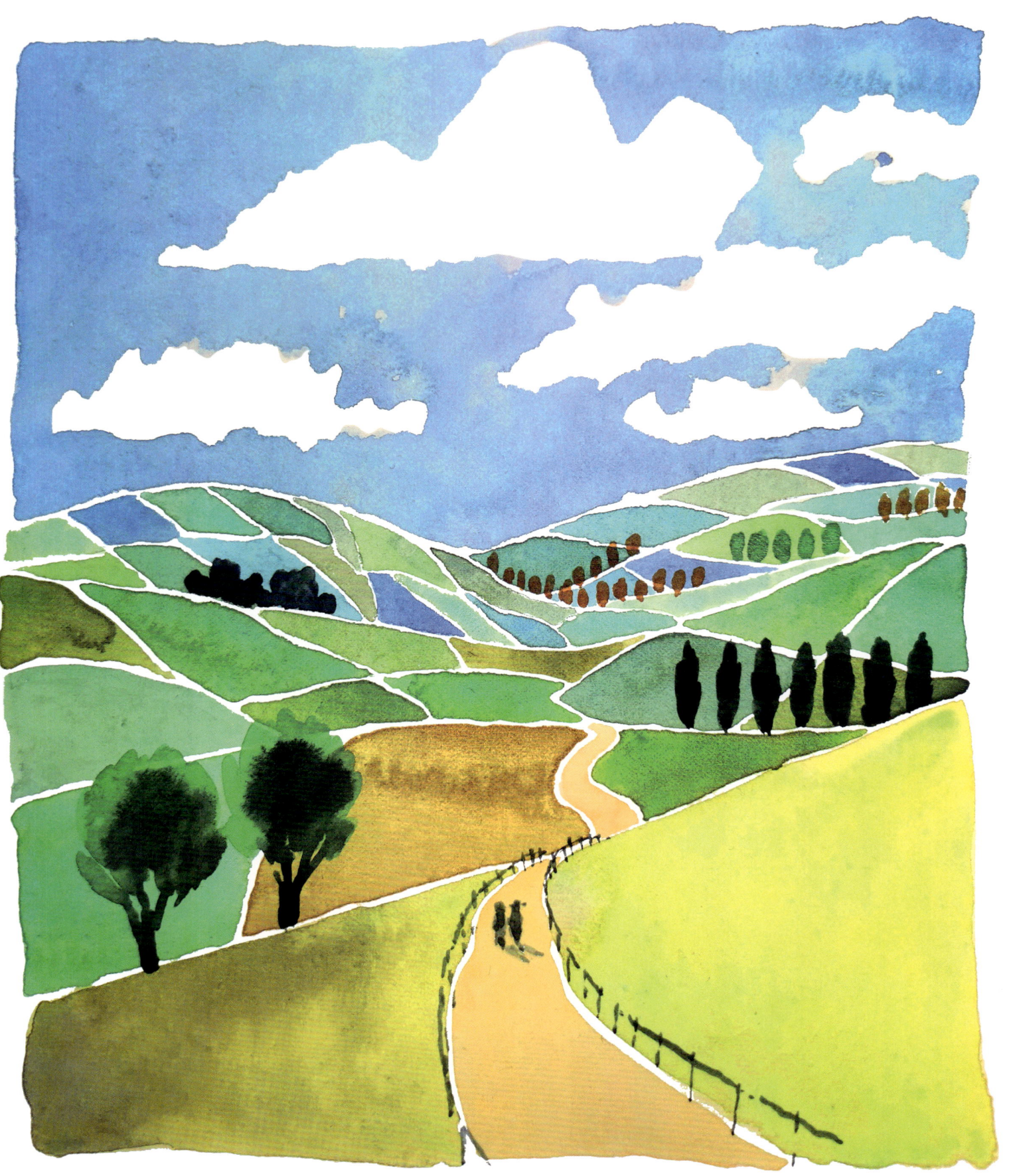

Week 6

Painting on Wet Paper

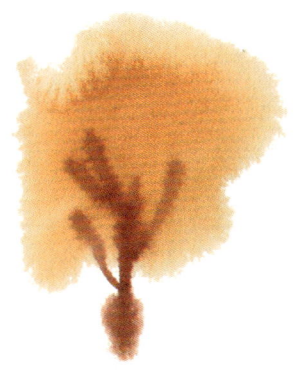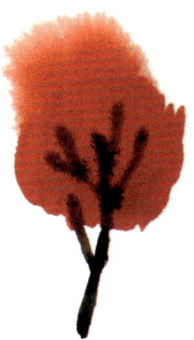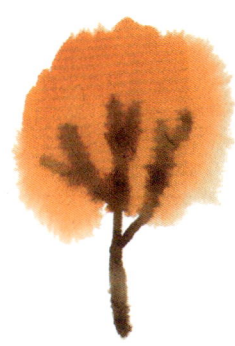

Let's return to my love: wet paper!

First, wet the paper with a large brush drenched with pure water. Wait for the paper to dry a little. The surface must not be shiny or matte, just moist. Then draw some blurry trees.

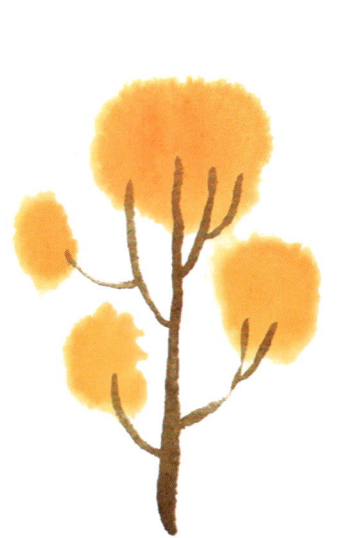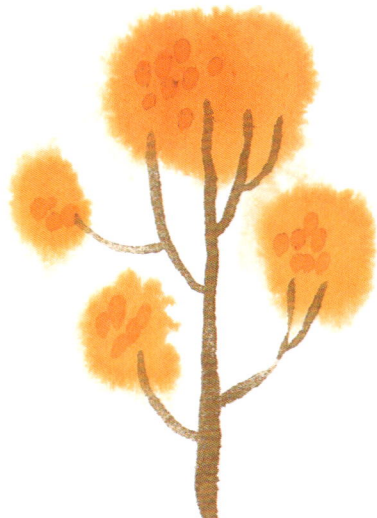

Here are some autumn trees drawn on the wet paper. By placing the strokes of watercolor on the damp paper, the color diffuses and comes to life.

You can wait for the paper to dry before painting the trunk and some reddening leaves in the foliage. But you don't have to. Try it both ways.

For this tree, draw the foliage on dry paper. Then immediately paint some red leaves in the wet paint.

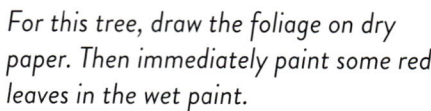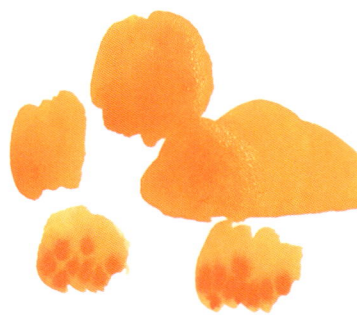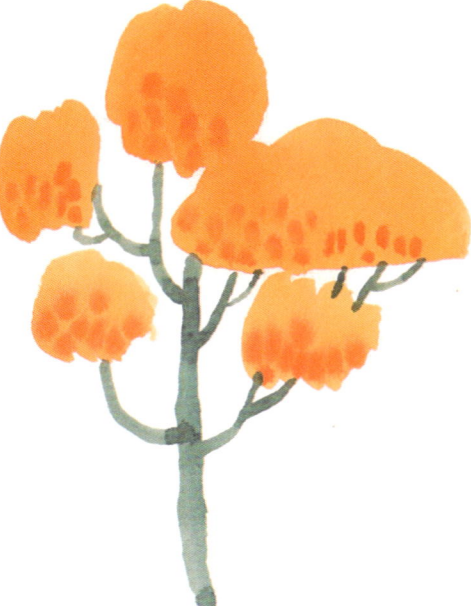

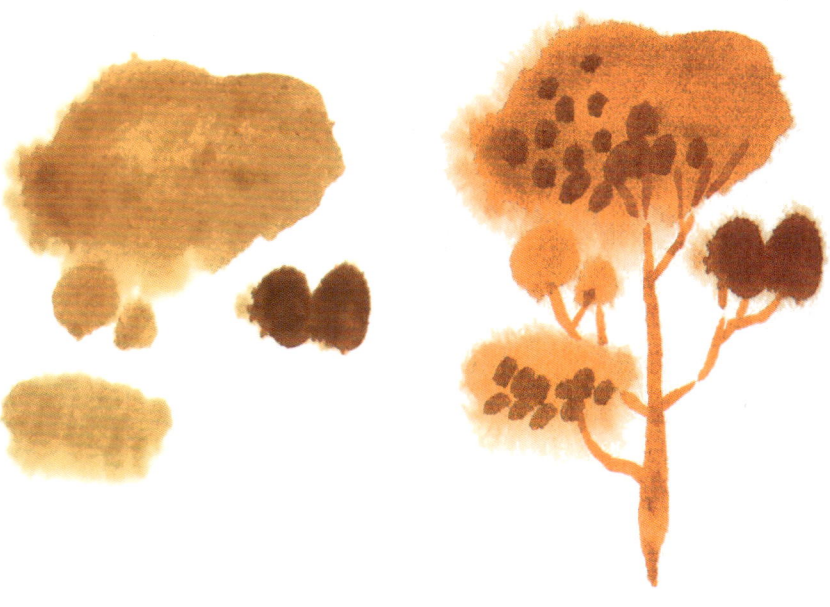

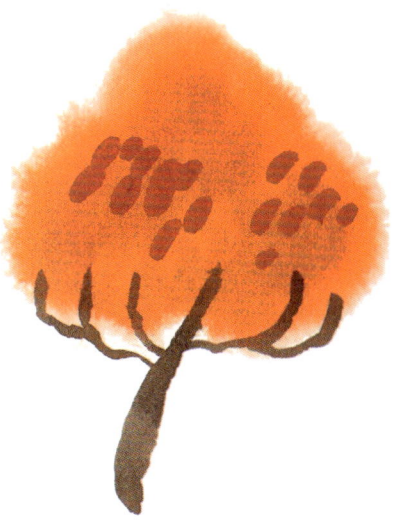

Notice the effects of blurring and diffusion when dabbing color in the wet paint. A painter doesn't control this. The water decides!

To make the trees disappear in the distance, draw them on the wet paper, in monochrome. Once everything is dry, draw the trees in the foreground. The blurry grove softens, and the more defined, darker trees seem close—which is perfect for creating some depth.

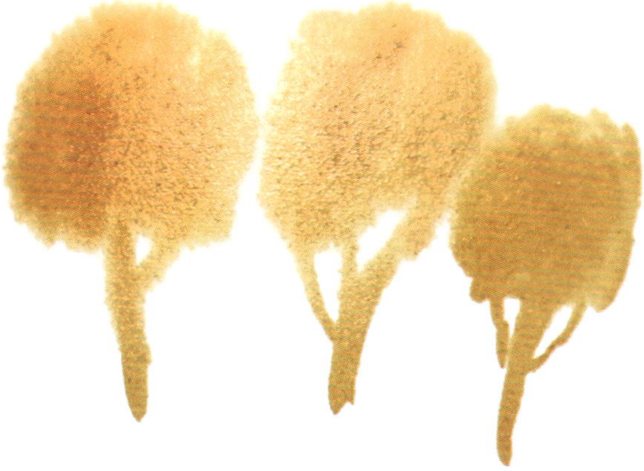

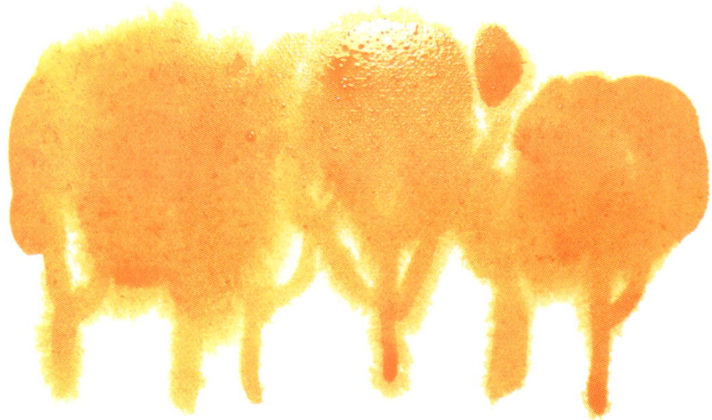

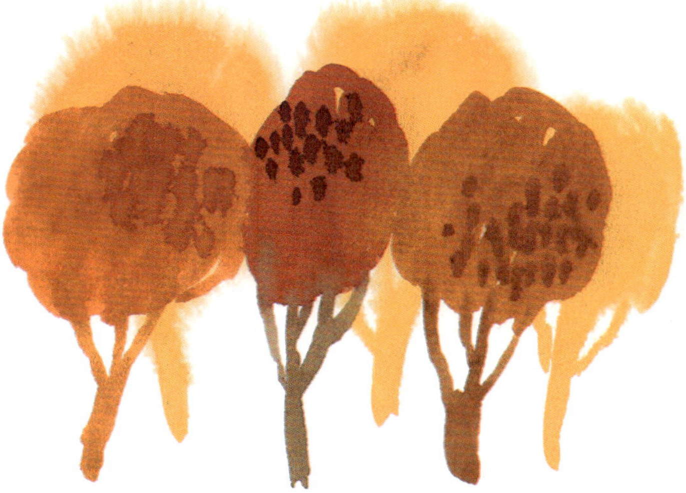

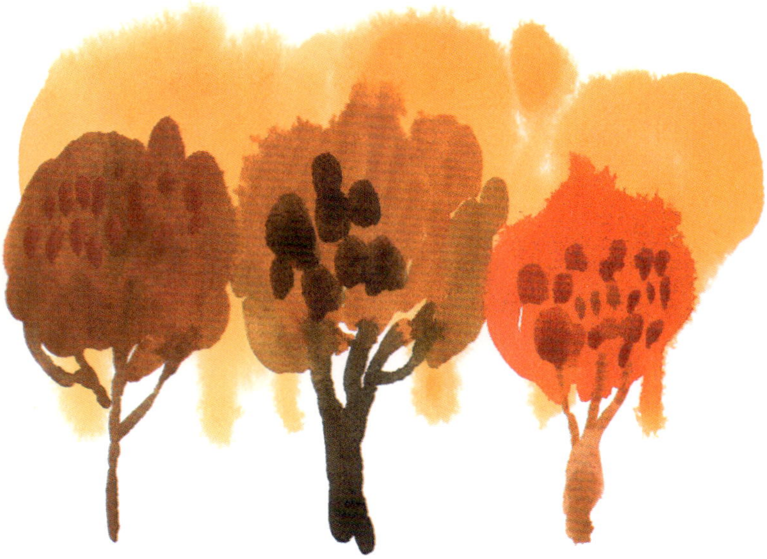

Week 7
Strokes on Wet Watercolor

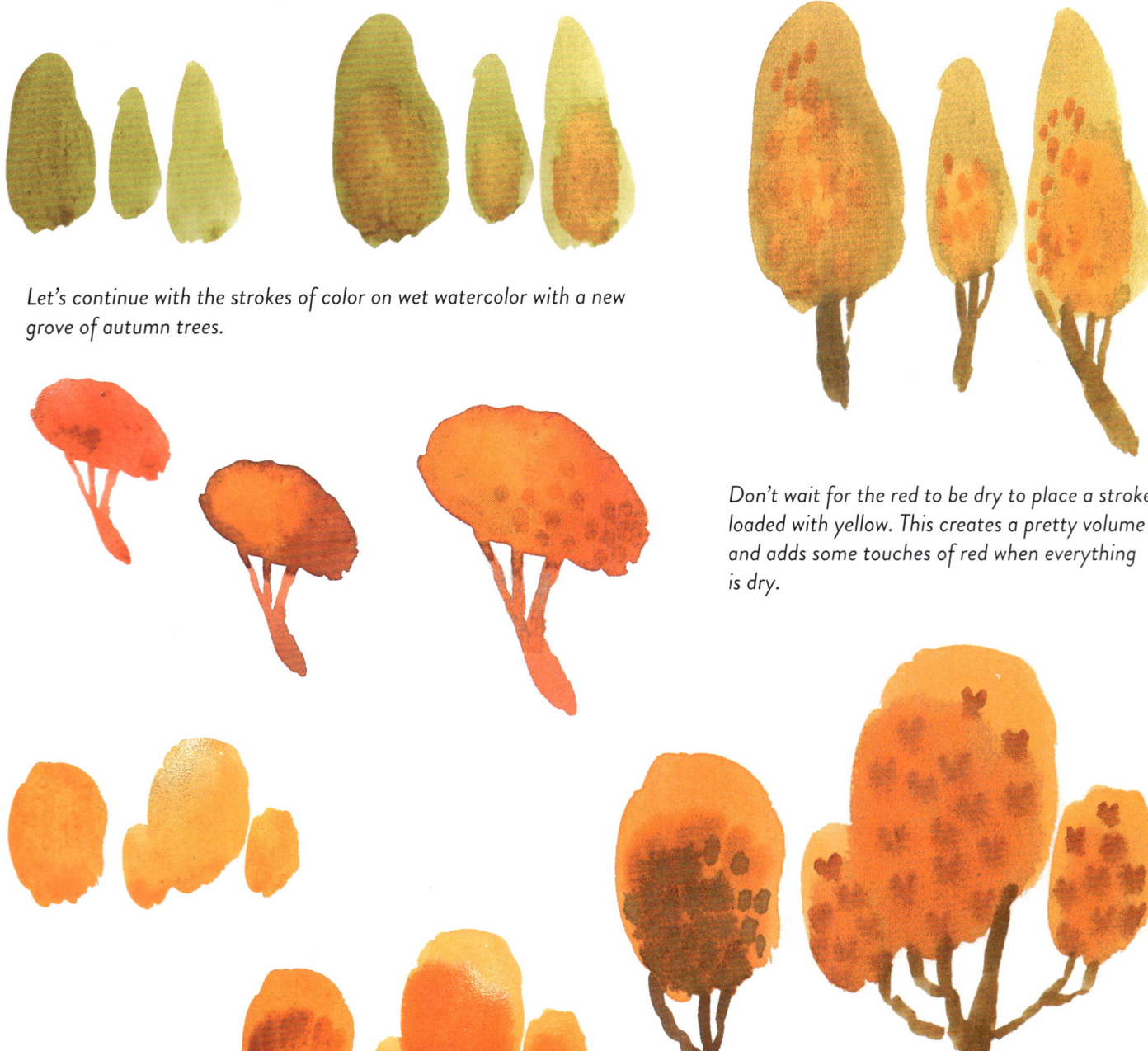

Let's continue with the strokes of color on wet watercolor with a new grove of autumn trees.

Don't wait for the red to be dry to place a stroke loaded with yellow. This creates a pretty volume and adds some touches of red when everything is dry.

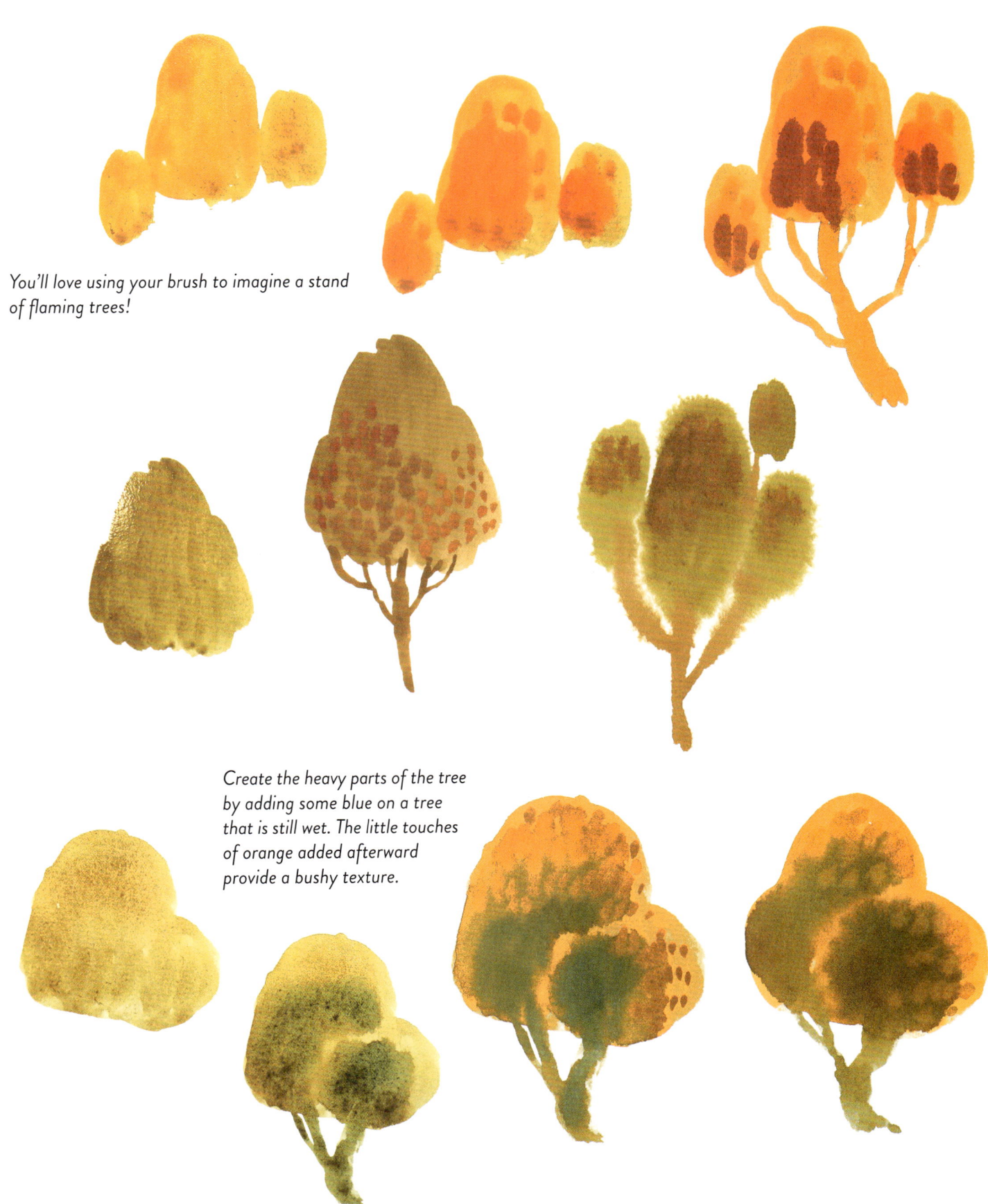

You'll love using your brush to imagine a stand of flaming trees!

Create the heavy parts of the tree by adding some blue on a tree that is still wet. The little touches of orange added afterward provide a bushy texture.

For More Practice

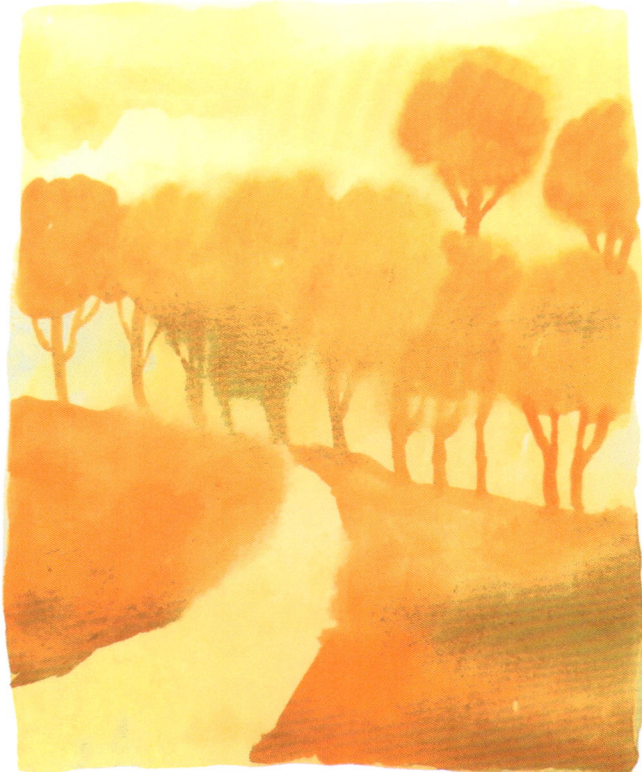

For this stroll reminiscent of the song "Autumn Leaves" (music by Joseph Kosma, English lyrics by Johnny Mercer), start with a yellow wash, as discussed in Week 5.

Without waiting for the wash to dry, define a road and paint a distant grove, in monochrome.

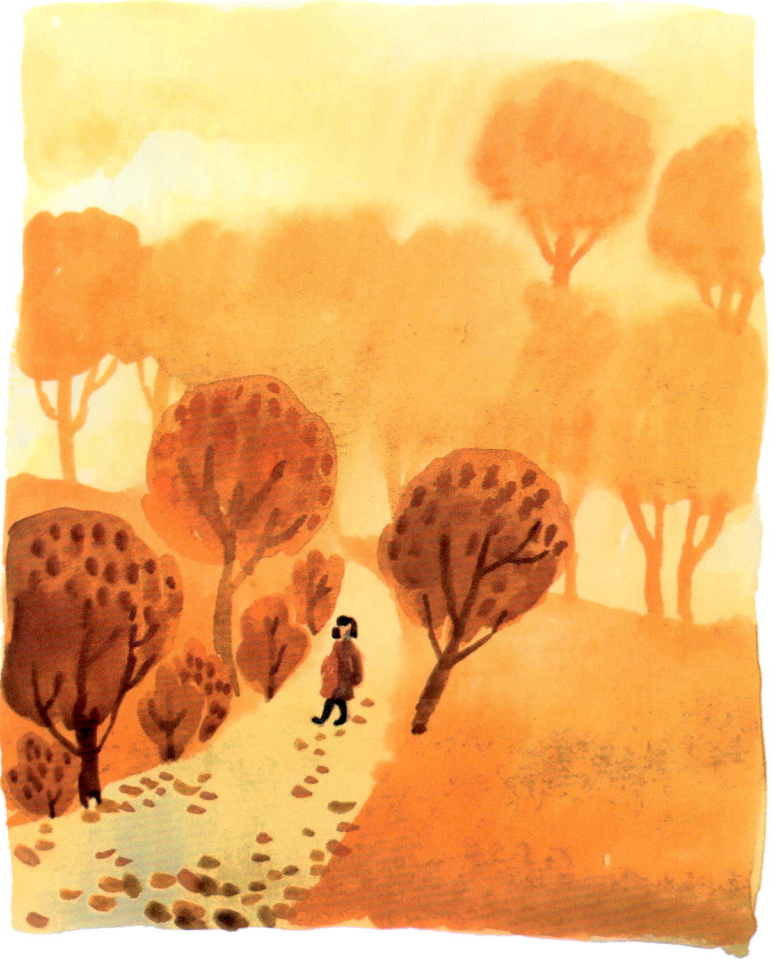

Once the Indian summer background is dry, paint some darker trees, a little silhouette, and some fallen leaves, with colors and textures drawn in the wet watercolor, as discussed in Week 7.

All that remains to draw are some branches and foliage—even darker and more contrasted—to create a foreground and some perspective. Add some bright red leaves fluttering down through the air for atmosphere!

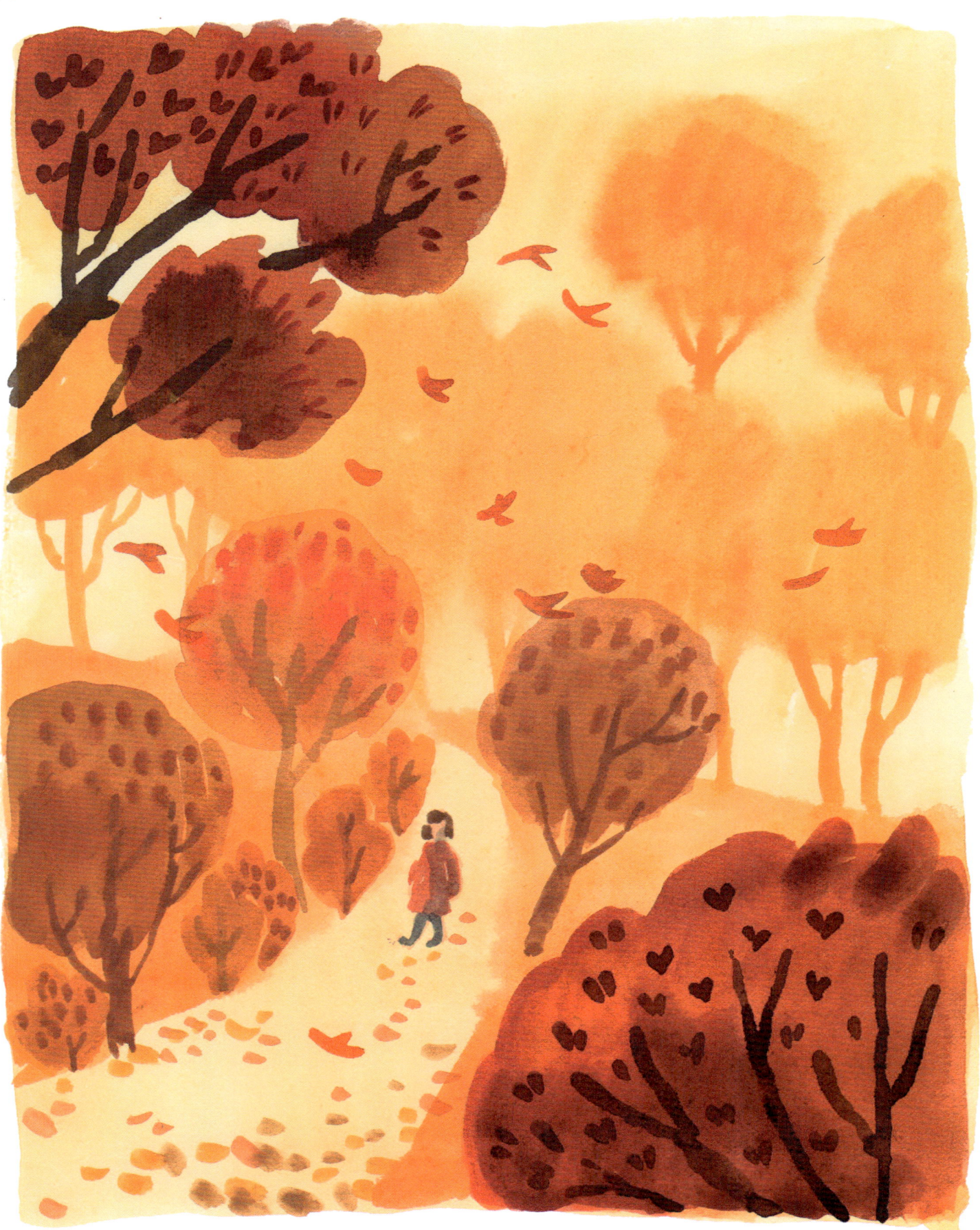

Week 8
—
Making Heavily Loaded Pigment Bloom in Wet Watercolor

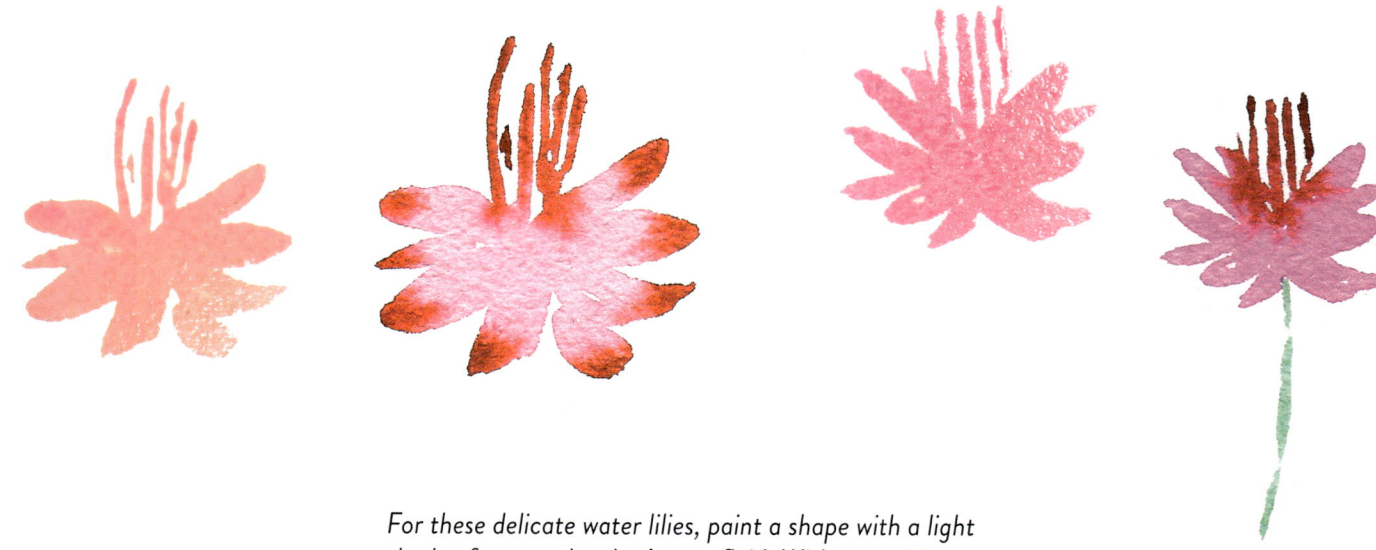

For these delicate water lilies, paint a shape with a light shade of watercolor that's very fluid. Without waiting for it to dry, load your brush with generous amounts of water and pigment. Gently touch the ends of the shapes with the tip of the brush. The pigment will follow the shape, seep into it, and diffuse.

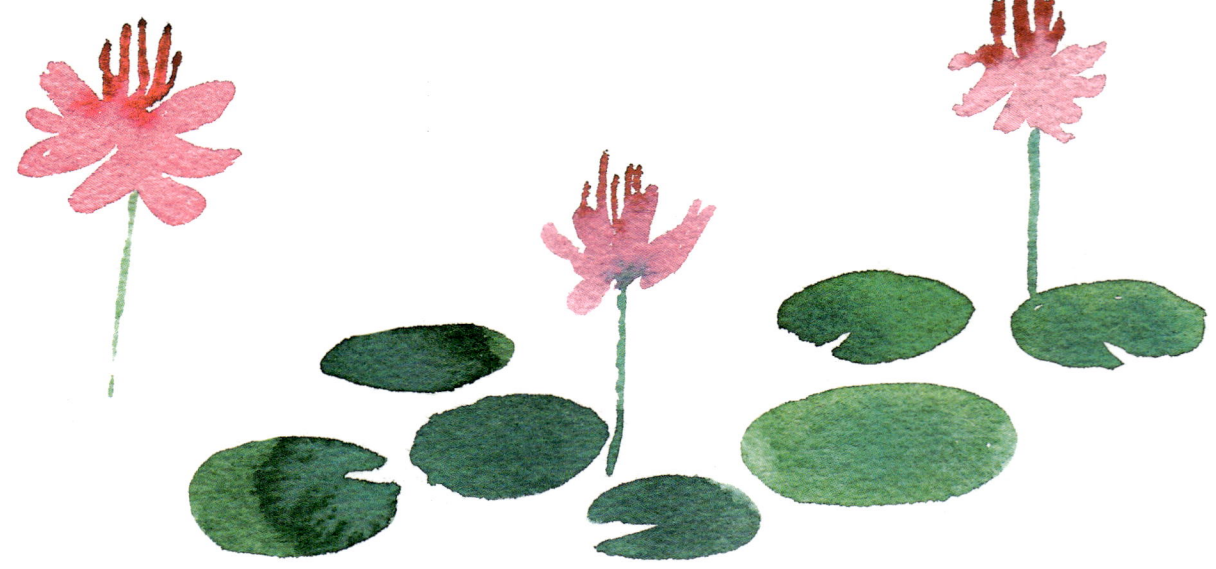

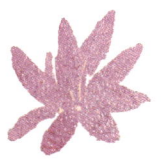
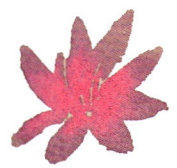
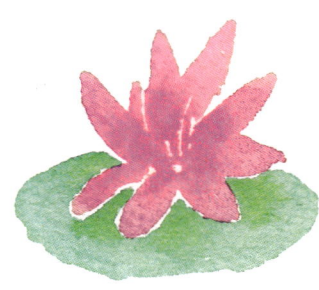

You can place the pigments in the middle of the flower to create a center that is more pronounced.

For the water lilies, wait for the flower to be completely dry. Surround it precisely with a green leaf, keeping a narrow white space between the flower and the leaf. This is your reserve. Without waiting for the green paint mix to be dry, place pigments to shade its color and give it depth.

Week 9
Blooms of Pigments Between Two Wet Strokes

To animate your compositions, try this technique. Paint a
first shape with a generously loaded brush. Juxtapose a second
shape with another color. The point of contact between
the two shapes serves as a bridge between the two colors.
One diffuses into the other.

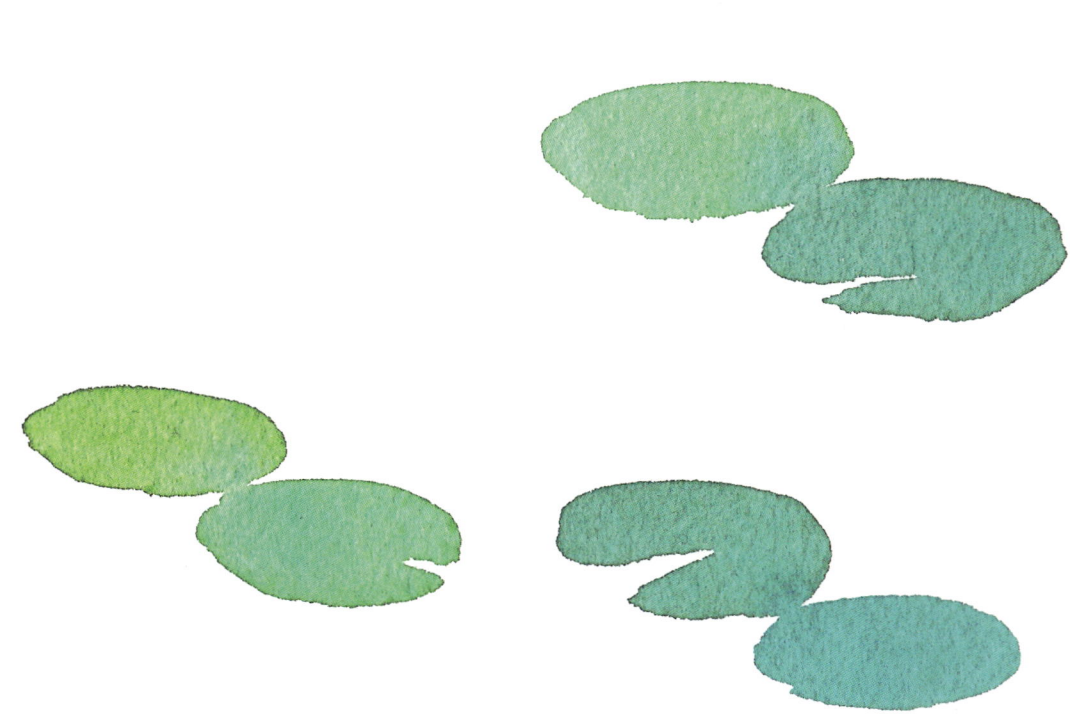

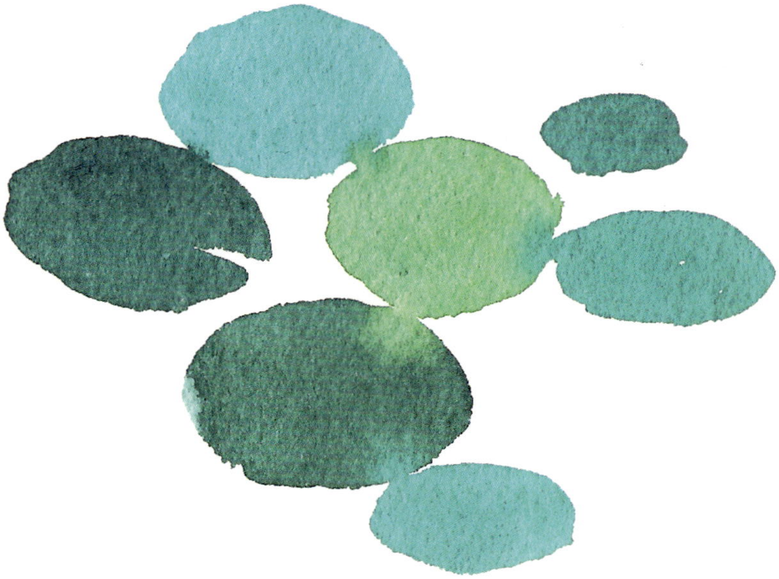

It is difficult to know which color will overflow onto the other. It's a surprise! It depends on the pigments—which ones are more or less volatile, heavy, or opaque.

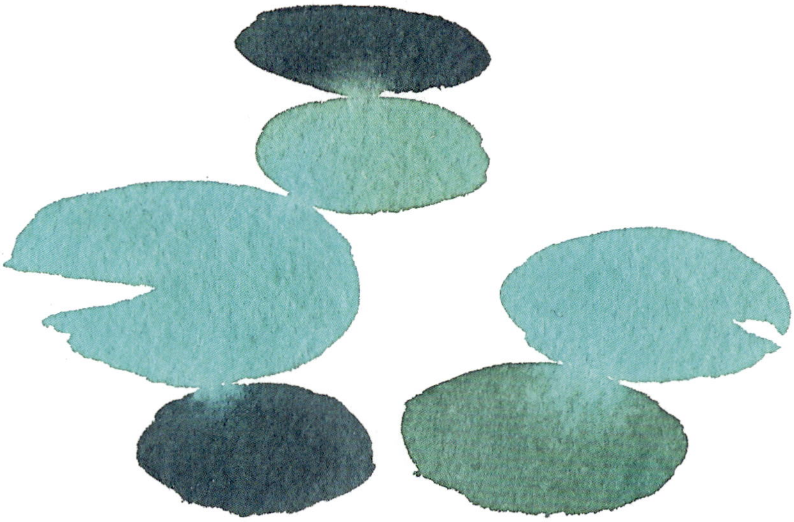

Play around with inventing aquatic plants in various shades.

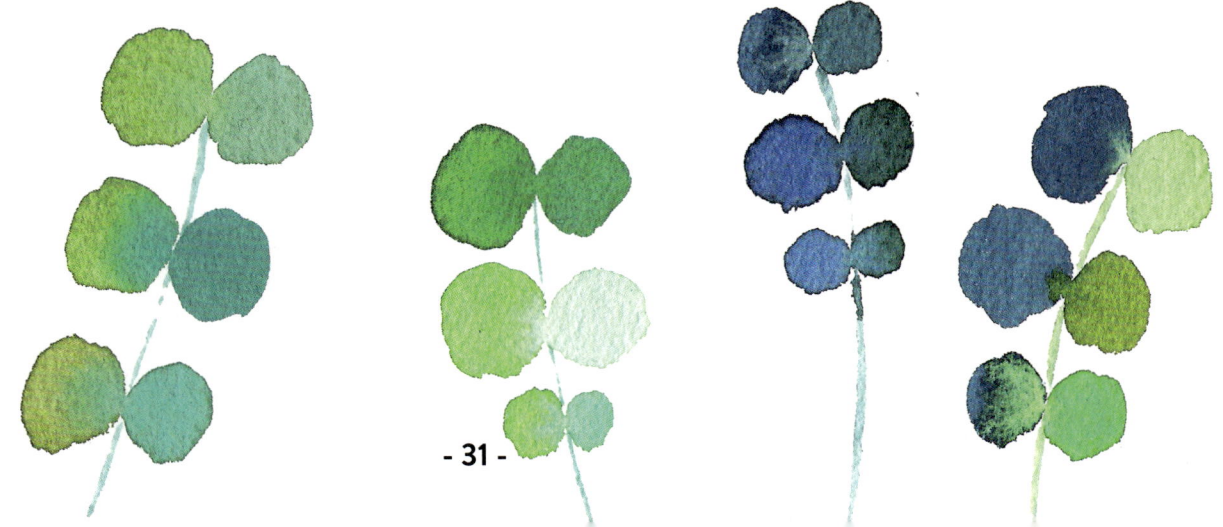

For More Practice

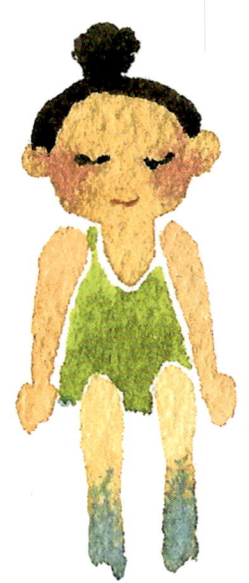

Wouldn't you love to be in a little greenhouse, sitting next to this pretty pond? To draw the lucky heroine, do a simple sketch of her body with a flesh-toned paint mix. Before it dries, place some blue paint on her feet, to give the impression that they are immersed in the water, and some pink paint on her cheeks. Next, dress her in a green dress, give her a brown bun, and draw eyelashes and a mouth.

Practice painting the blue background of the water by leaving a thin white space around the water lilies, with the rapid wash technique, as explained in Week 5.

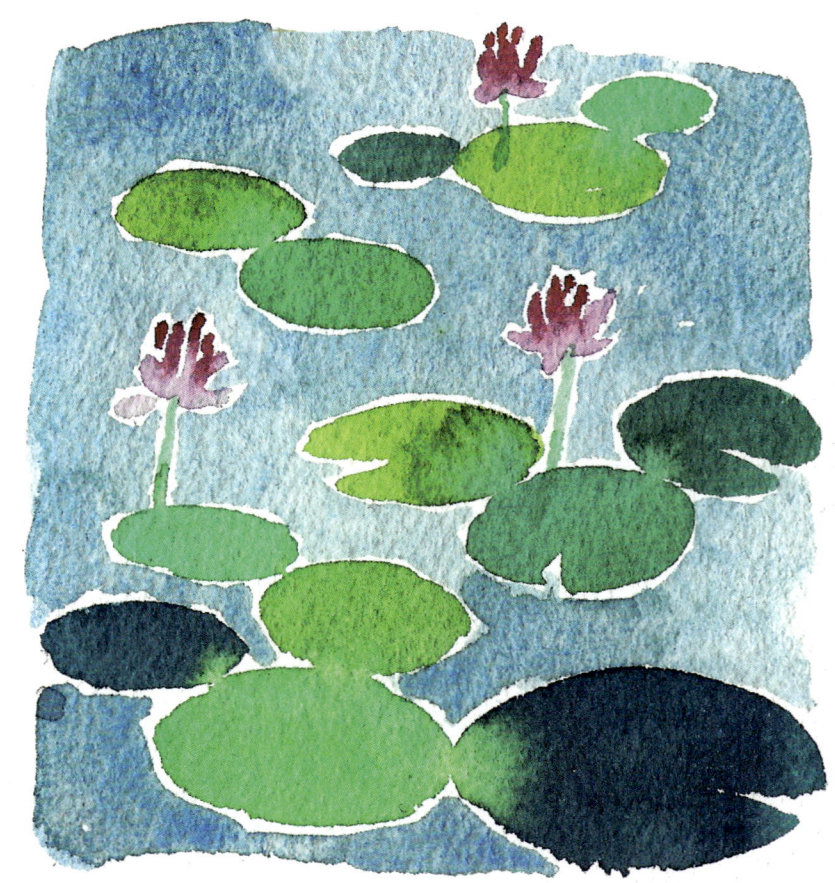

Paint blue rectangles in washes, separating each wash with a narrow white space to suggest the window frames of a greenhouse in the background.

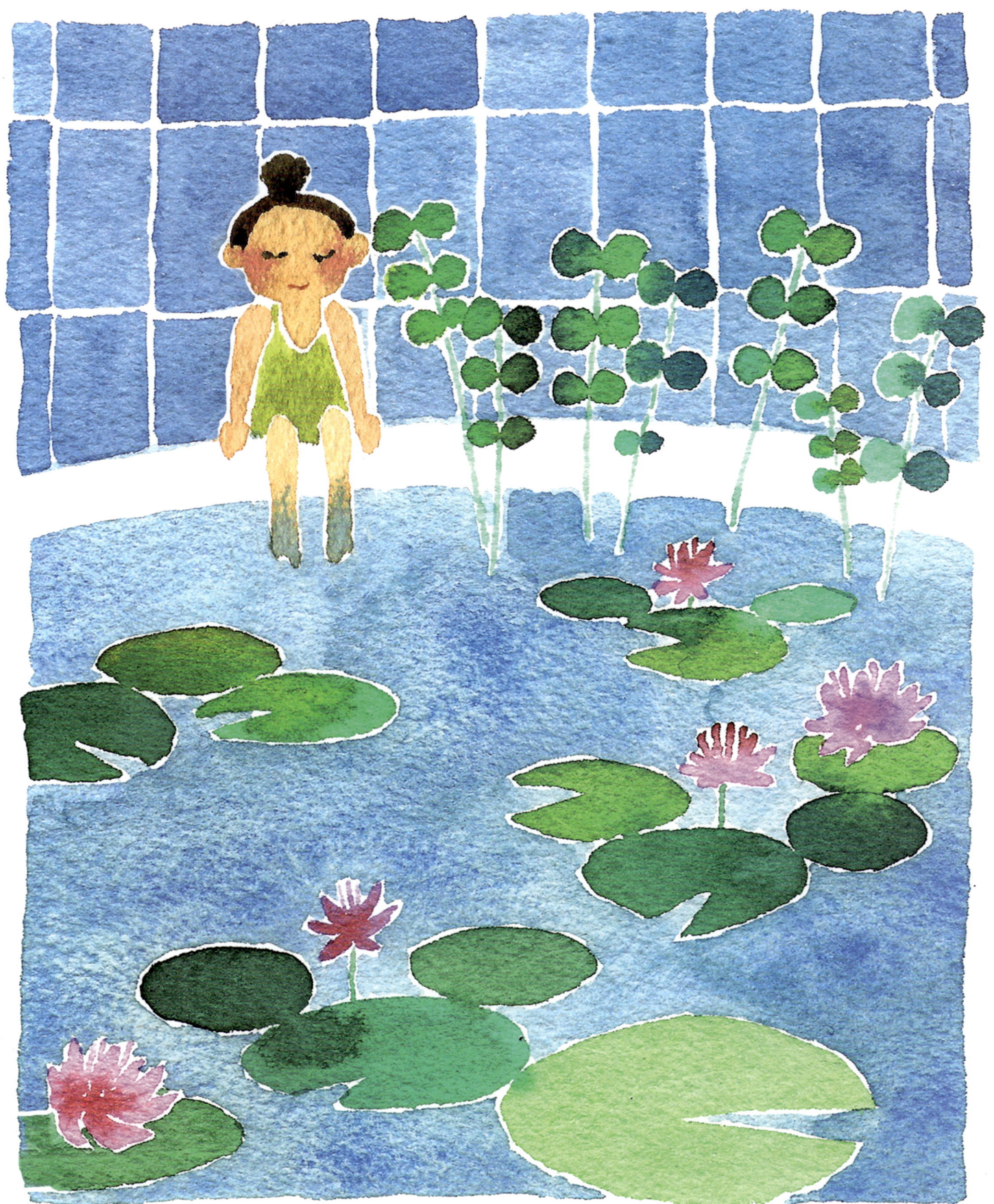

Week 10

Pushing Back the Wet Pigments by Adding Pure Water

This technique is very useful. Sketch a silhouette of a whale with paint and water. Without waiting for it to dry, let a drop of water fall from a brush to push back the pigments, revealing the white belly of the whale.

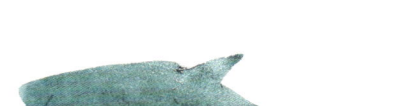

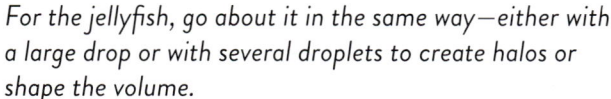

For the jellyfish, go about it in the same way—either with a large drop or with several droplets to create halos or shape the volume.

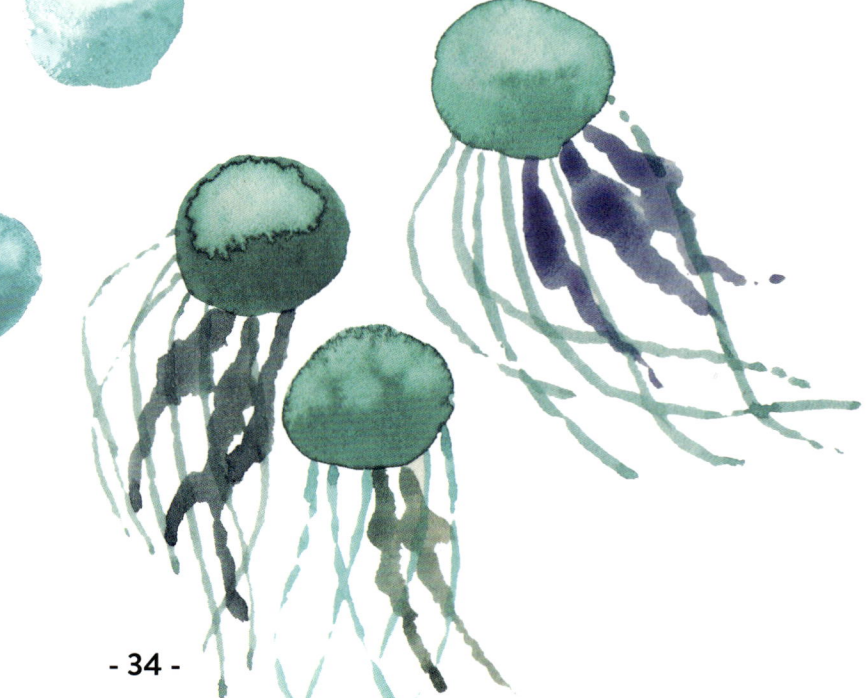

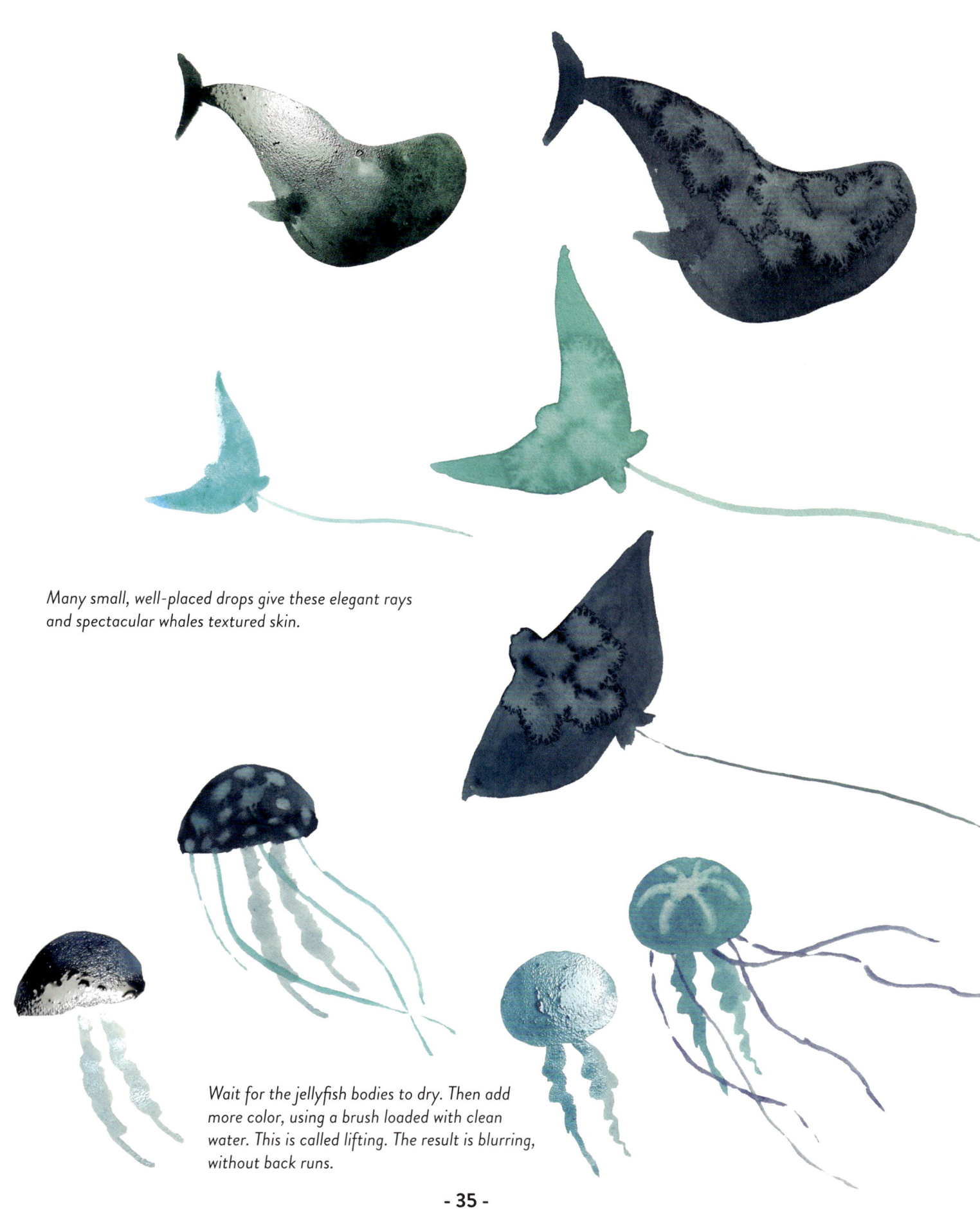

Many small, well-placed drops give these elegant rays and spectacular whales textured skin.

Wait for the jellyfish bodies to dry. Then add more color, using a brush loaded with clean water. This is called lifting. The result is blurring, without back runs.

Week 11

Pushing Back the Wet Pigments with Wet Pigments

To bring these sharks to life, paint their silhouettes in a light wash. Then place a darker paint mix on their still-wet back. As if by magic, their volume appears!

Place a drop of clean water on the wet body to give this celadon shark a white belly. Draw his stripes while the paint is still wet.

Place colored drops on their wet backs. The pigments push each other back and diffuse, and the back runs make their skins materialize.

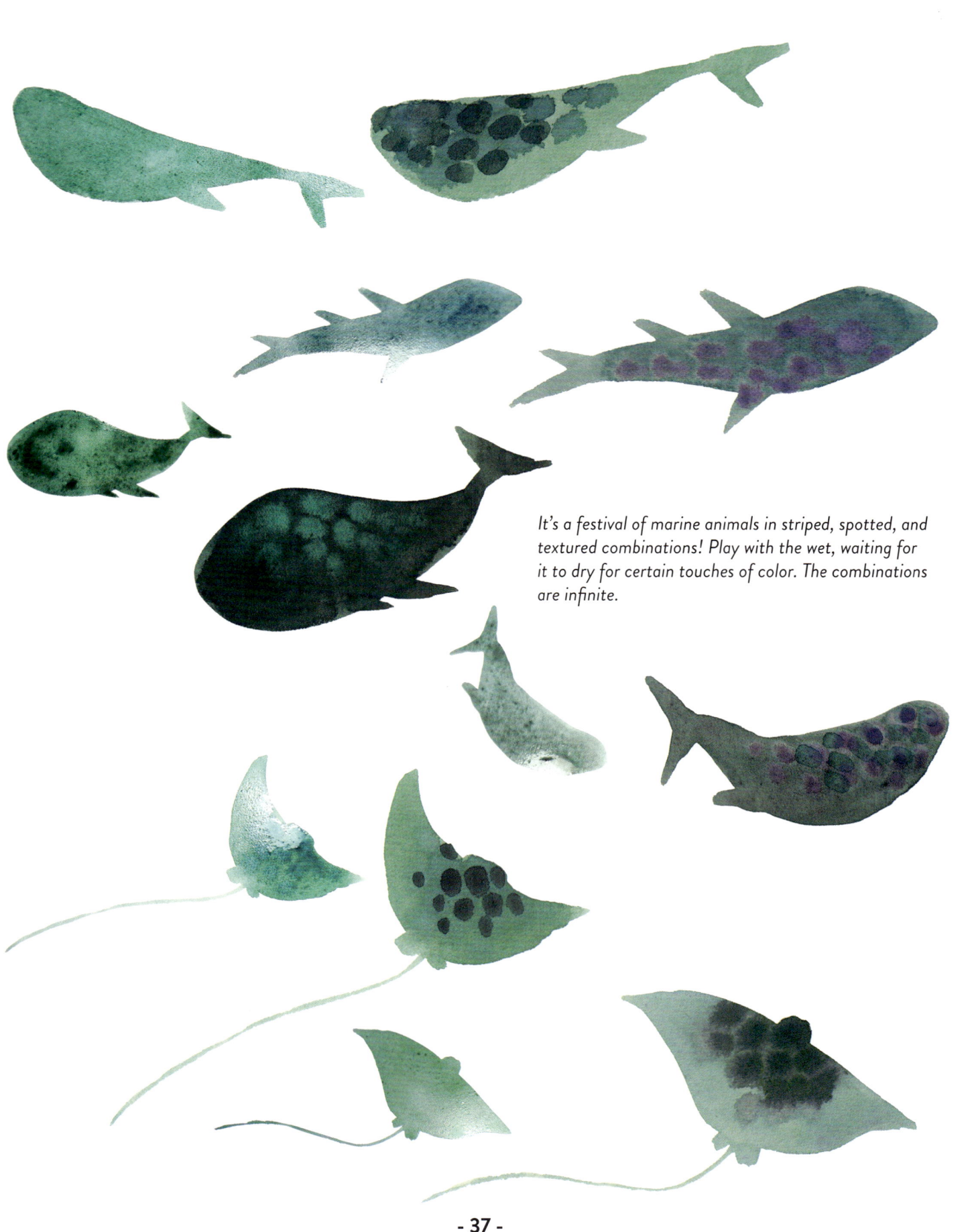

It's a festival of marine animals in striped, spotted, and textured combinations! Play with the wet, waiting for it to dry for certain touches of color. The combinations are infinite.

For More Practice

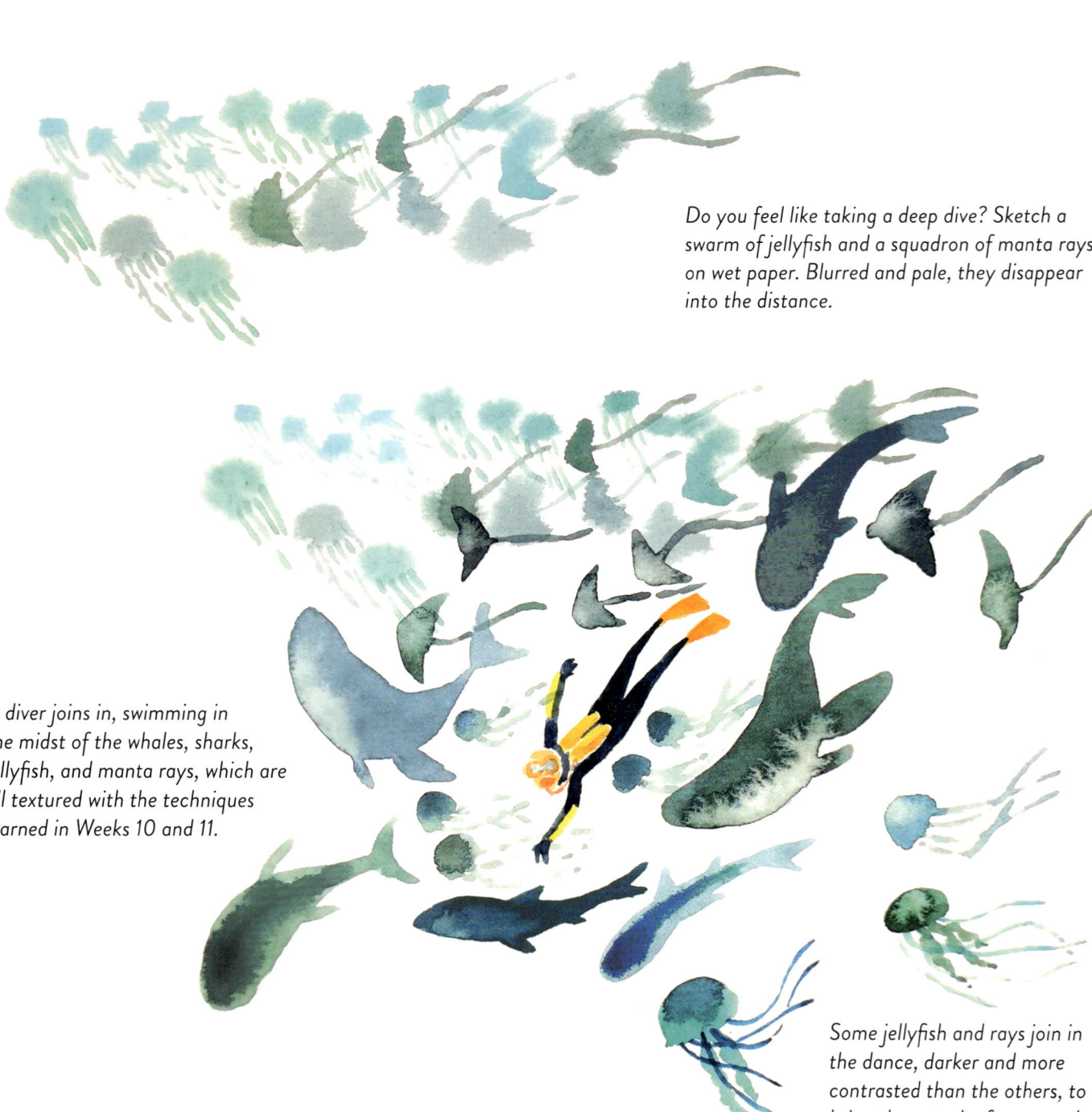

Do you feel like taking a deep dive? Sketch a swarm of jellyfish and a squadron of manta rays on wet paper. Blurred and pale, they disappear into the distance.

A diver joins in, swimming in the midst of the whales, sharks, jellyfish, and manta rays, which are all textured with the techniques learned in Weeks 10 and 11.

Some jellyfish and rays join in the dance, darker and more contrasted than the others, to bring them to the foreground.

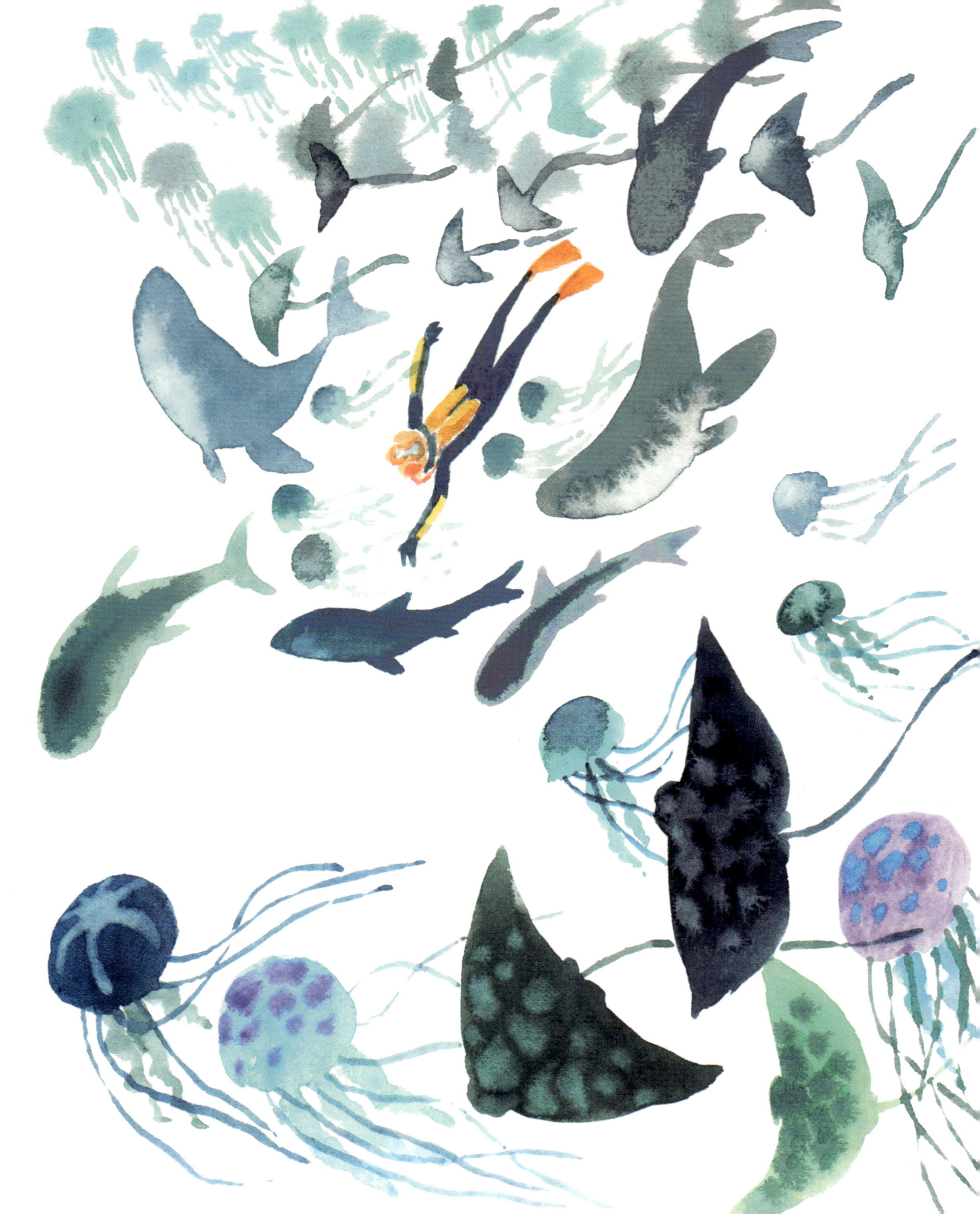

Week 12
Creating Gradations by Wetting the Paper

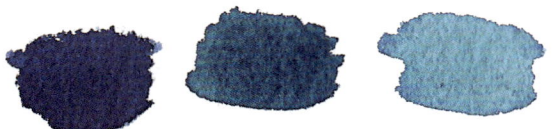

To paint a regular gradation, choose the two colors you want to make the gradation between. Prepare very diluted paint mixes in the wells in your watercolor box: the pale cyan, the indanthrone blue, and a transition, which is the mixture of the first two colors. Also prepare a fourth, very diluted blue paint mix.

Paint the final form with the very diluted paint mix. Without waiting for it to dry, place the lightest color (pale cyan) with the brush. Rinse the brush, and load it with the transition color. Then apply this color mix next to and touching the first color. Do this again with the darkest color. The three dilutions mix harmoniously, creating soft transitions.

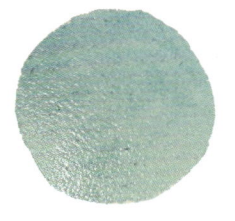 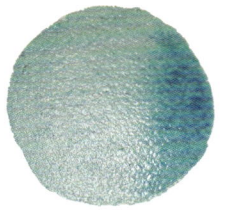 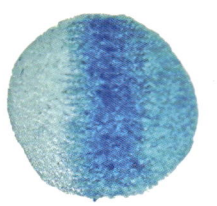 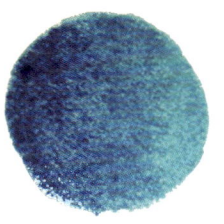 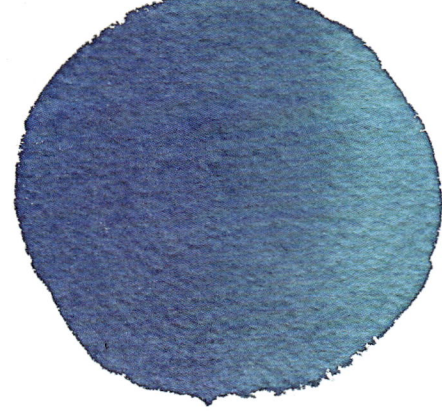

You can use this technique of gradation in any direction—for example, in concentric circles, in waves, diagonally, or with more than three colors. As long as you start with the most diluted color and paint in the wet, anything is possible!

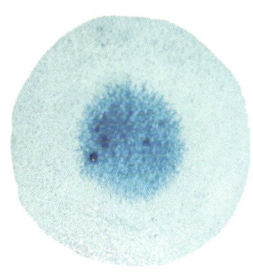 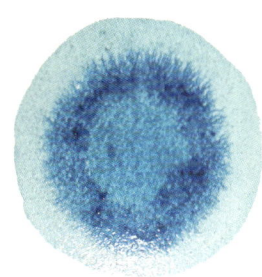 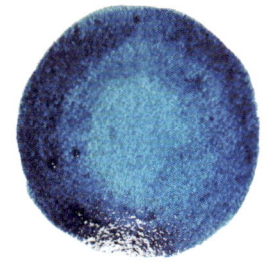 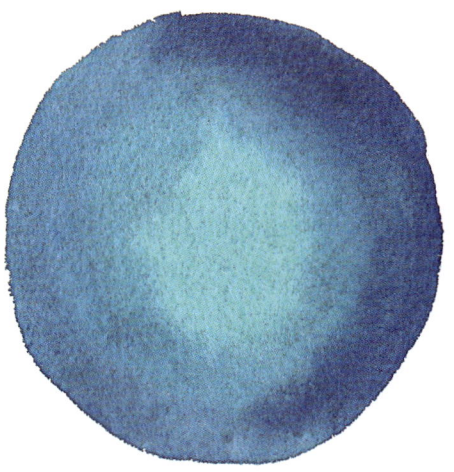

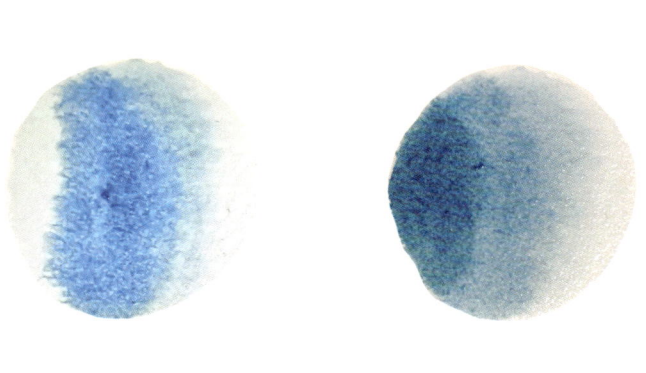
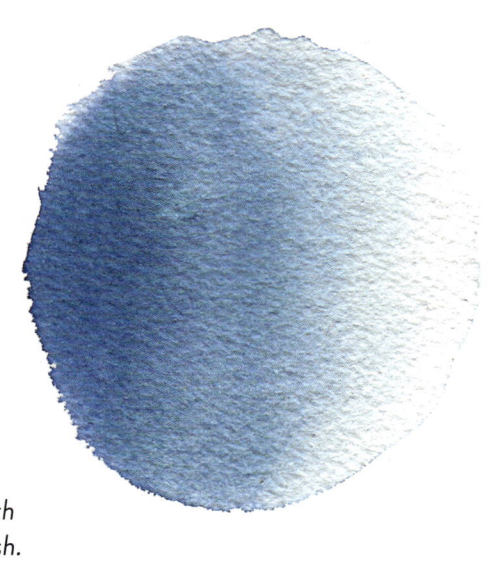

For a gradation from white to color, prepare two mixes in the wells in your watercolor box: a more saturated mix and a transition mix between this color and clear water. Paint the final form with a wet brush, but without color—just with water. Without waiting for the paper to dry, place the transition color with a brush. Then add the saturated color mix.

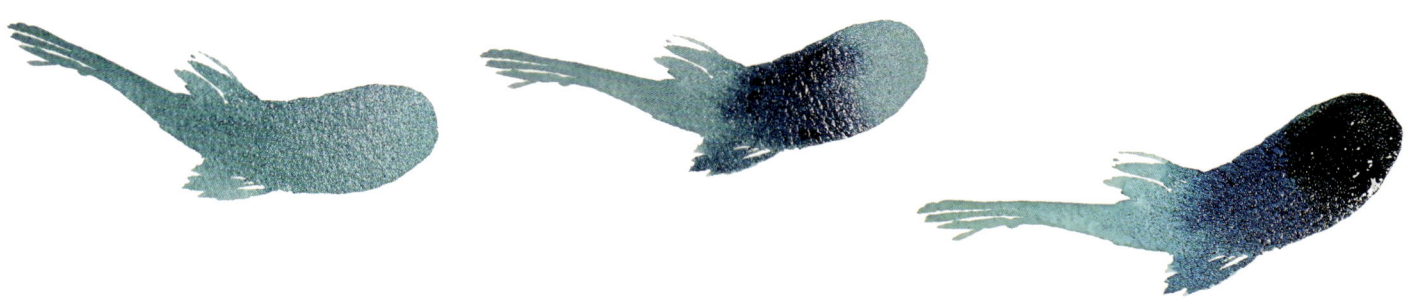

Here are some fish to practice with, in gradations that wriggle!

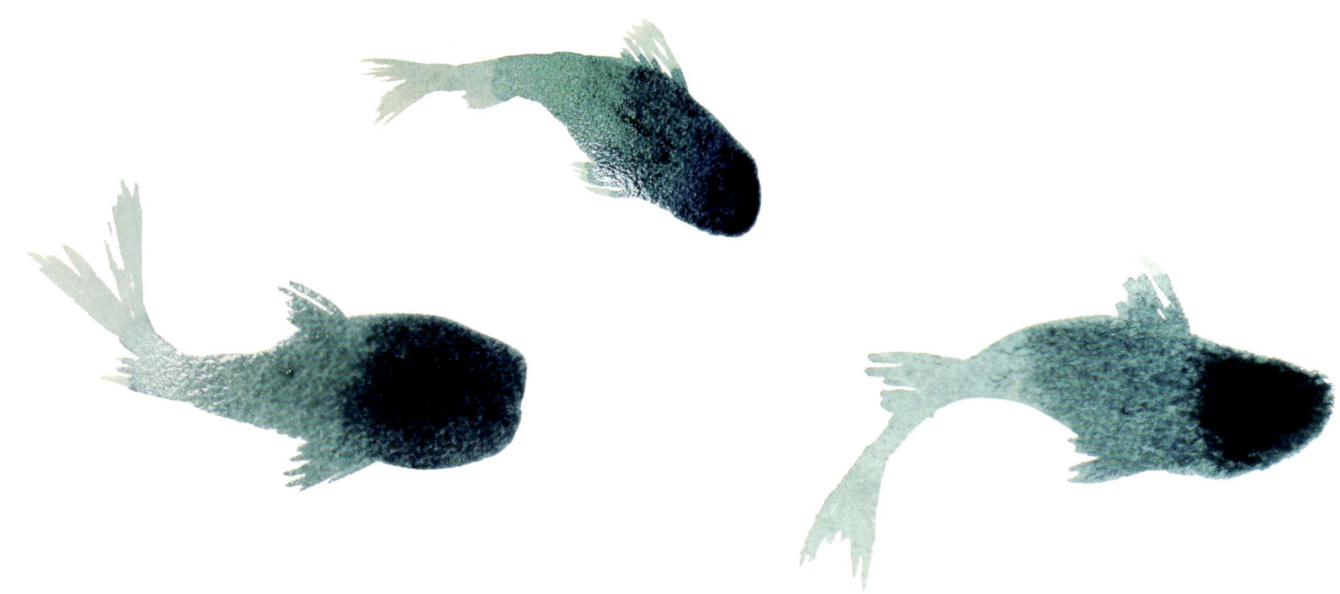

Week 13

Gradation by Colored Wet Strokes

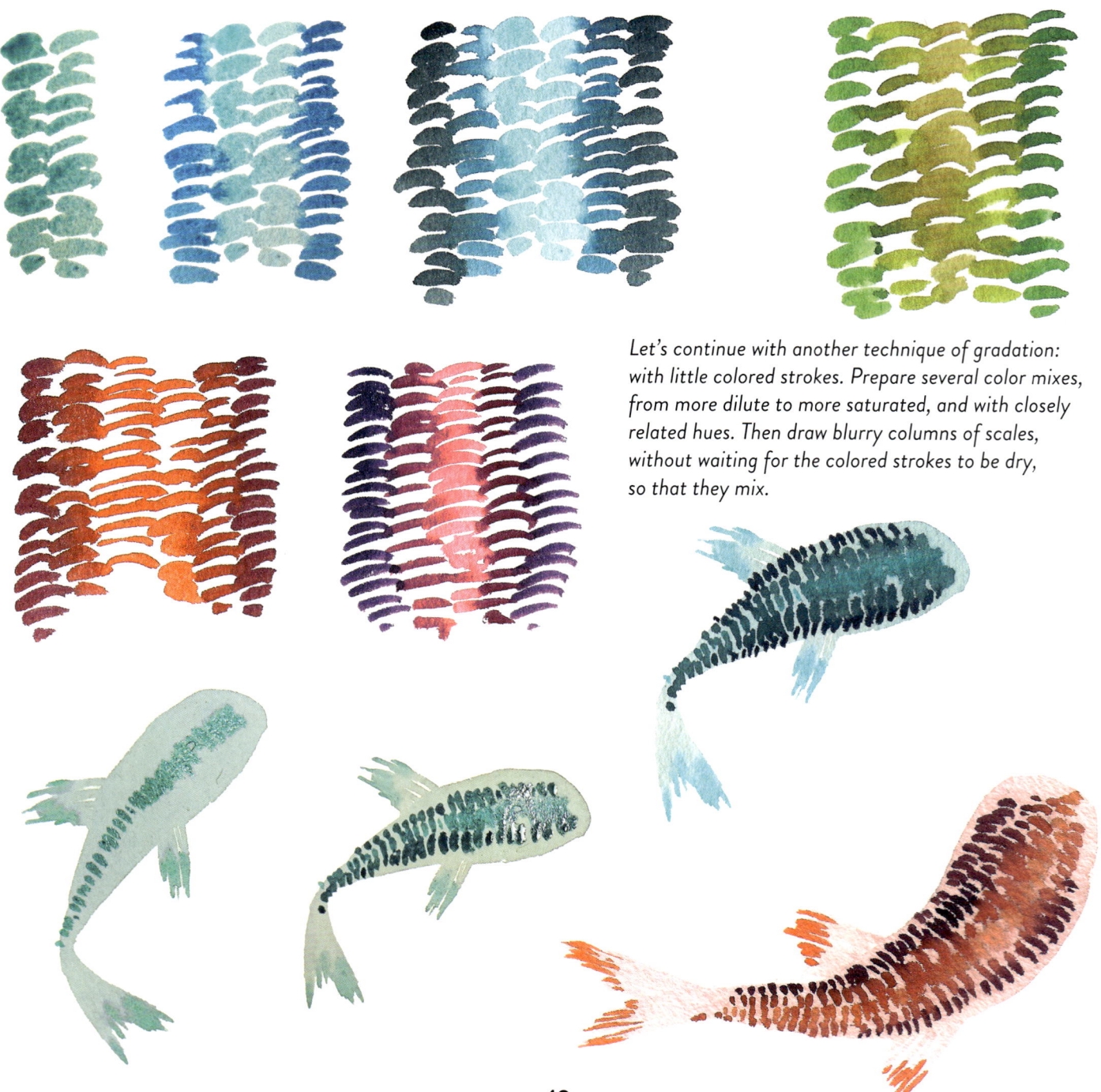

Let's continue with another technique of gradation: with little colored strokes. Prepare several color mixes, from more dilute to more saturated, and with closely related hues. Then draw blurry columns of scales, without waiting for the colored strokes to be dry, so that they mix.

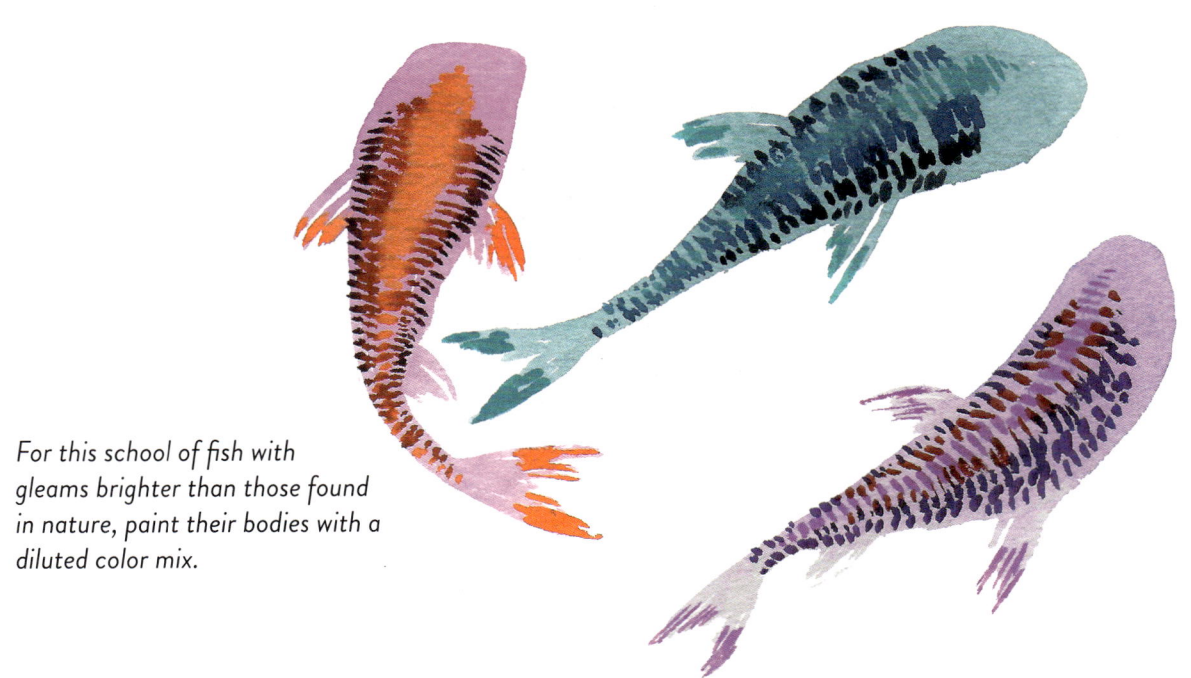

For this school of fish with gleams brighter than those found in nature, paint their bodies with a diluted color mix.

You can get a blended effect by not waiting for the bodies to dry before drawing the scales in gradation.

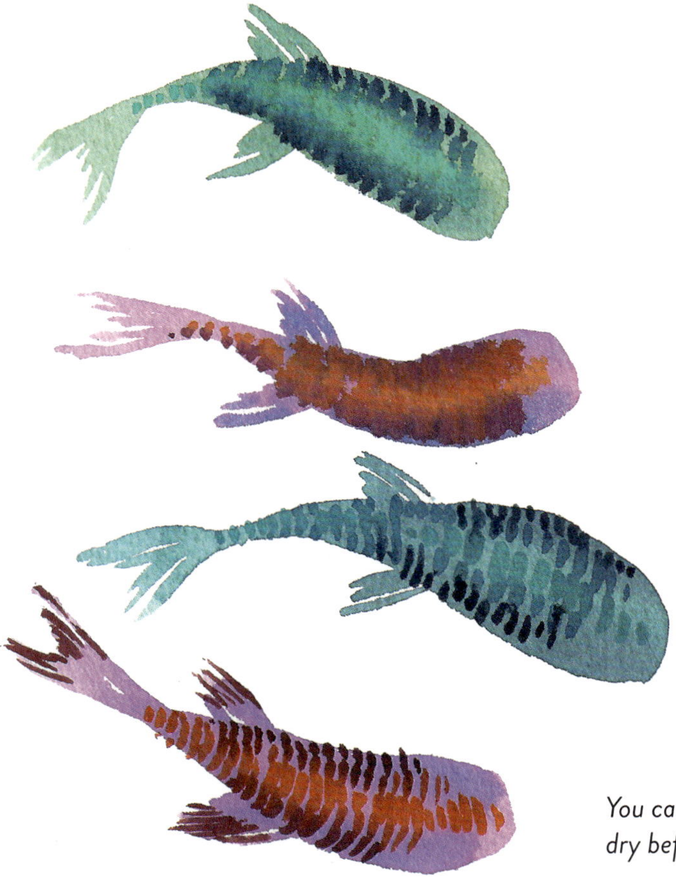

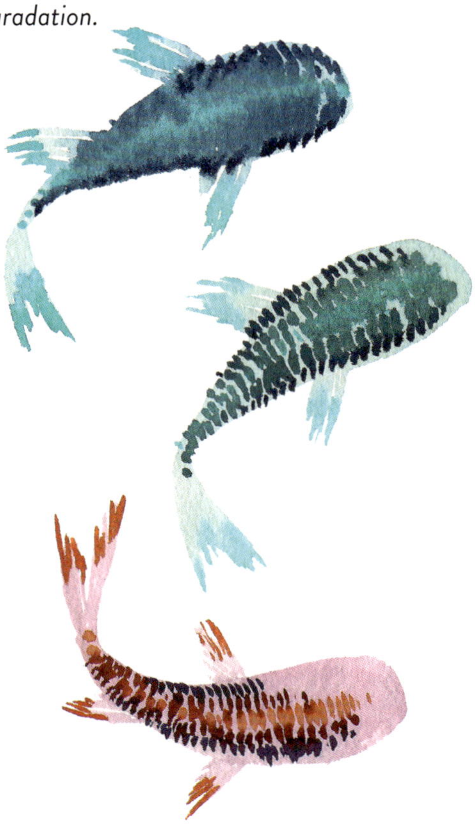

You can get a sharper effect by waiting for the body to dry before drawing the scales in gradation.

For More Practice

To illustrate this miraculous school of fish—which is worthy of a Japanese engraving—start with a gradation between the white of the paper and the blue.

Once the gradation is dry, paint some carp in two colors—the diluted color for the body and a darker paint mix to give the fish volume—without waiting for the bodies to dry.

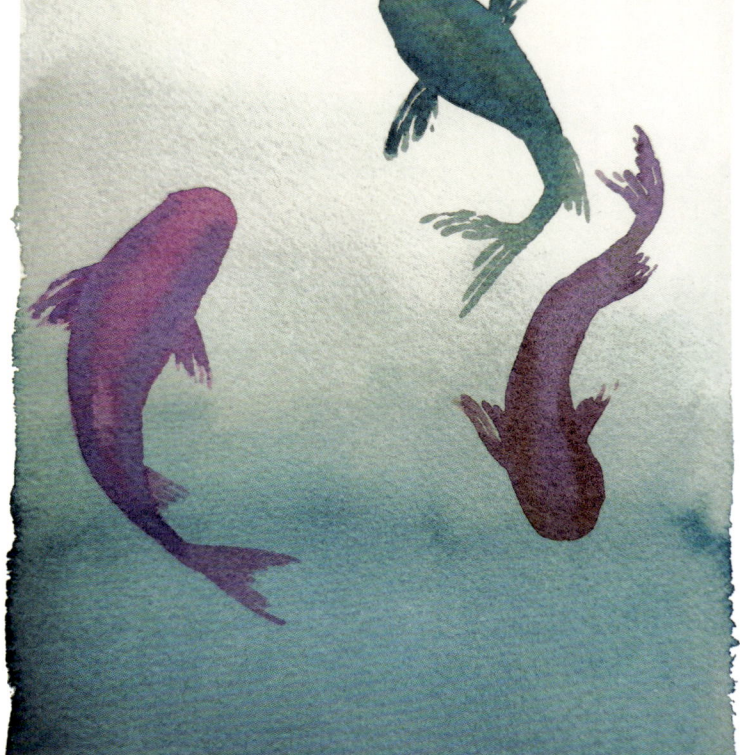

Finally, add some smaller, less detailed carp, animated by gradations in three colors. The fish look so vibrant!

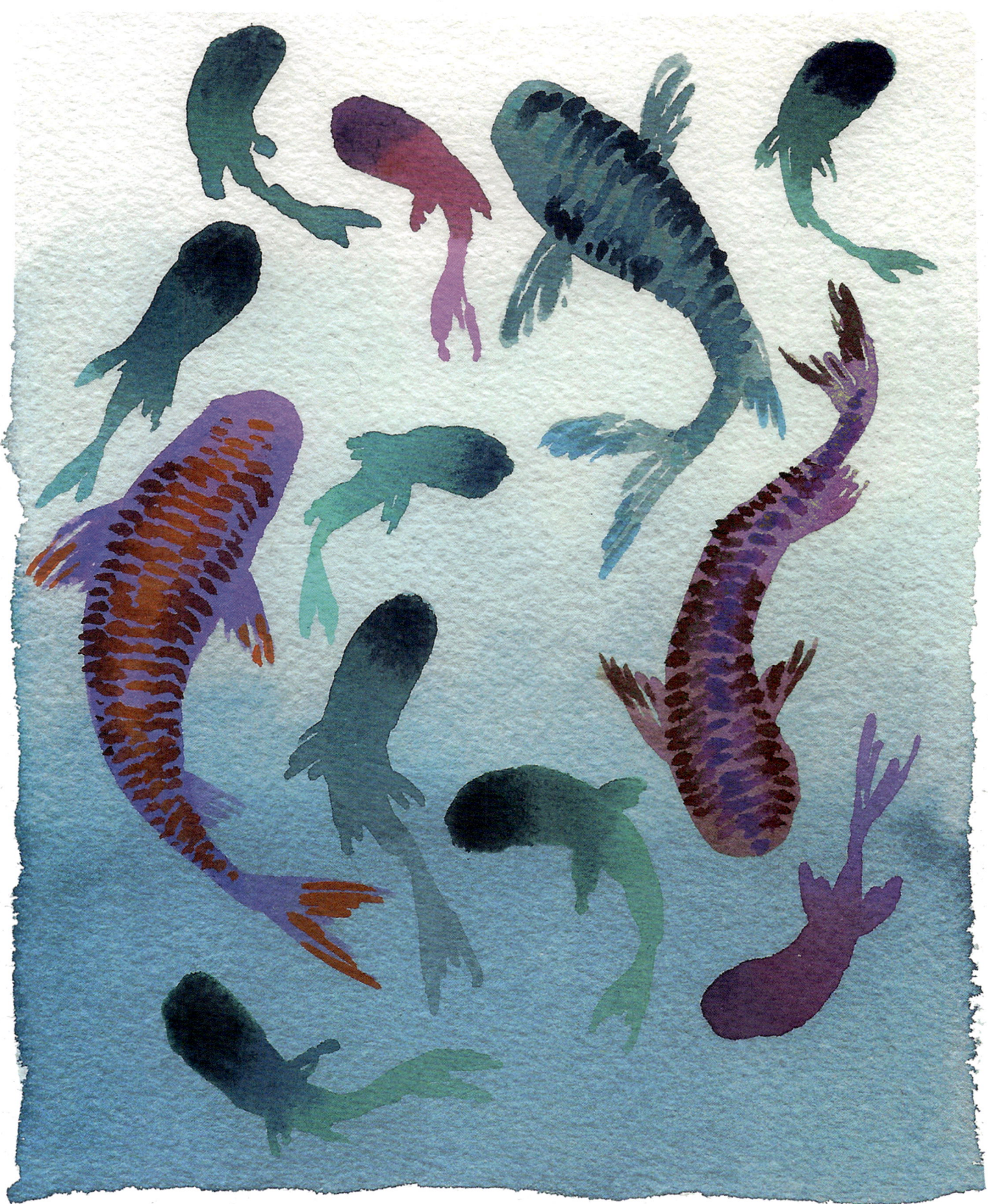

Week 14

Gradation on Dry Paper, Part 1

Decide on the two colors between which to make the gradation. Prepare the color pools quite diluted in the wells in your watercolor box: the yellow, the turquoise, and a third one—the transition, which is a mixture of the first two colors.

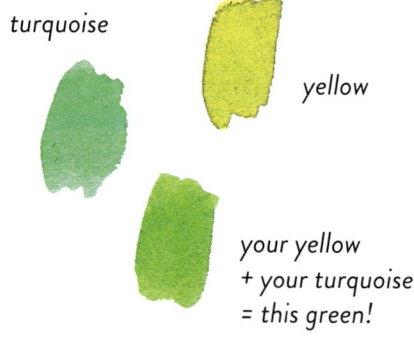

turquoise

yellow

your yellow + your turquoise = this green!

Place your first color.

Place the last color in the same way, always before the color dries.

Before it dries, rinse the brush, soak it in your transition color, and start the gradation by picking up the drop of the preceding color on the point of the brush. This avoids demarcations, and the transition is very soft.

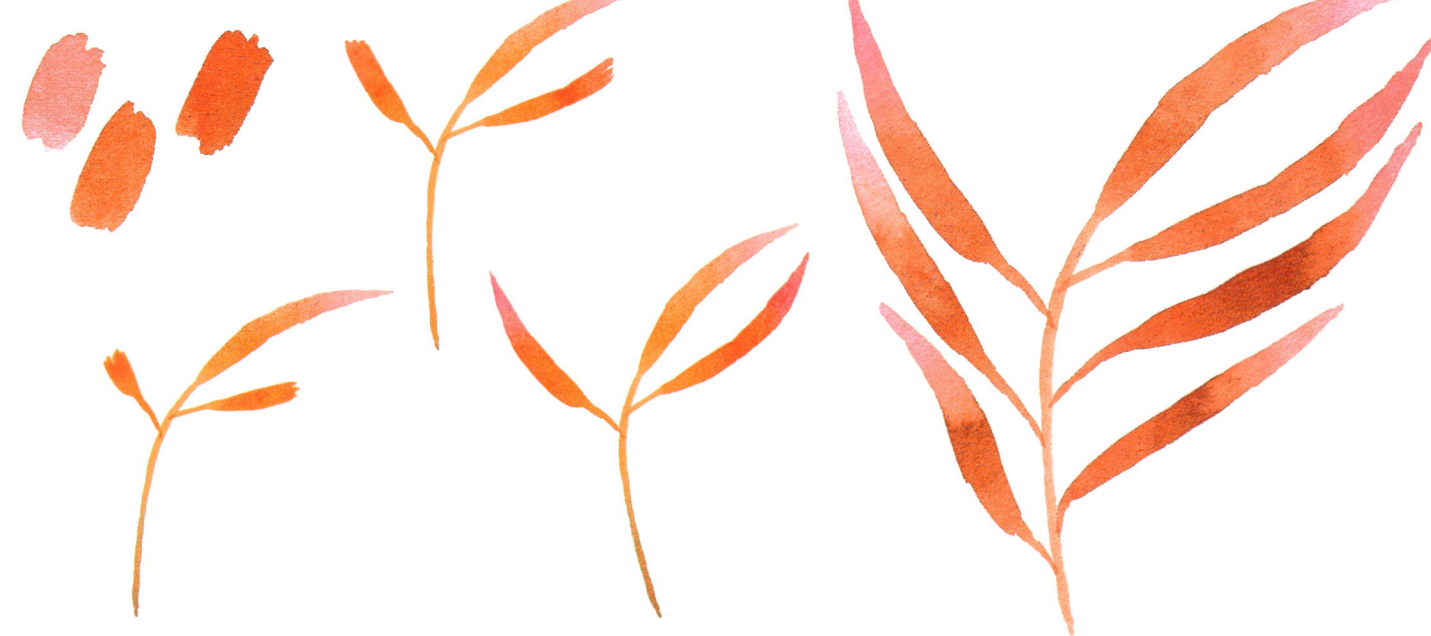

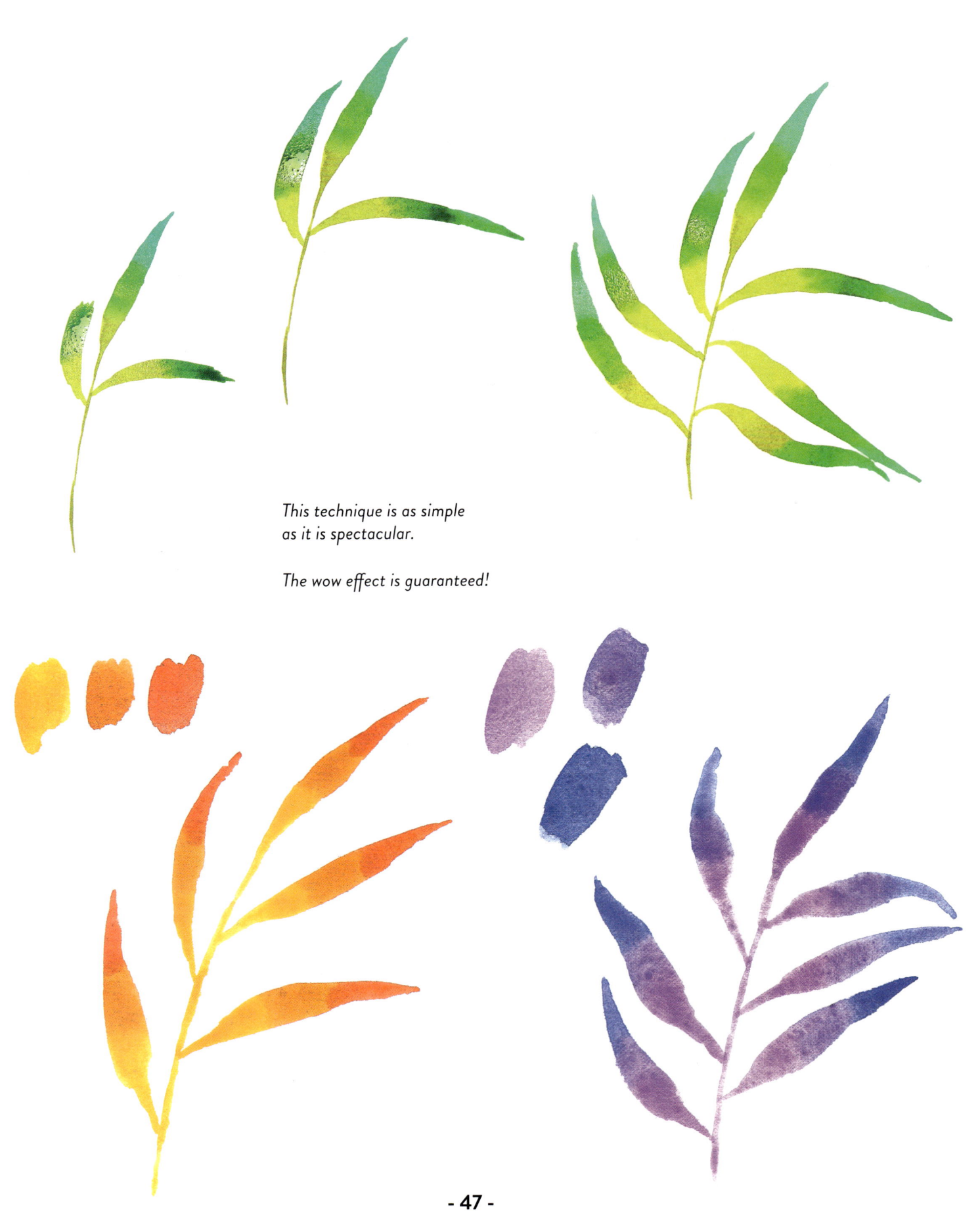

This technique is as simple
as it is spectacular.

The wow effect is guaranteed!

Week 15
Gradation on Dry Paper, Part 2

Let's continue practicing gradations!
Prepare your colors for the beaks
of these flamboyant toucans.
Start painting a beak.

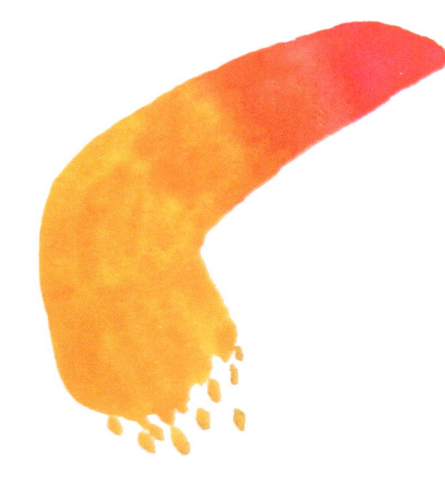

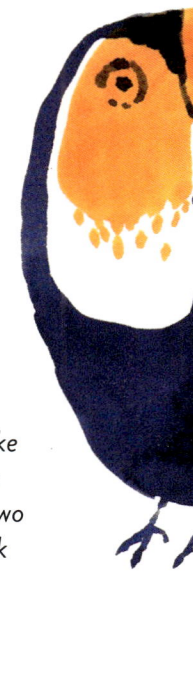

Once each bird's beak is dry, a stroke
of dark blue or somber violet makes
the bird's body appear, along with two
feet, a simple eye, and the little dark
spot at the end of the beak.

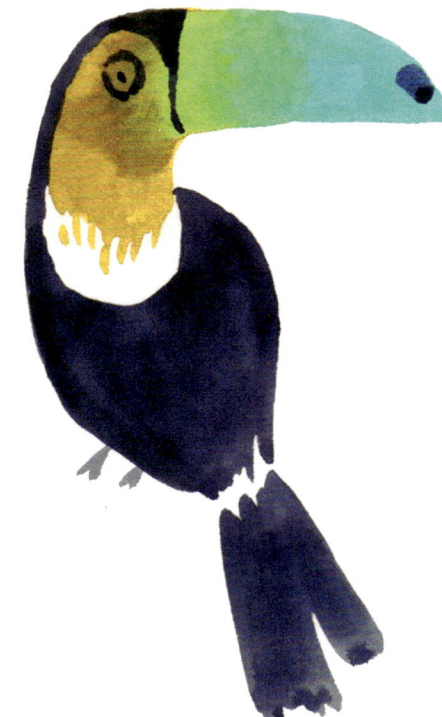

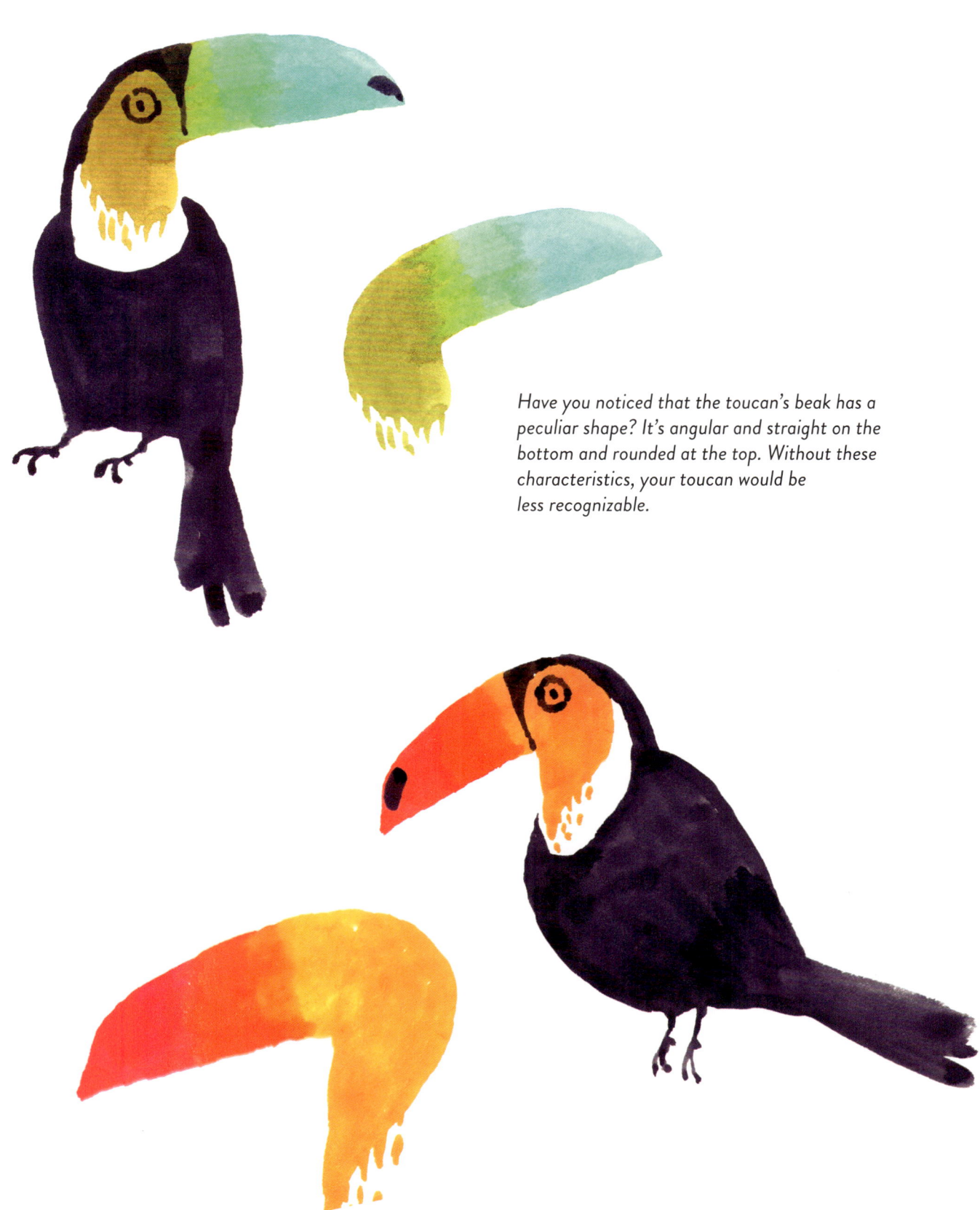

Have you noticed that the toucan's beak has a peculiar shape? It's angular and straight on the bottom and rounded at the top. Without these characteristics, your toucan would be less recognizable.

For More Practice

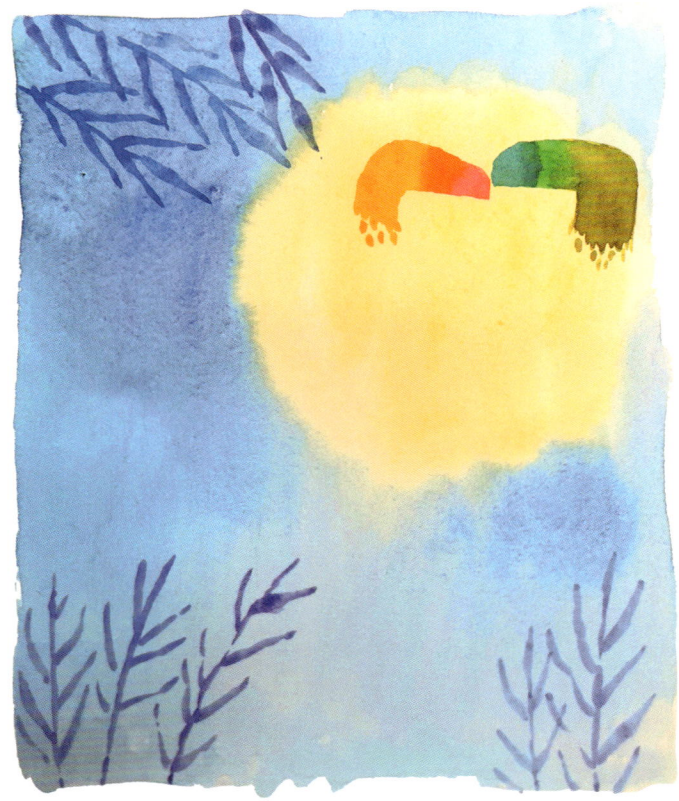

To illustrate this tropical scene, wet the paper. Cover the sheet with a light blue paint mix, leaving a circular shape blank. Place yellow paint mix in the circle before everything dries. Let it dry before painting some bluish palm fronds and the beaks of the toucan lovers.

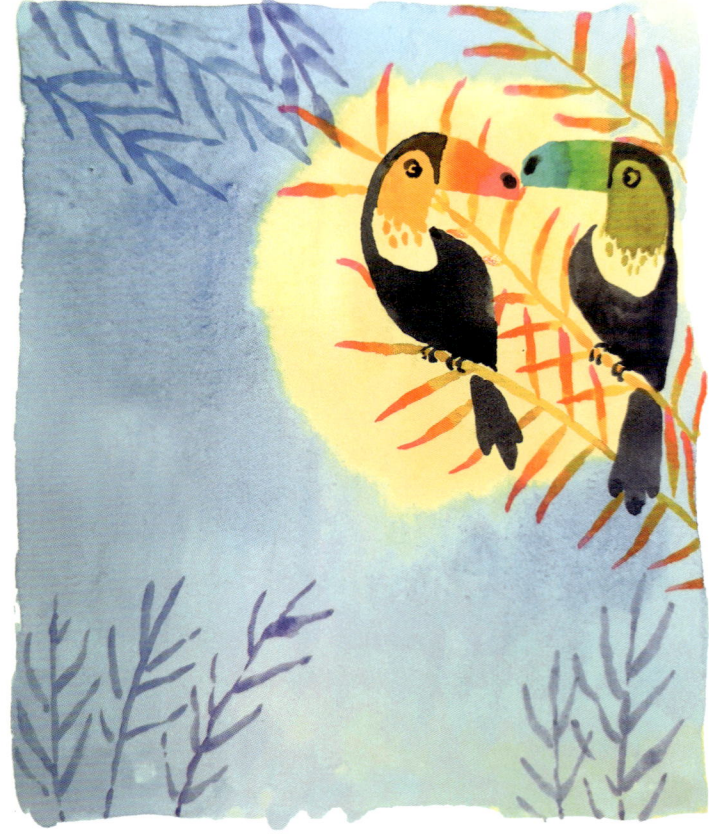

Paint the bodies of the toucans on the very dry background, perched on palm fronds that are painted with gradation.

Paint larger and darker palm fronds around the toucans, to complete their love nest!

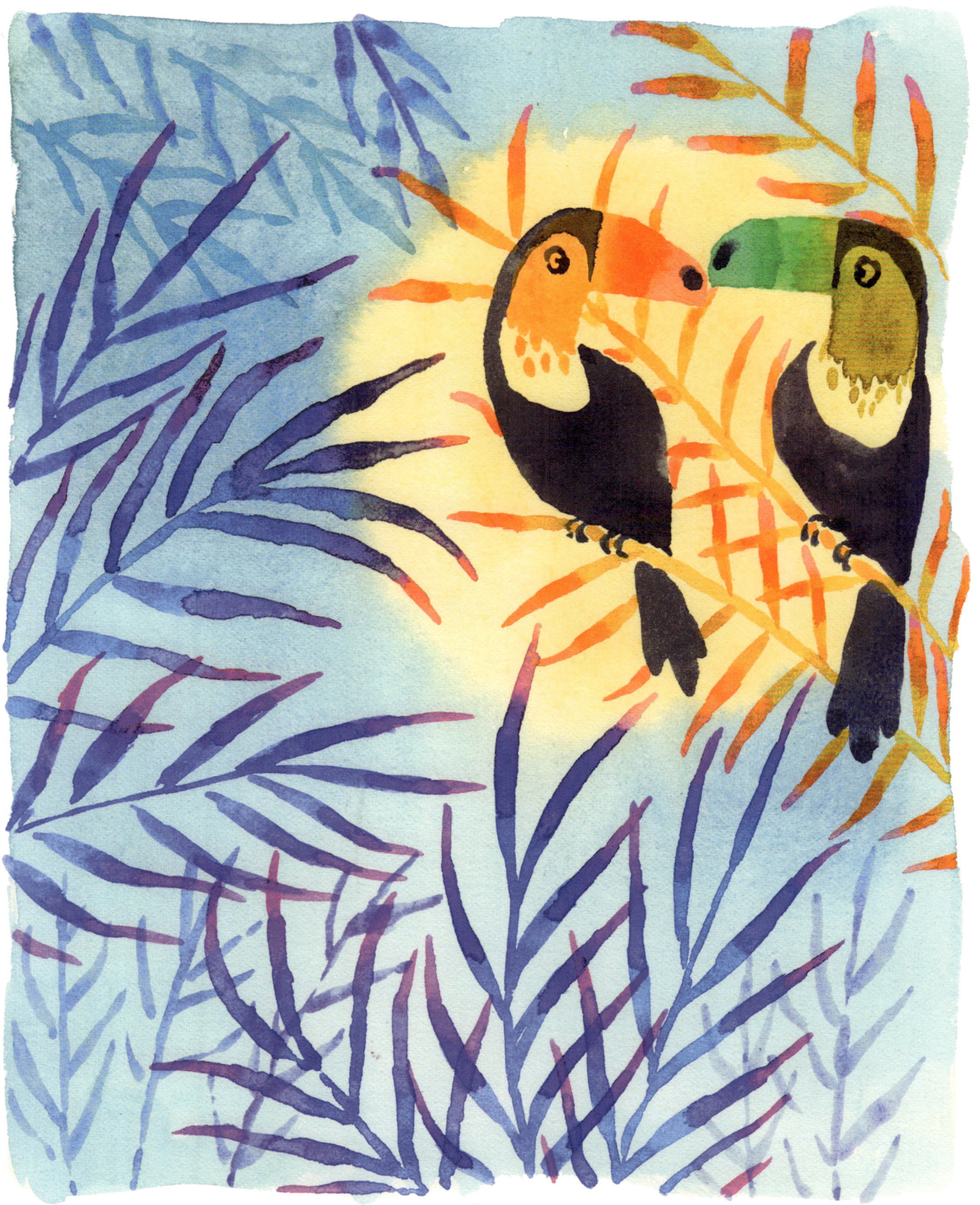

Week 16

Creating Depth with Blurriness and Sharpness

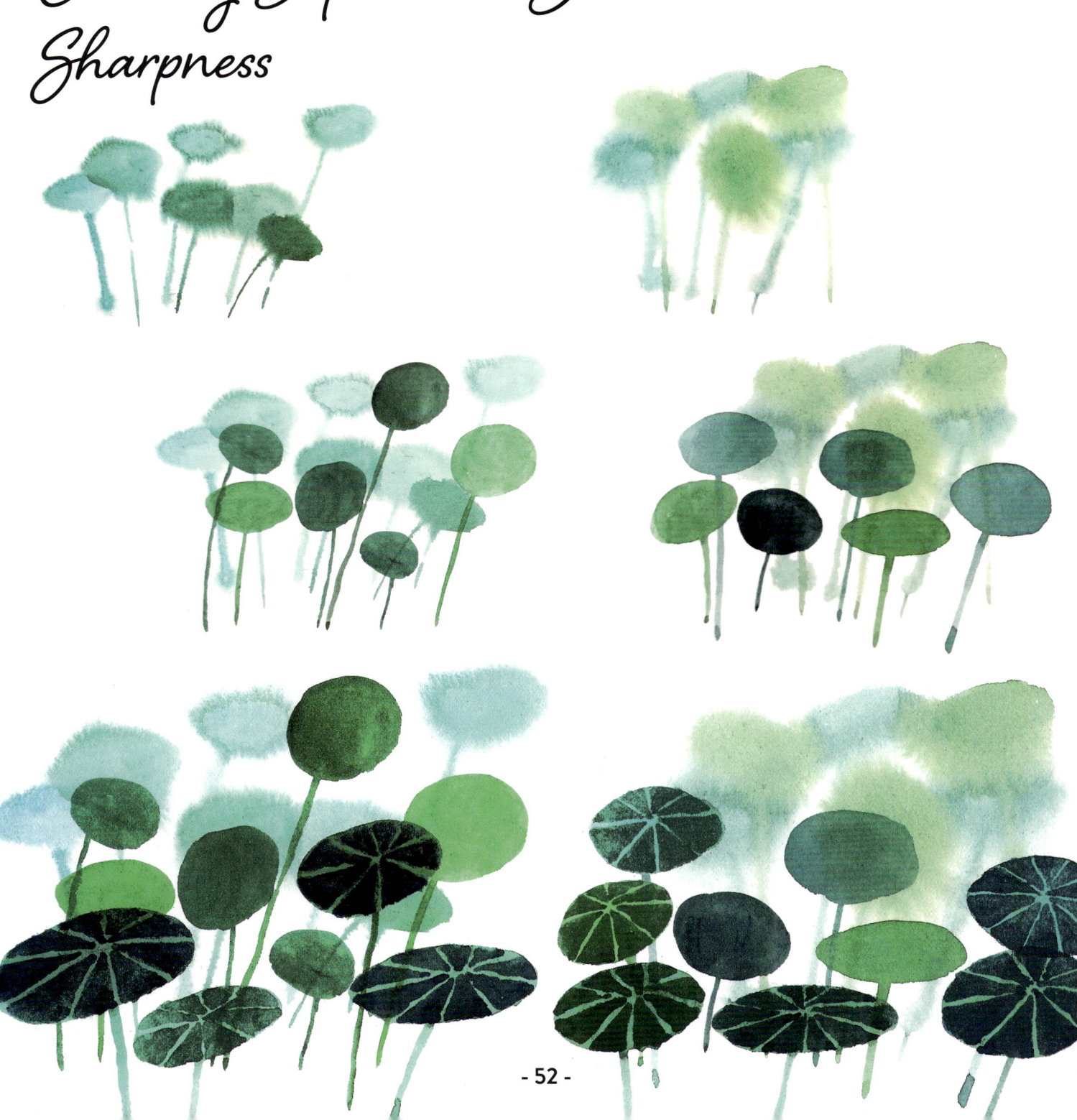

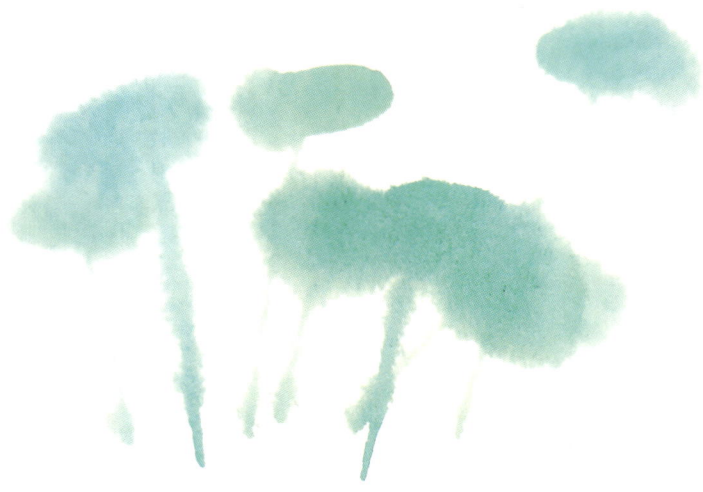

There's nothing better than playing with blurriness and sharpness to lend depth to a composition! Wet the paper to draw the first water lilies, with a diluted paint mix.

Once the first row of water lilies dries, paint the next one, in a darker color and on dry paper. They are quite sharp, and they appear to be closer.

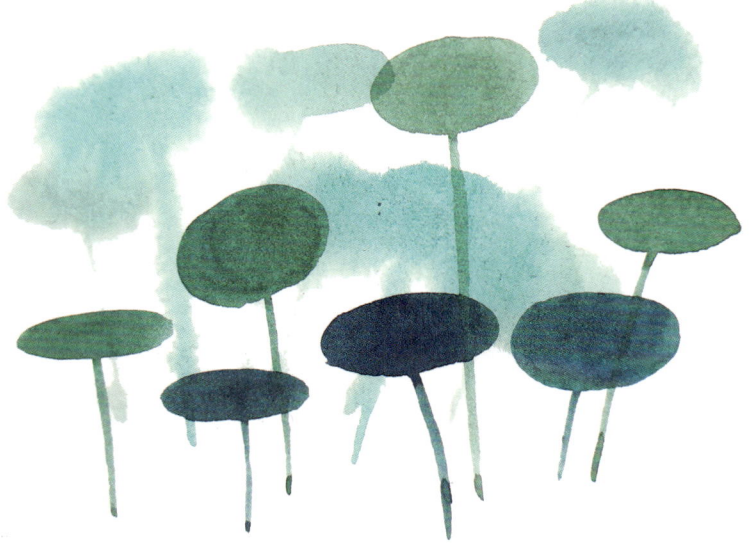

Finish with the water lilies closest to you. They are very contrasted: drawn with a diluted and lively paint mix, but accentuated with a dark paint mix.

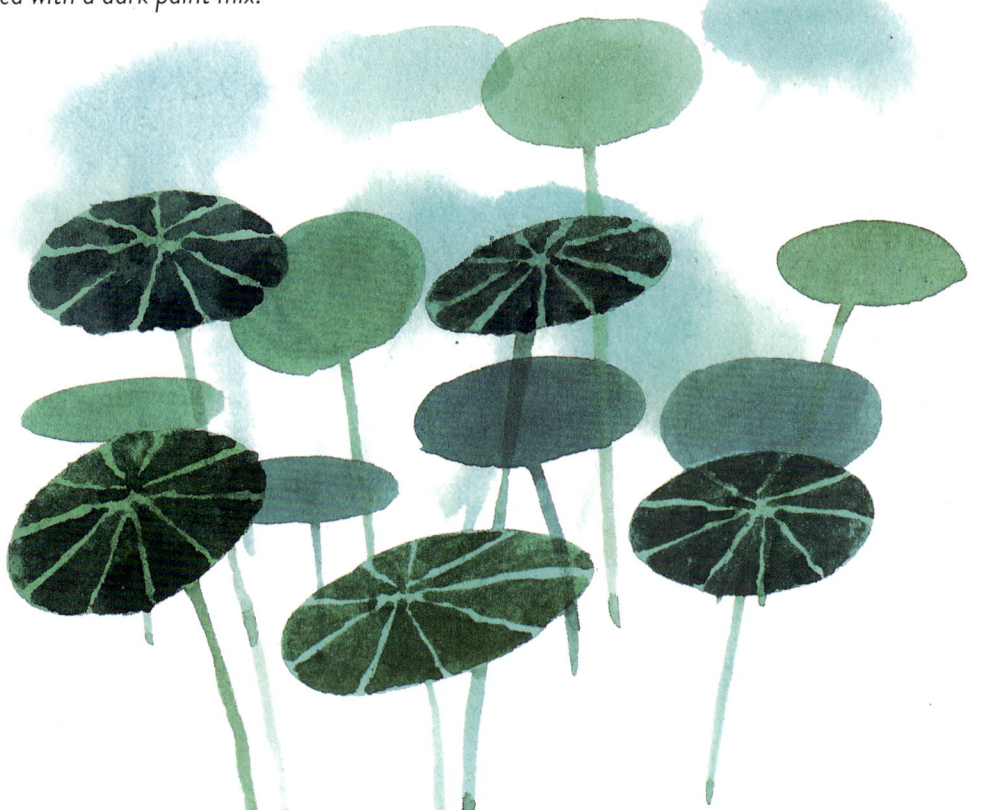

Week 17
—
Creating Depth with Contrasting Harmonies

Let's continue our pursuit of depth! To push an element toward the background, it must present a soft color harmony. To bring an element to the foreground, it must be bold and contrasted.

Paint the plant in the background with a pale pink paint mix. Don't wait for it to dry before adding some strokes of pale purple. The color harmony is soft and blurry.

The plant in the foreground is painted with a bright pink. The addition of strokes of dark blue offers an even stronger contrast since they are drawn on dry paper. Therefore, they are quite sharp.

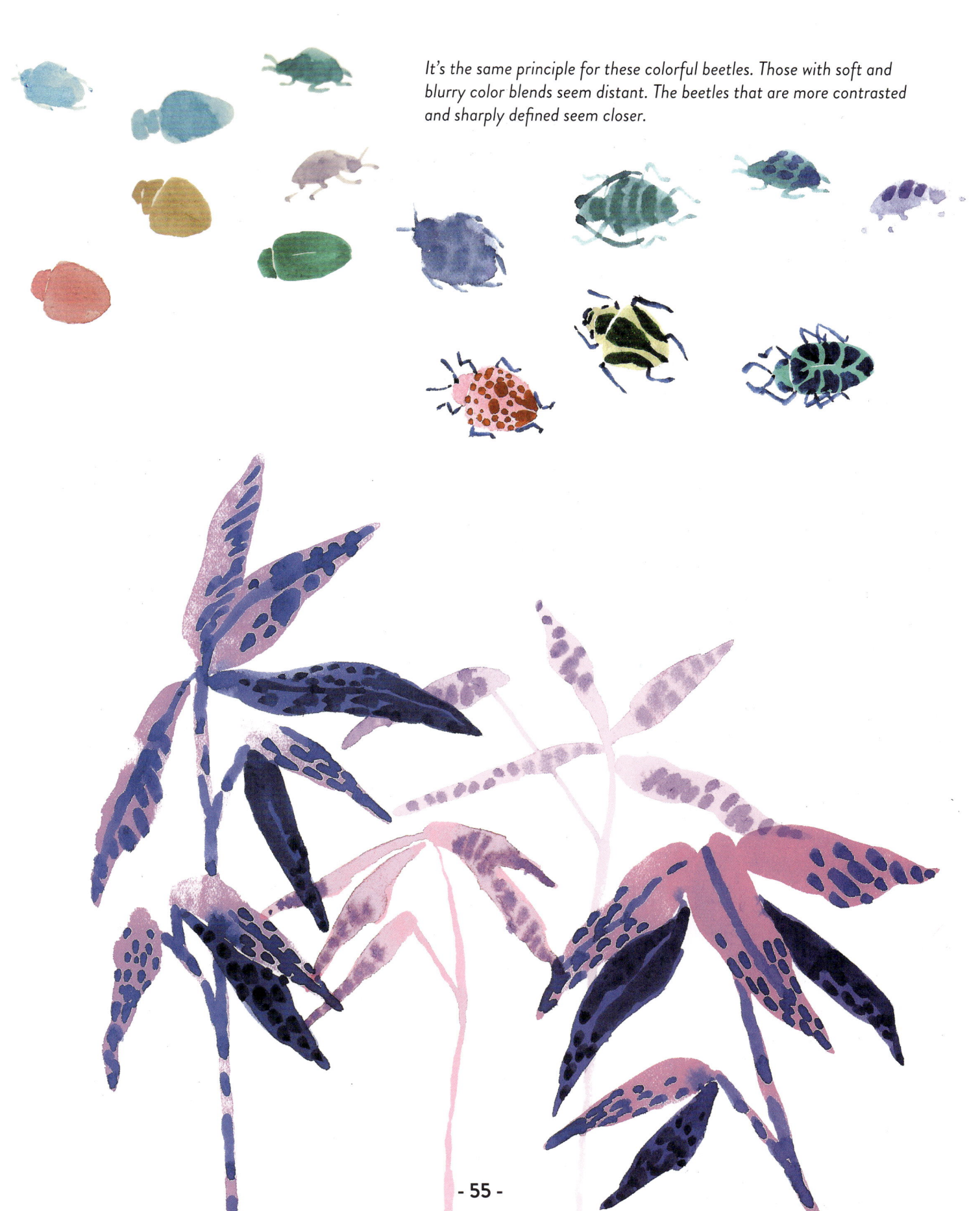

It's the same principle for these colorful beetles. Those with soft and blurry color blends seem distant. The beetles that are more contrasted and sharply defined seem closer.

For More Practice

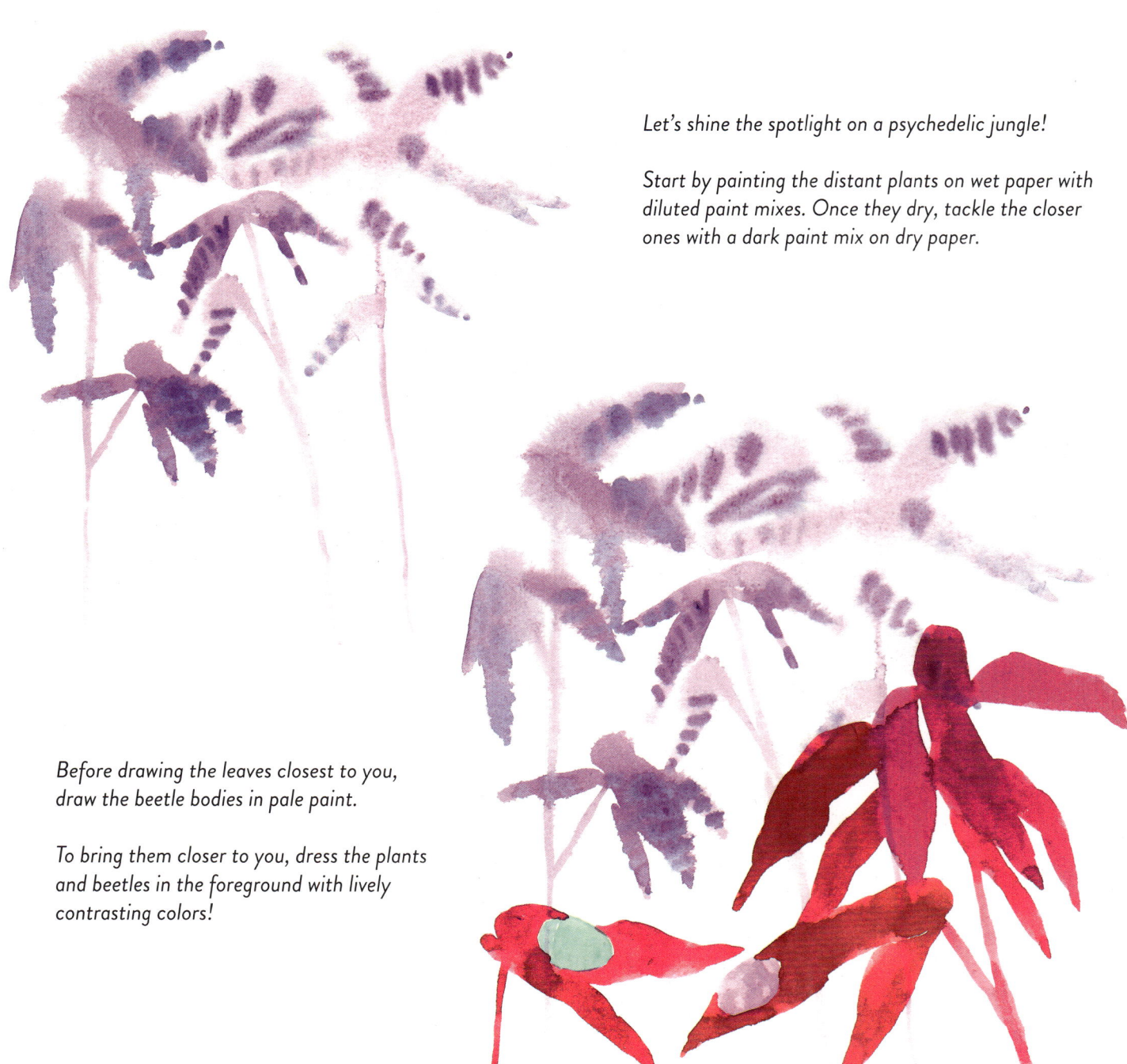

Let's shine the spotlight on a psychedelic jungle!

Start by painting the distant plants on wet paper with diluted paint mixes. Once they dry, tackle the closer ones with a dark paint mix on dry paper.

Before drawing the leaves closest to you, draw the beetle bodies in pale paint.

To bring them closer to you, dress the plants and beetles in the foreground with lively contrasting colors!

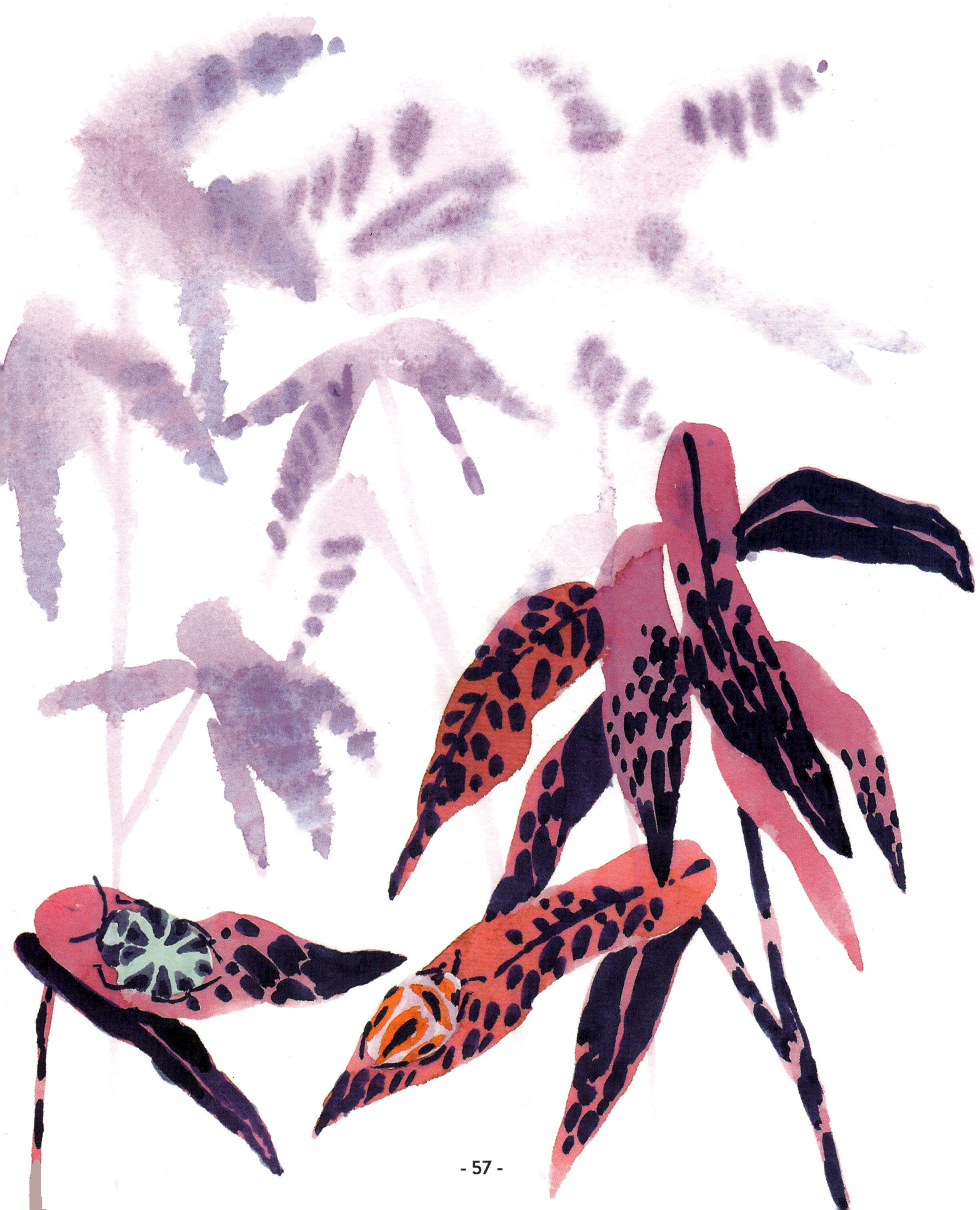

Week 18
Creating a Luminous Atmosphere on Wet Paper, Part 1

Alert! Alert! This is the most important technique in the book. This is the one that counts the most. Impressive effect guaranteed!

To create a luminous atmosphere—or simply an ambience—in your paintings, wet the paper with a diluted color. Then paint the large, colored masses, defined by light and shadow, on the wet paper.

Once the background is dry, paint the elements of your composition. Like magic, your watercolor has an atmosphere!

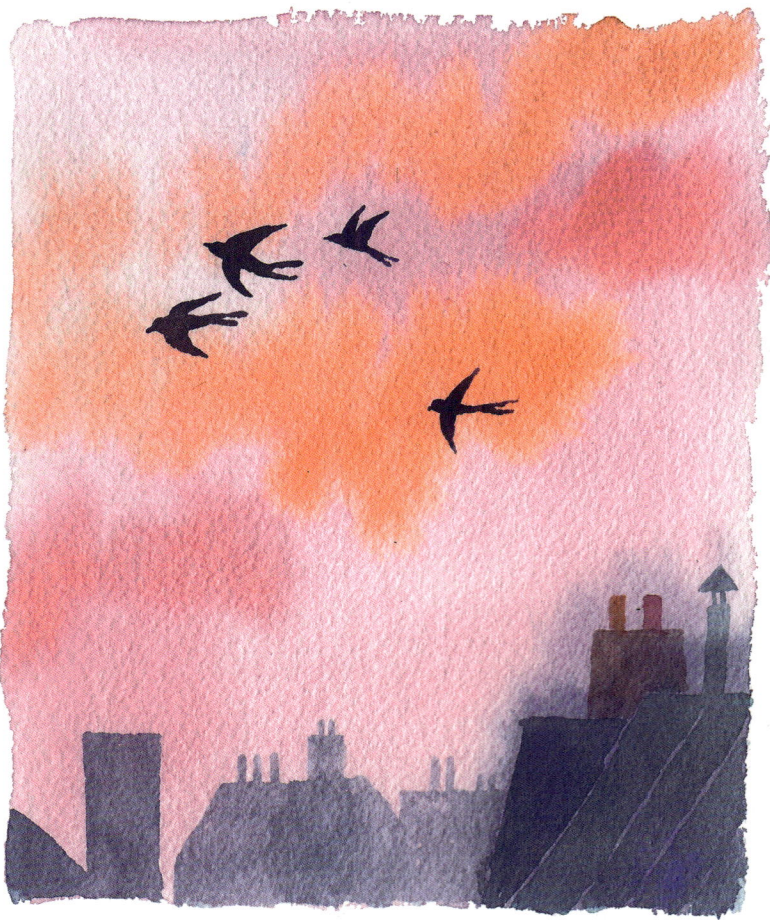

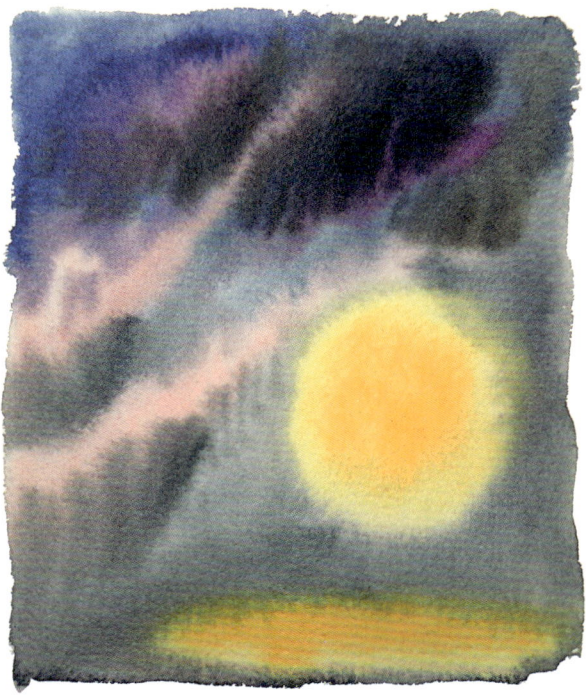

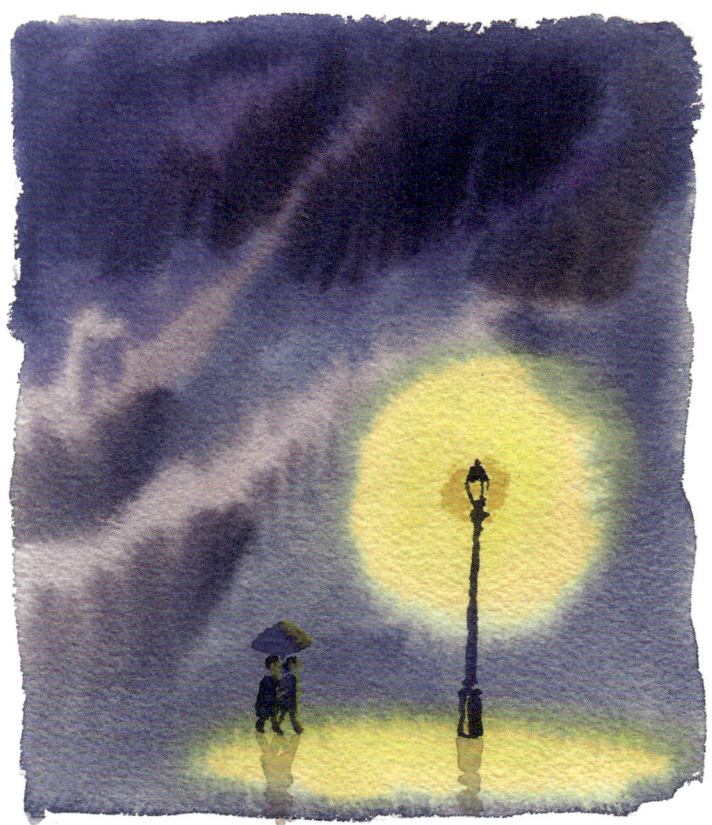

Wait until the background is dry to draw the dark and well-defined elements.

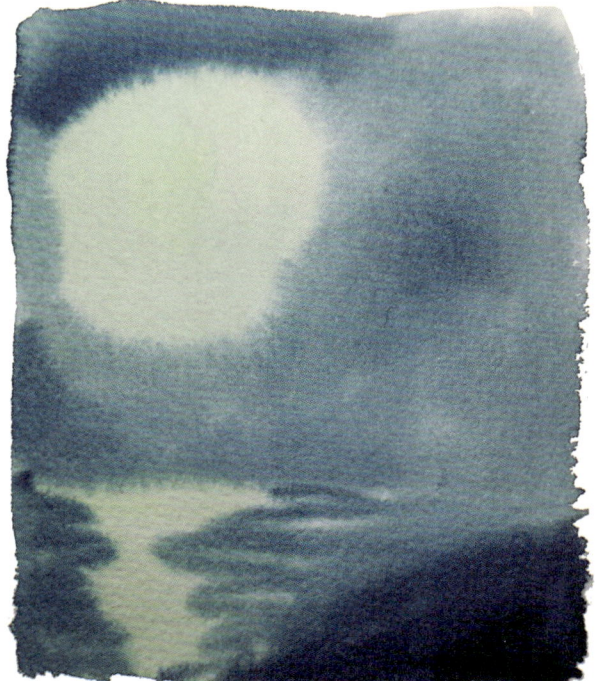

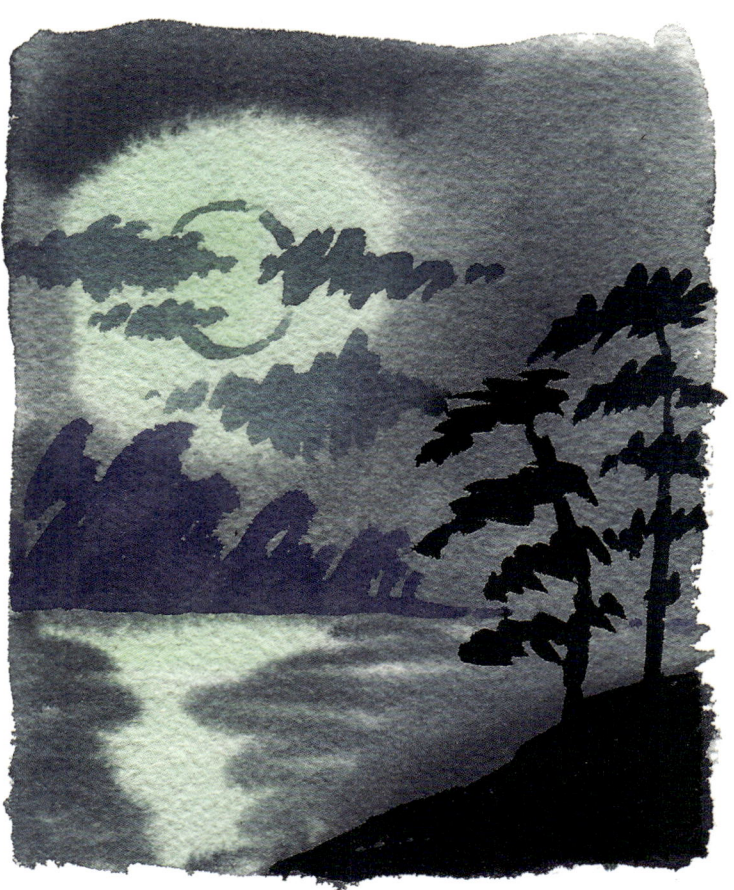

Practice painting different backgrounds on wet paper: sunset, stormy or rainy sky, moonlight, etc.

Week 19
Creating a Luminous Atmosphere on Wet Paper, Part 2

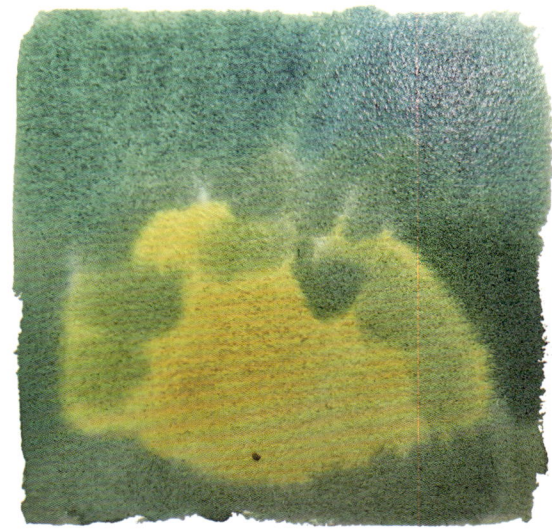

Let's make my favorite technique a bit more complex!

To create a luminous atmosphere, paint the large masses of colors, of light and shadow, on very wet paper.

When the paper is less wet, but still damp, refine the large masses. Continue painting to make the shapes and colors more precise.

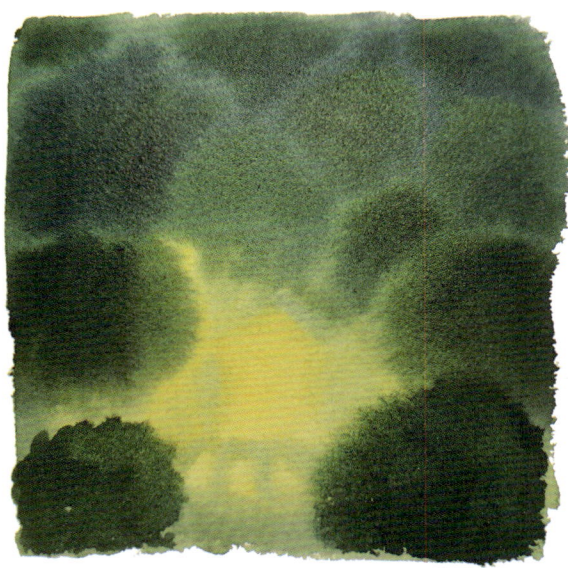

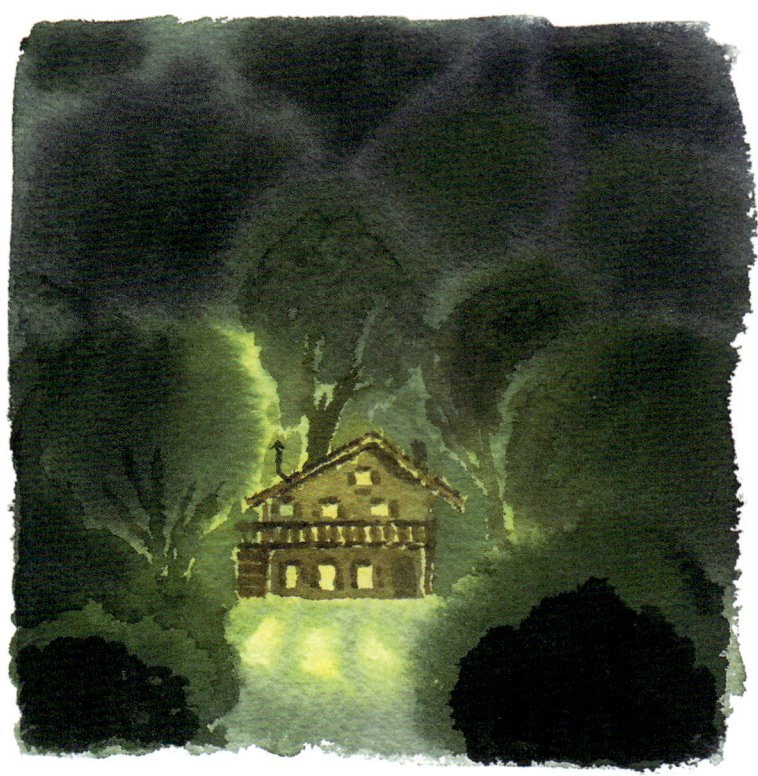

Once everything is dry, draw the sharp details and the darker elements. And here is a little house that lights up a mysterious forest!

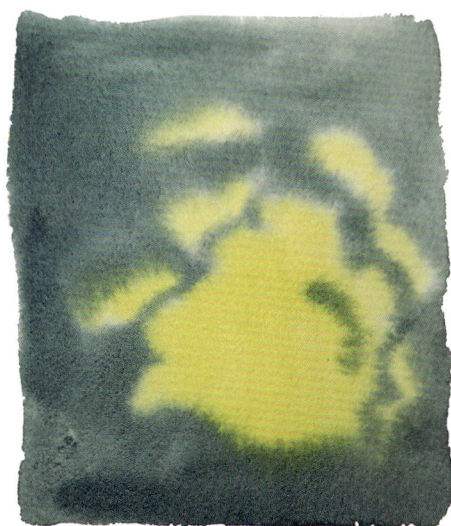

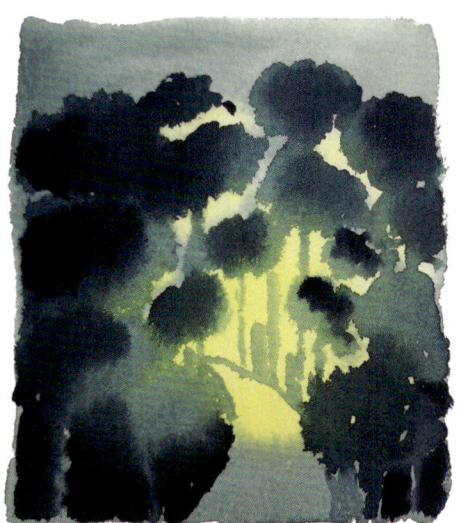

This technique is my favorite because it gives life to all the luminous atmospheres, whether it is the halo of the headlights in the dark or the glow of an open refrigerator in the night!

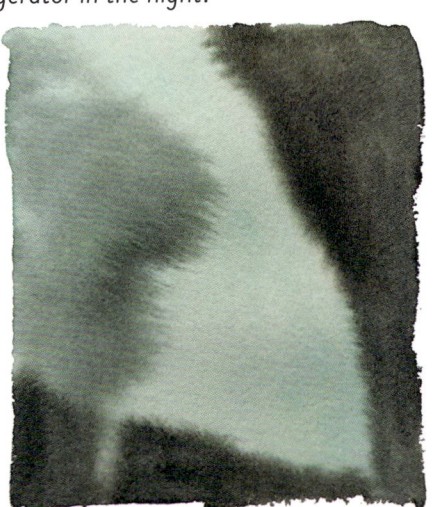

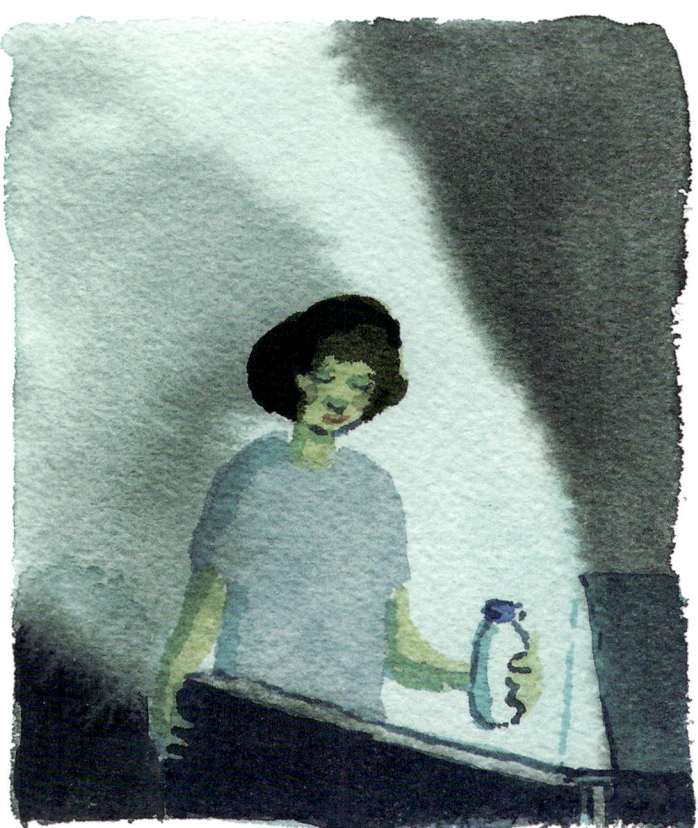

For More Practice

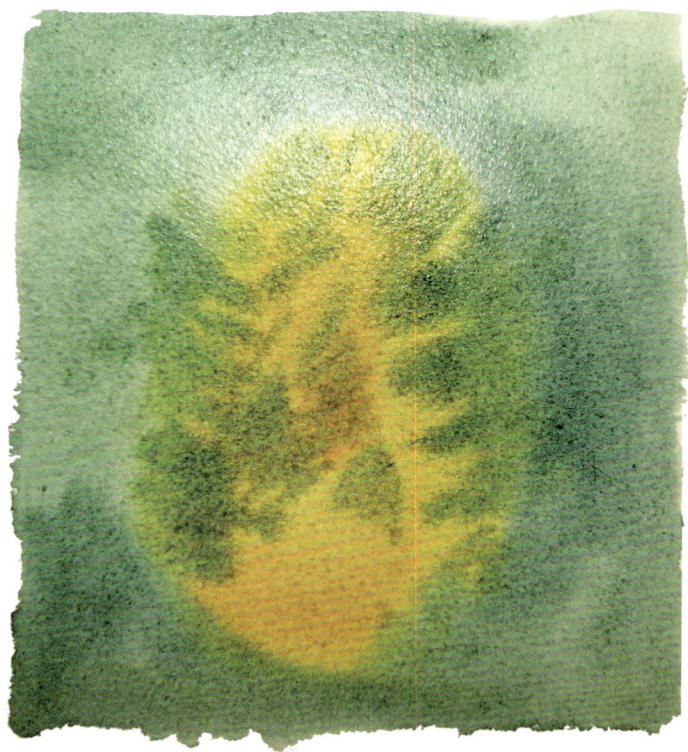

Wet the paper. Then paint a large mass of golden yellow and lots of green for the fir trees.

While the background is still moist but less wet, sketch the silhouettes of the fir trees in dark green and some branches of conifers that come in to "lick" the yellow halo.

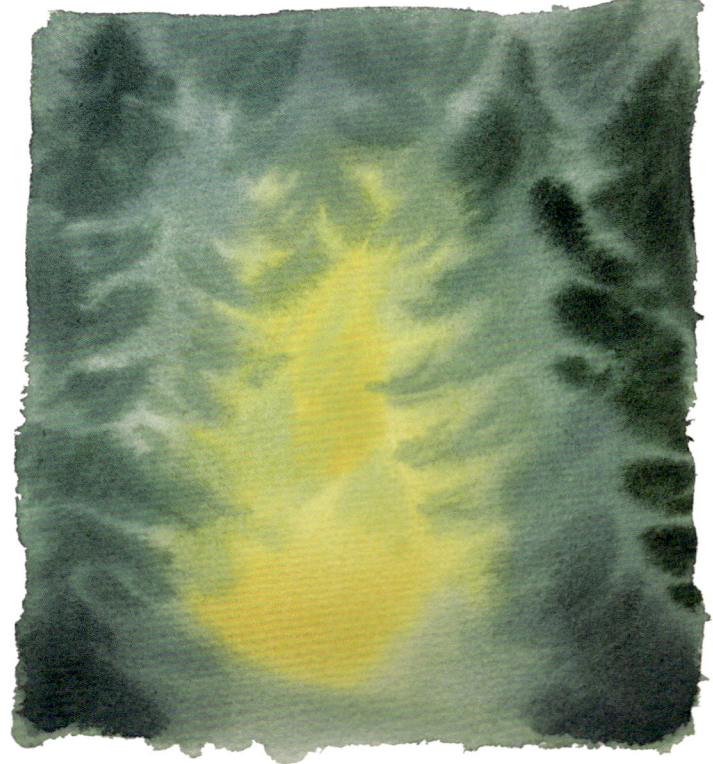

Once the background is totally dry, it's time for the details: the conifers that surround the reddening campfire, some yellow reflections in the branches, the campers and their tent, the fir trees, dark and well-defined in front.

To breathe life into a composition in chiaroscuro, I swear by this technique—and this technique only!

Do you feel the heat of this campfire?

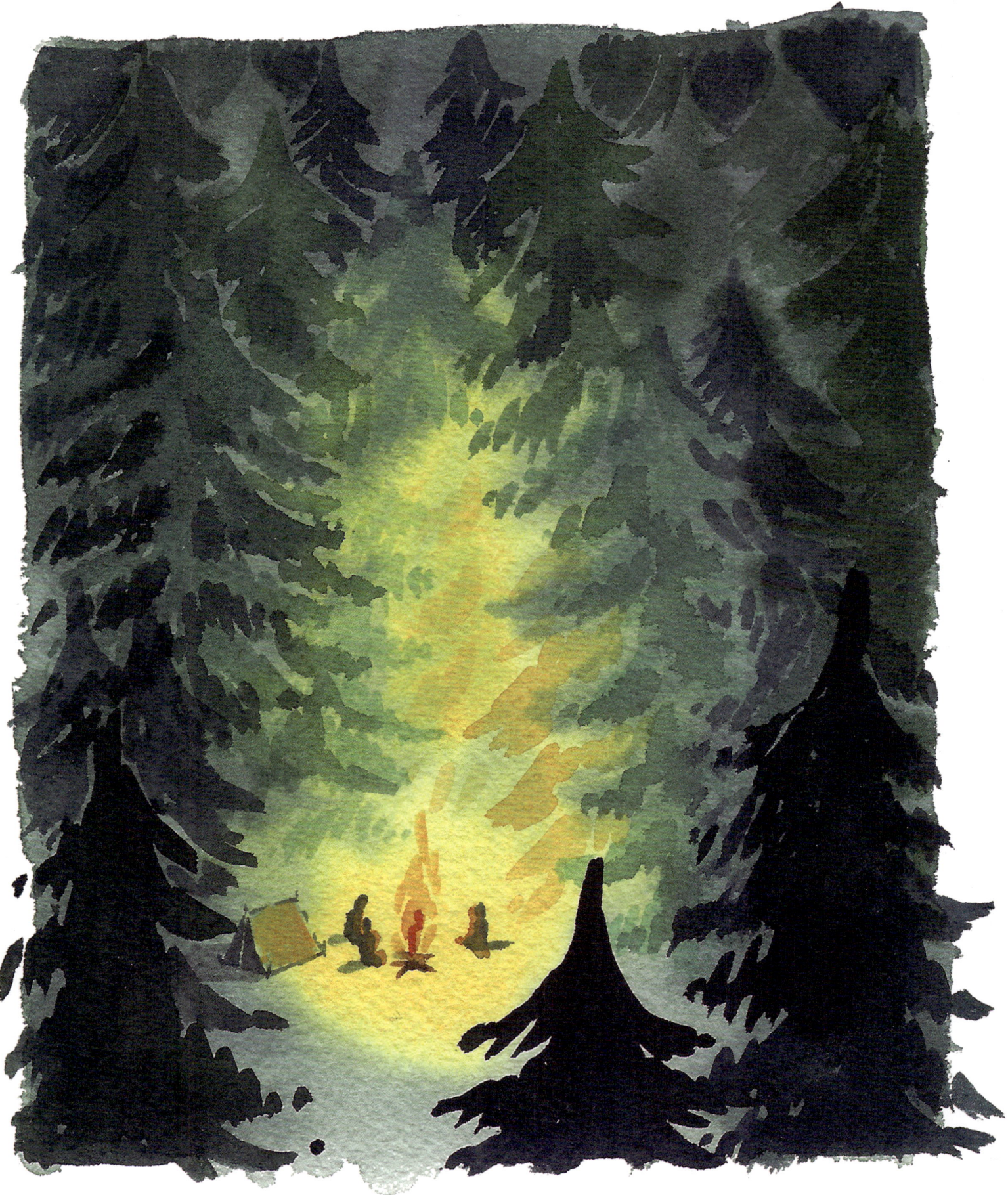

Week 20

Defining Depth by Light and Dark

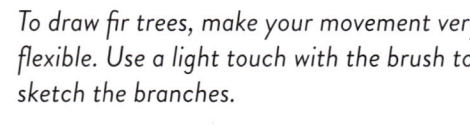

To draw fir trees, make your movement very flexible. Use a light touch with the brush to sketch the branches.

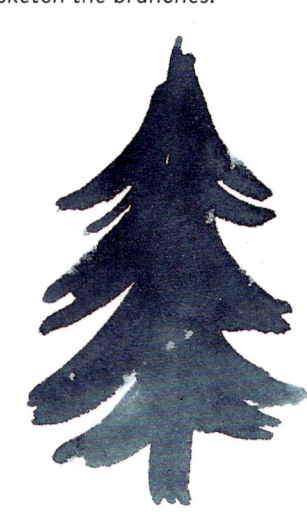

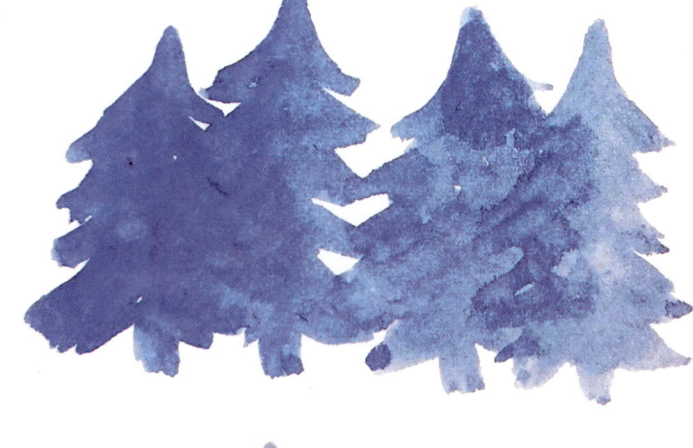

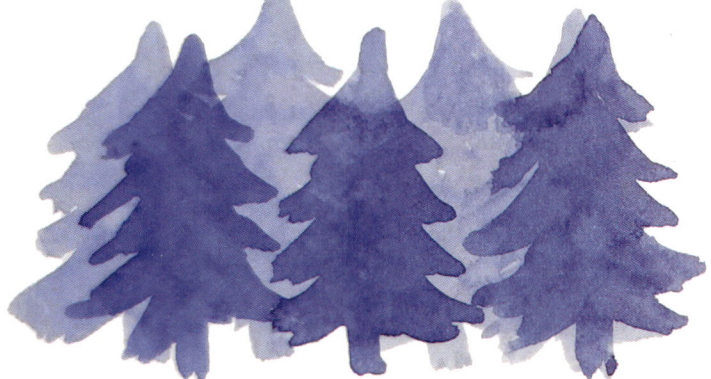

To give depth to the composition, go from the lightest (distant) to the darkest (close).

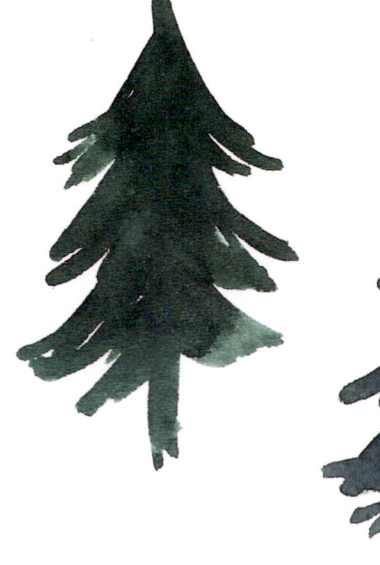

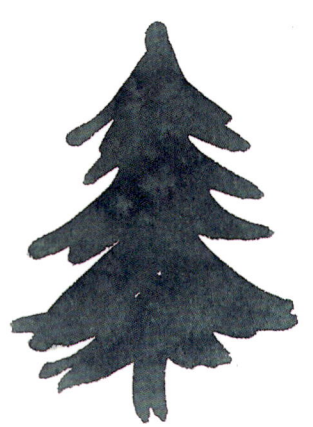

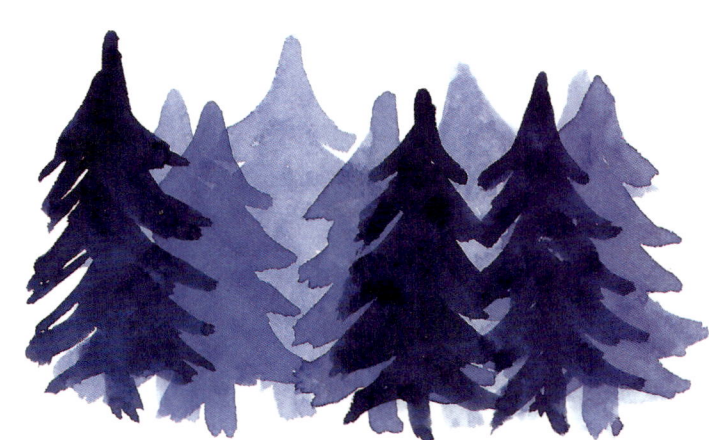

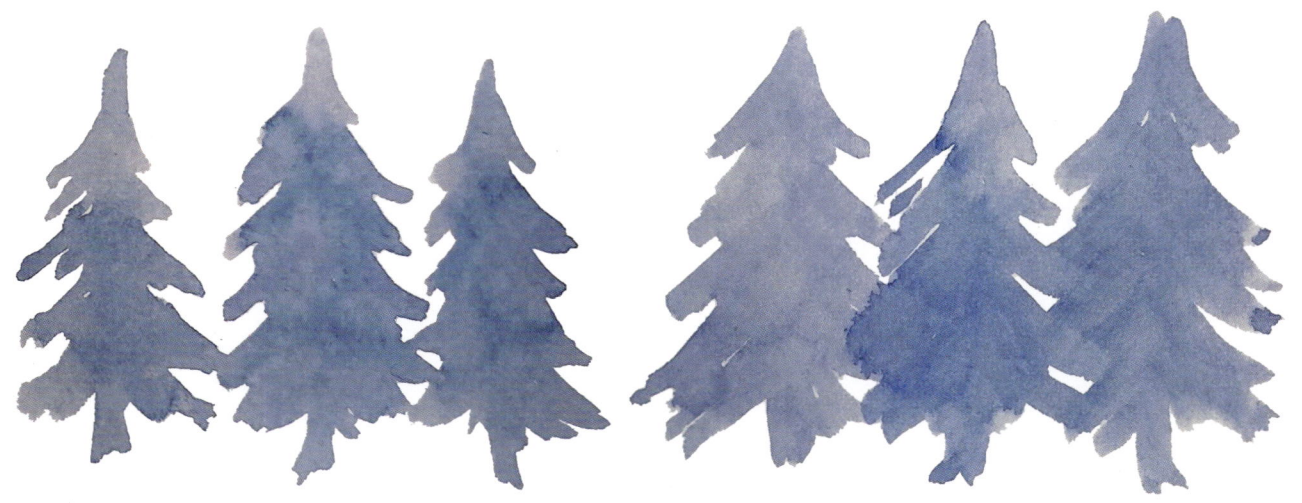

To lighten the elements in the distance, add pure water to your paint mix. Dilute it.

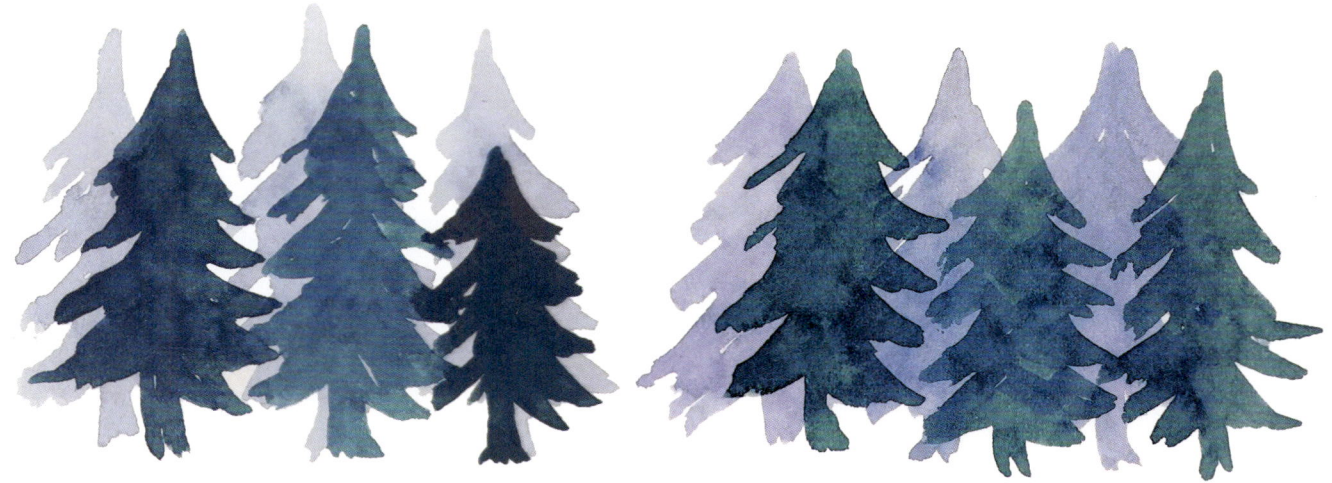

The distant elements tend to be more bluish. This is true for the fir trees as well. Add some blue to the diluted paint mix.

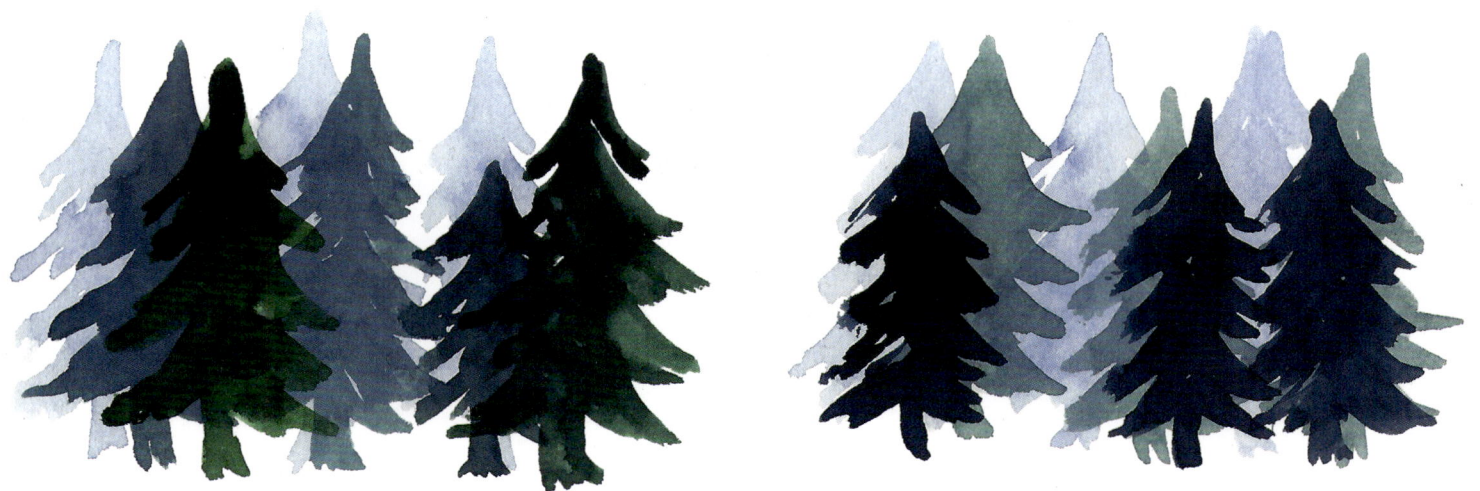

Week 21
Atmospheric Perspective

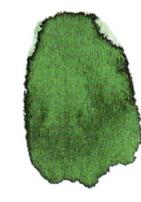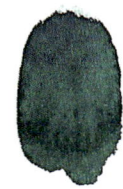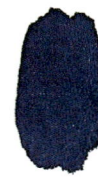

Prepare three paint mixes: the green of the mountain in the front, a blue for the most distant mountain, and a transitional paint mix between the green and the blue.

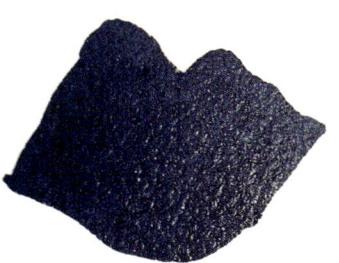

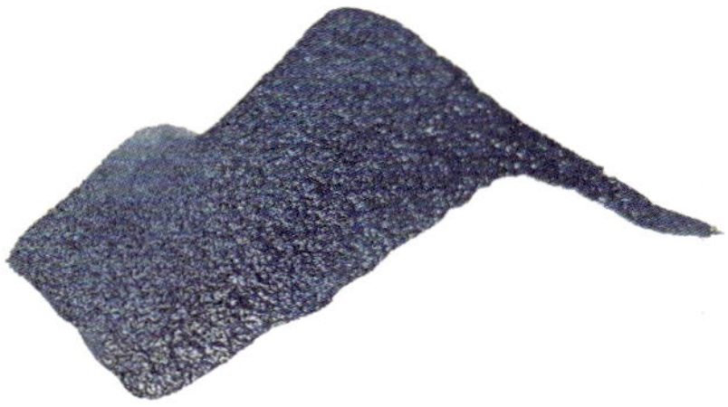

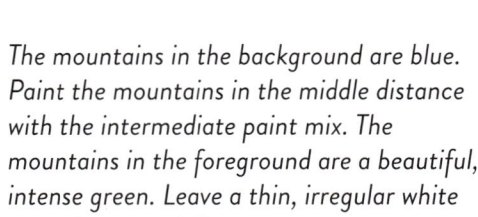

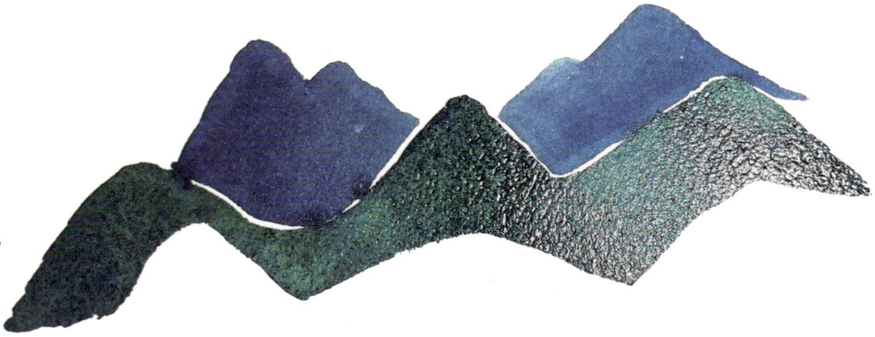

The mountains in the background are blue. Paint the mountains in the middle distance with the intermediate paint mix. The mountains in the foreground are a beautiful, intense green. Leave a thin, irregular white space between different mountain ranges. Don't worry whether each layer is dry.

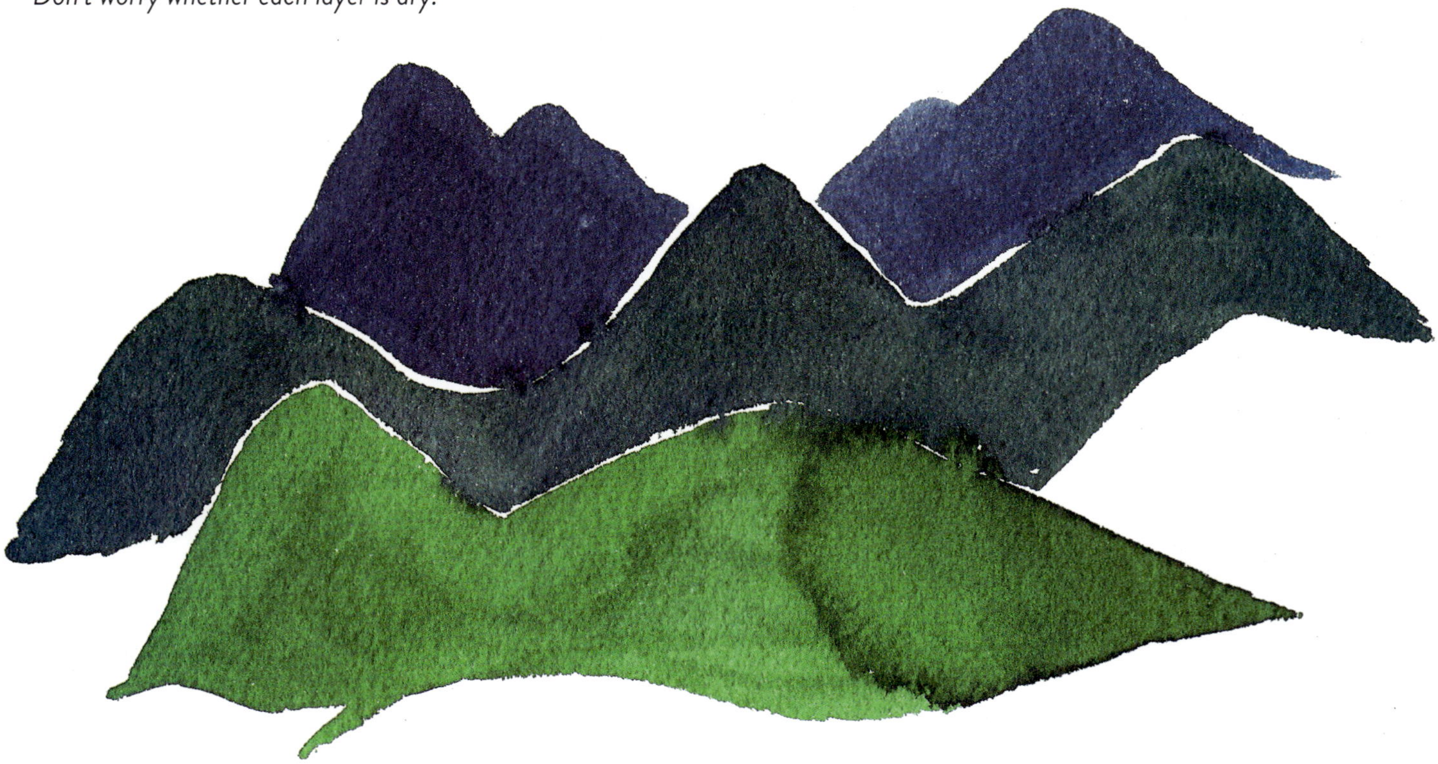

What makes distant objects take on a bluish hue? The atmospheric perspective! The more air there is between us and an object, the more it turns blue by this mass of oxygen that accumulates. Theorized by Leonardo da Vinci, this phenomenon is readily observable in the mountains.

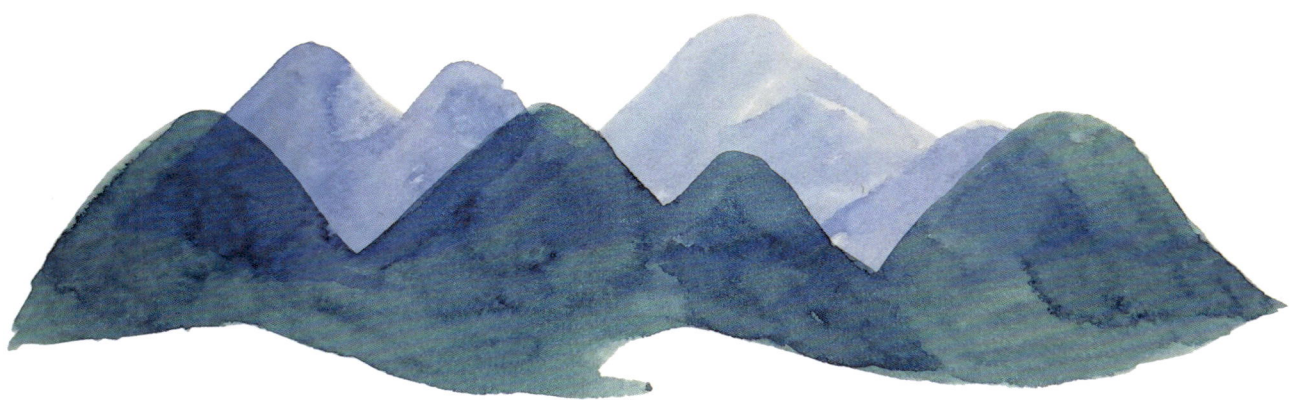

To give depth to your compositions, accentuate this effect.
Everything that is distant is bluish or definitively blue!

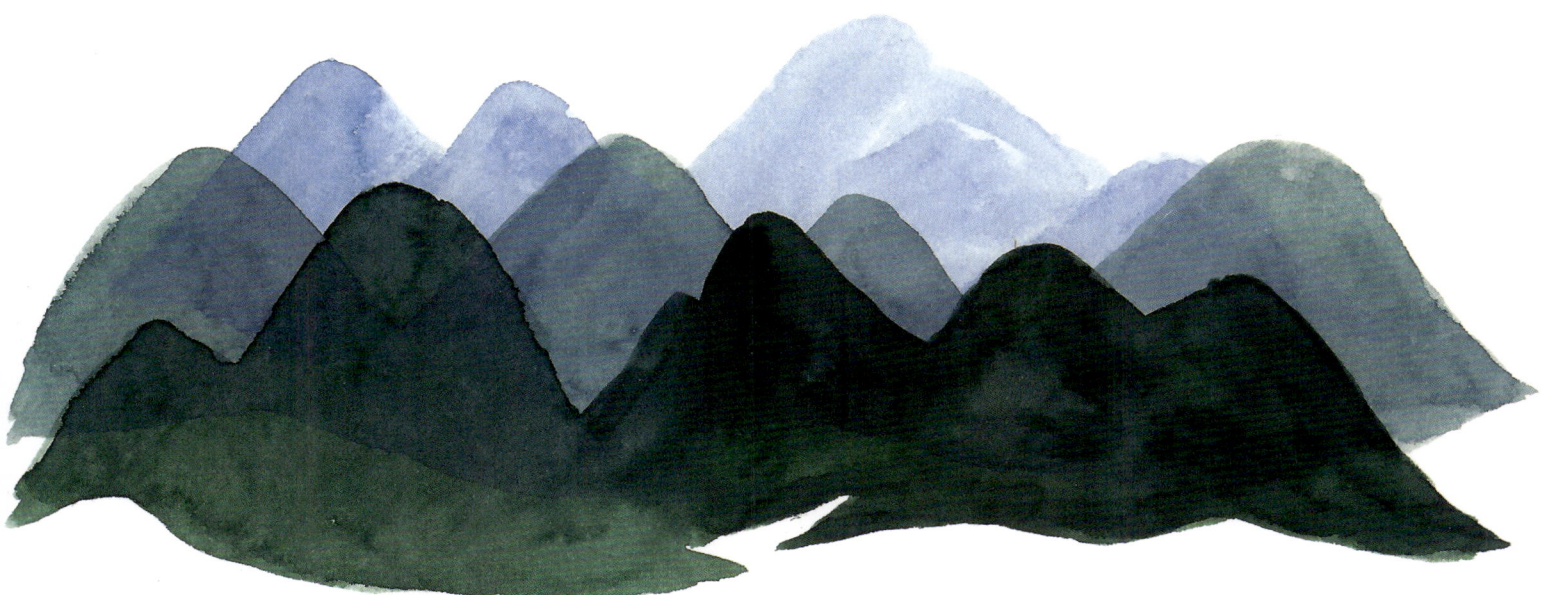

For More Practice

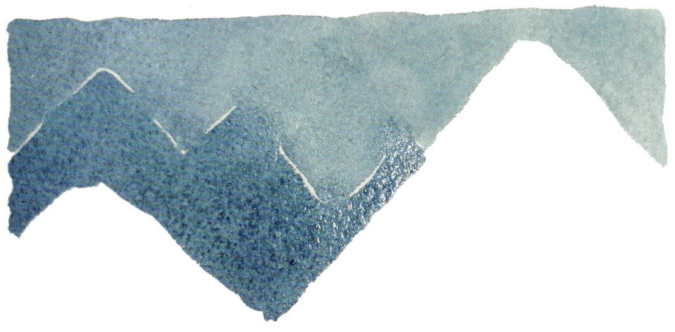

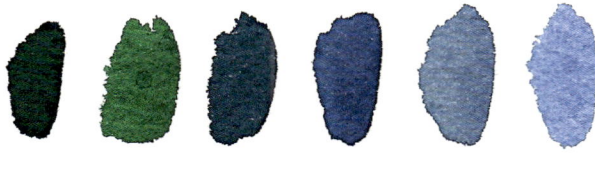

For this very oxygenated landscape, prepare the paint mixes—from dark green to bright green and then toward blue, from darker to lighter.

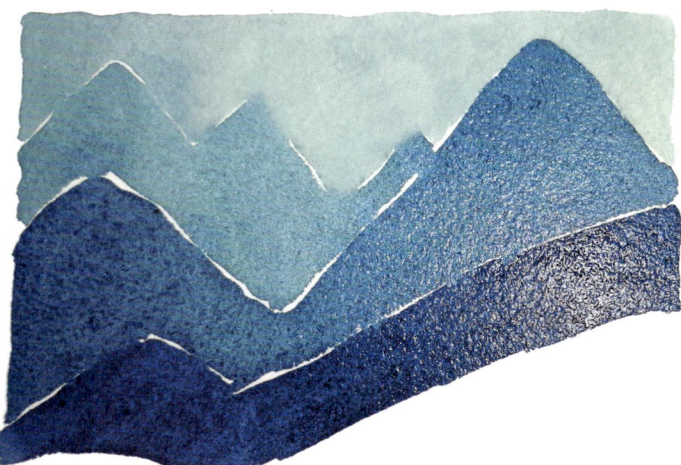

Between each mountain range, leave an irregular thin line of white. Don't worry whether each layer is dry. It is good for the colors to mix slightly.

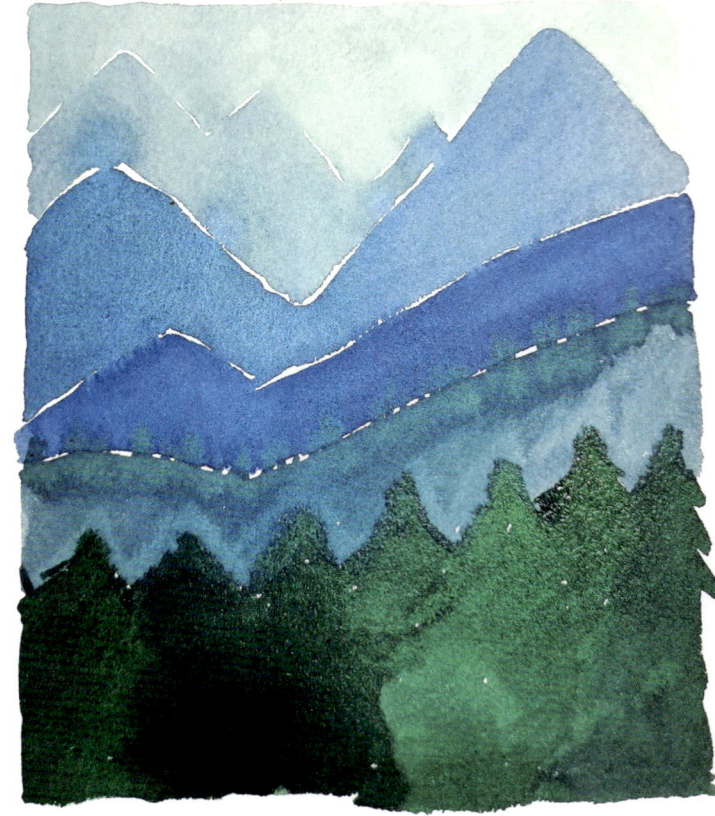

Finish with the fir trees in the foreground. They are very dark, drawn in the still damp but almost dry green.

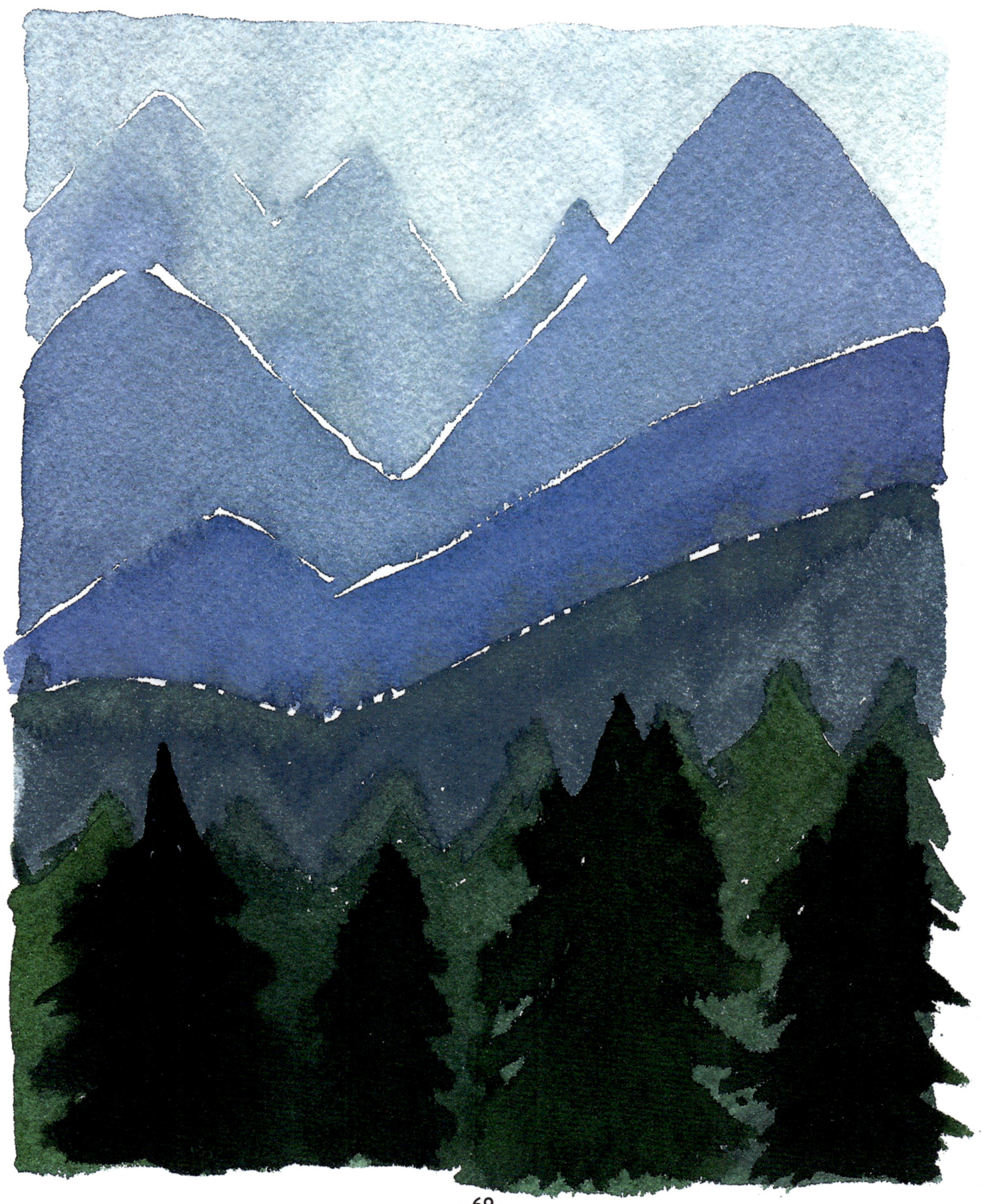

Week 22

Shadows with Blue

Without a shadow, an element floats in empty space. To anchor an element to the ground, attach a shadow to it—as in Peter Pan! Just as my mother taught me when I was little, always paint the shadows in blue, as for this tree.

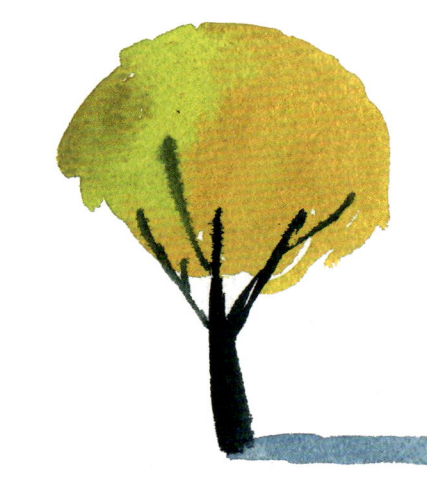

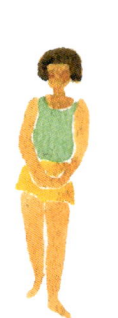
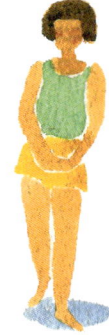
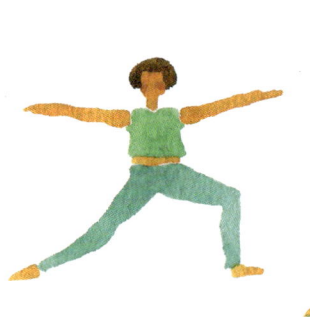
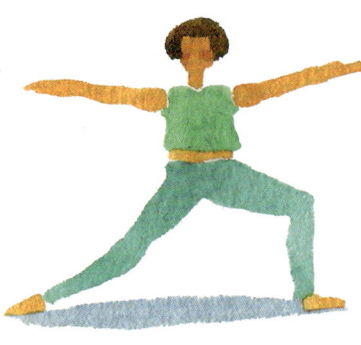
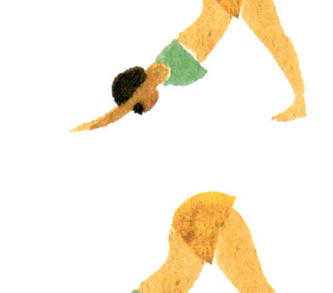

When the sun is high, above the yogi, the shadow is just under her. The shadow reproduces her volume, flattened under her. If the sun is low in the sky, it projects a shadow far away from the body that's deformed and lengthened.

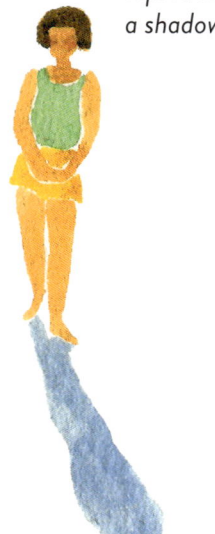
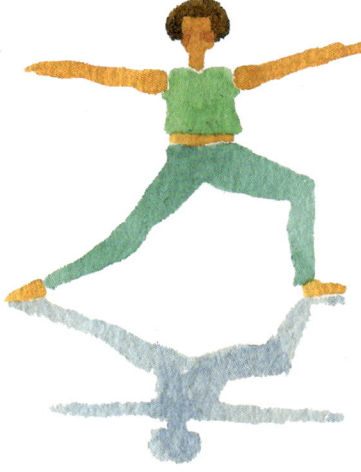
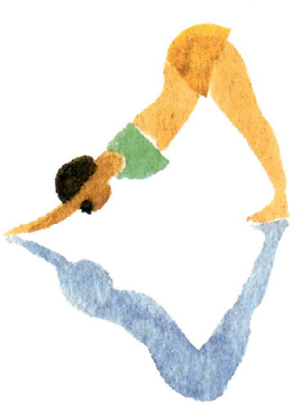

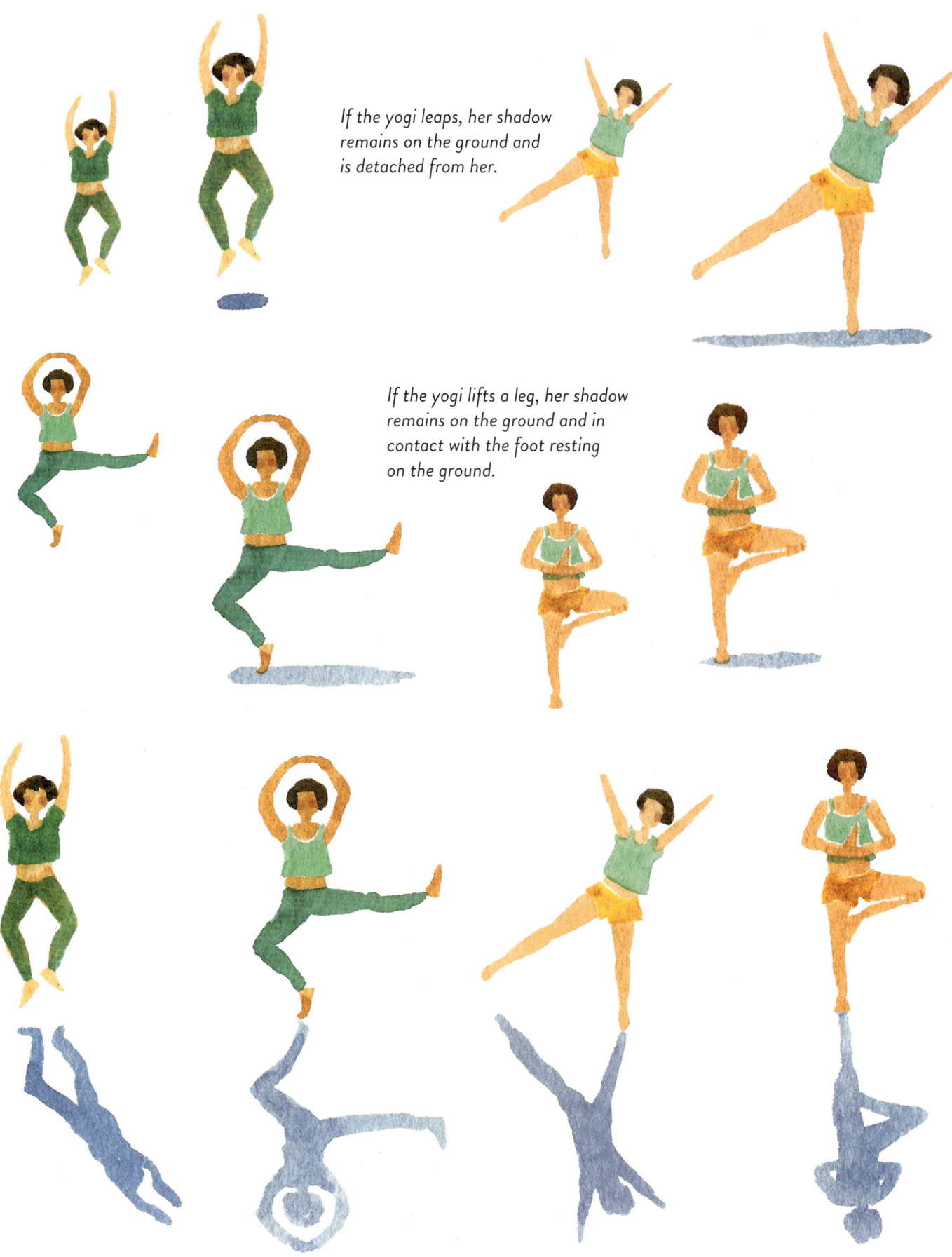

If the yogi leaps, her shadow remains on the ground and is detached from her.

If the yogi lifts a leg, her shadow remains on the ground and in contact with the foot resting on the ground.

Week 23
Splashes of Light and Shadow

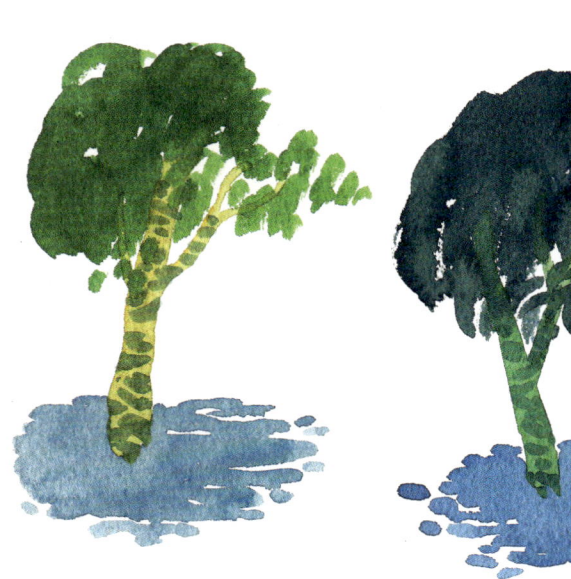
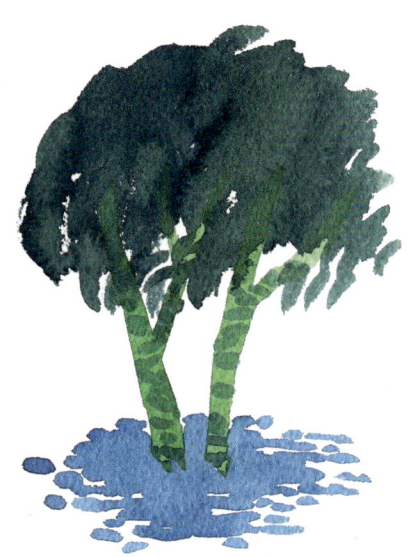
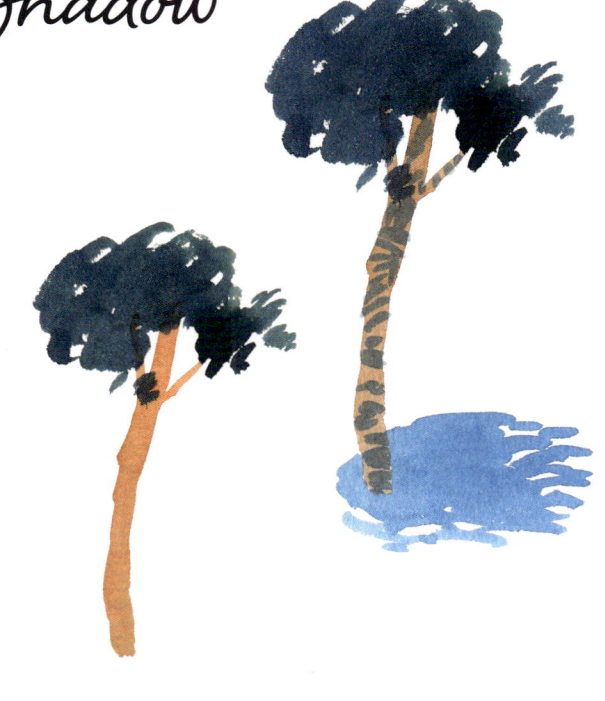

A shadow is not always solid. Under a tree, there are often splashes of light and shadow. You can also see this chiaroscuro under a tunnel, through a trellis, or in the undergrowth of a forest.

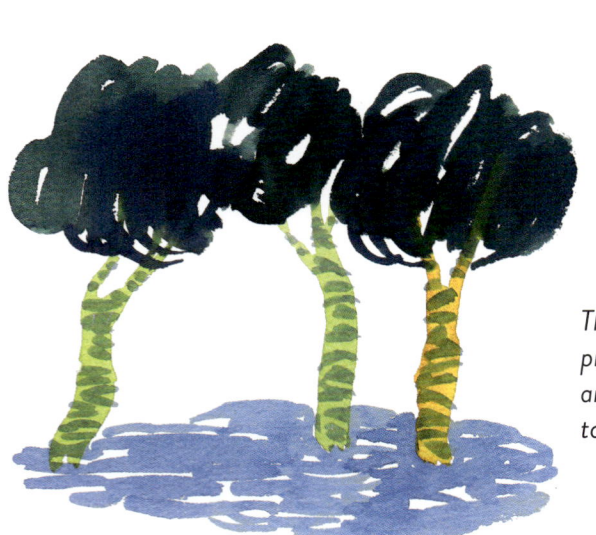
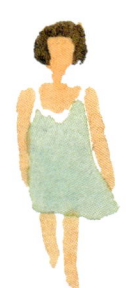
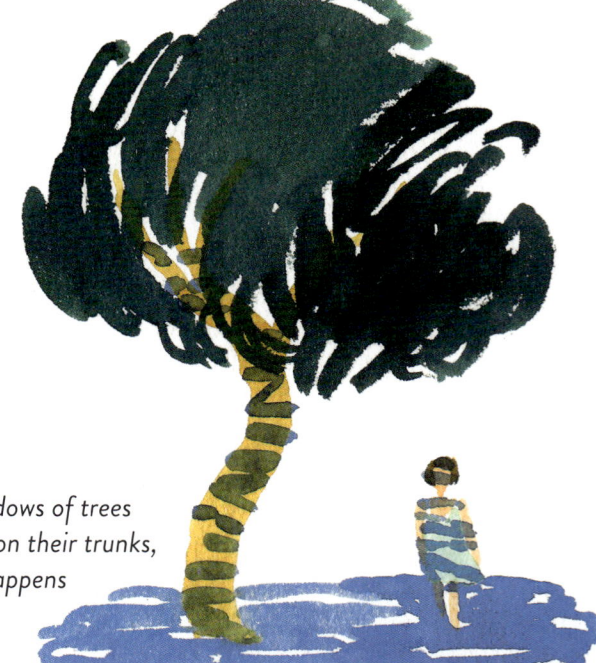

These "perforated" shadows of trees project on the ground, on their trunks, and on someone who happens to walk by.

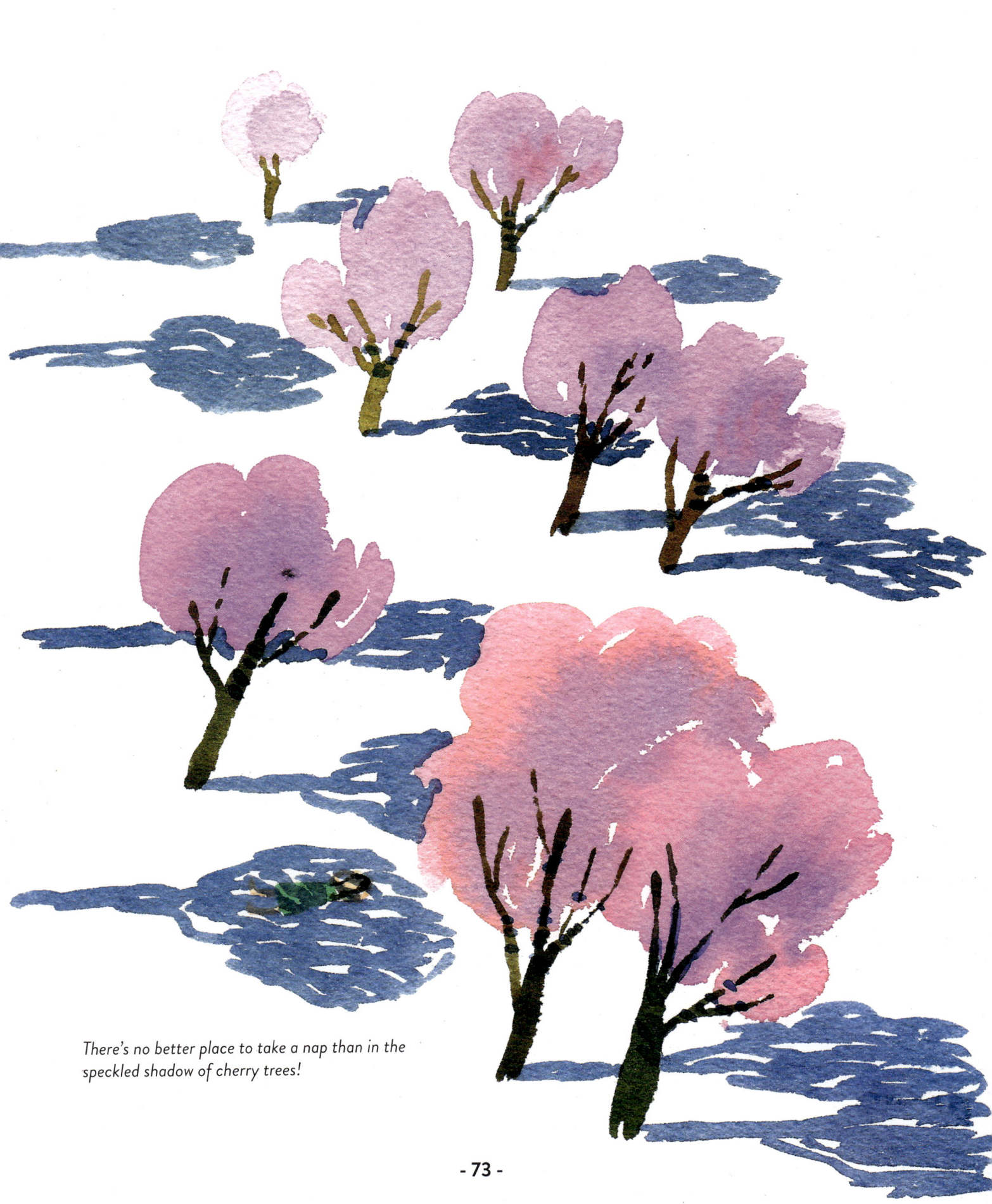

There's no better place to take a nap than in the speckled shadow of cherry trees!

For More Practice

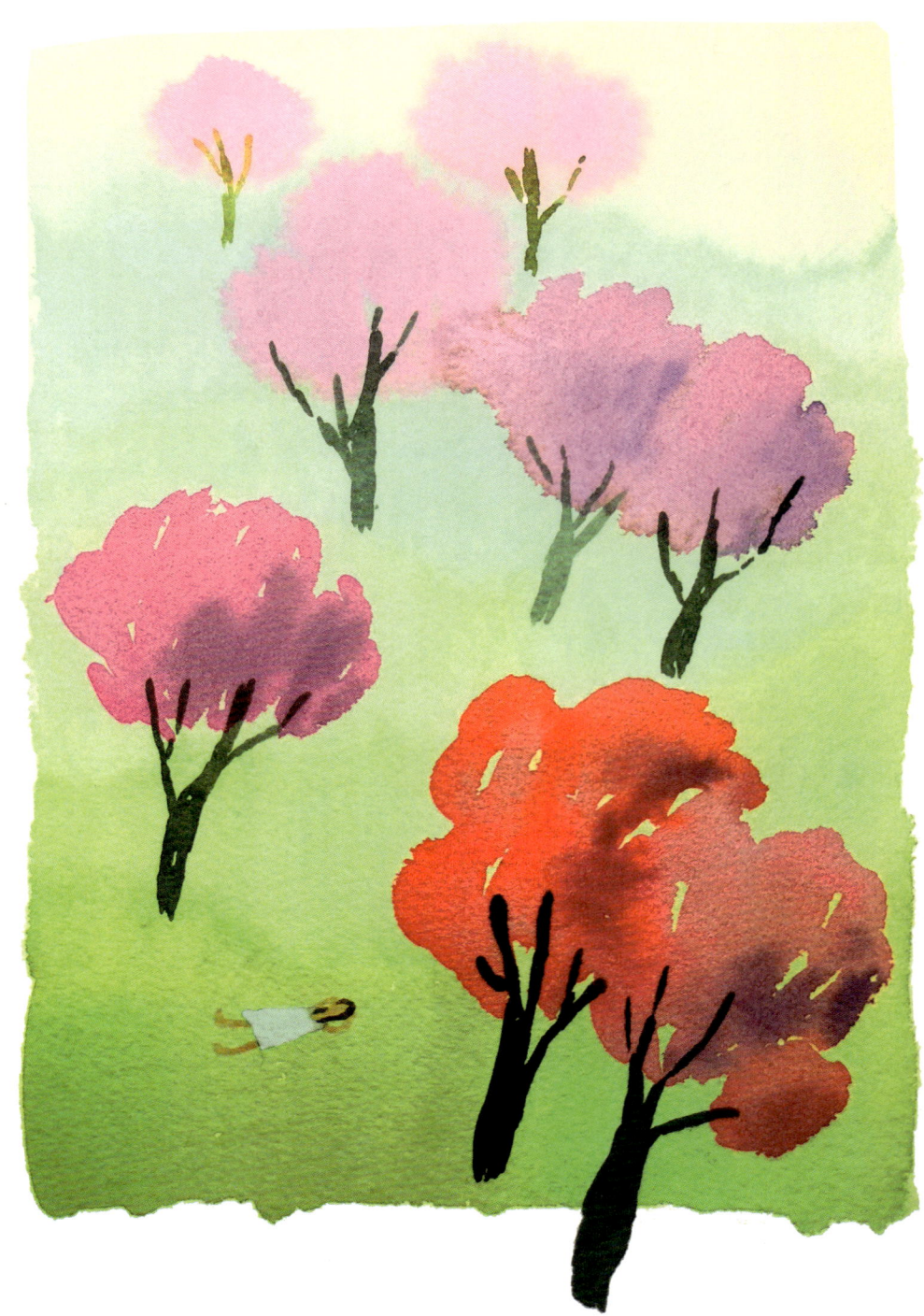

To include a breath of springtime, paint a wet-on-wet gradation of green as the background.

Without waiting for the gradation to dry, sketch some distant plum trees with a blurred effect.

Draw the flowering trees, the sleepyhead, and the trunks of the plum trees on dry paper. The more distant the trees, the lighter and blurrier they are!

To give a third dimension to the spring, add shadows—in blue, of course!

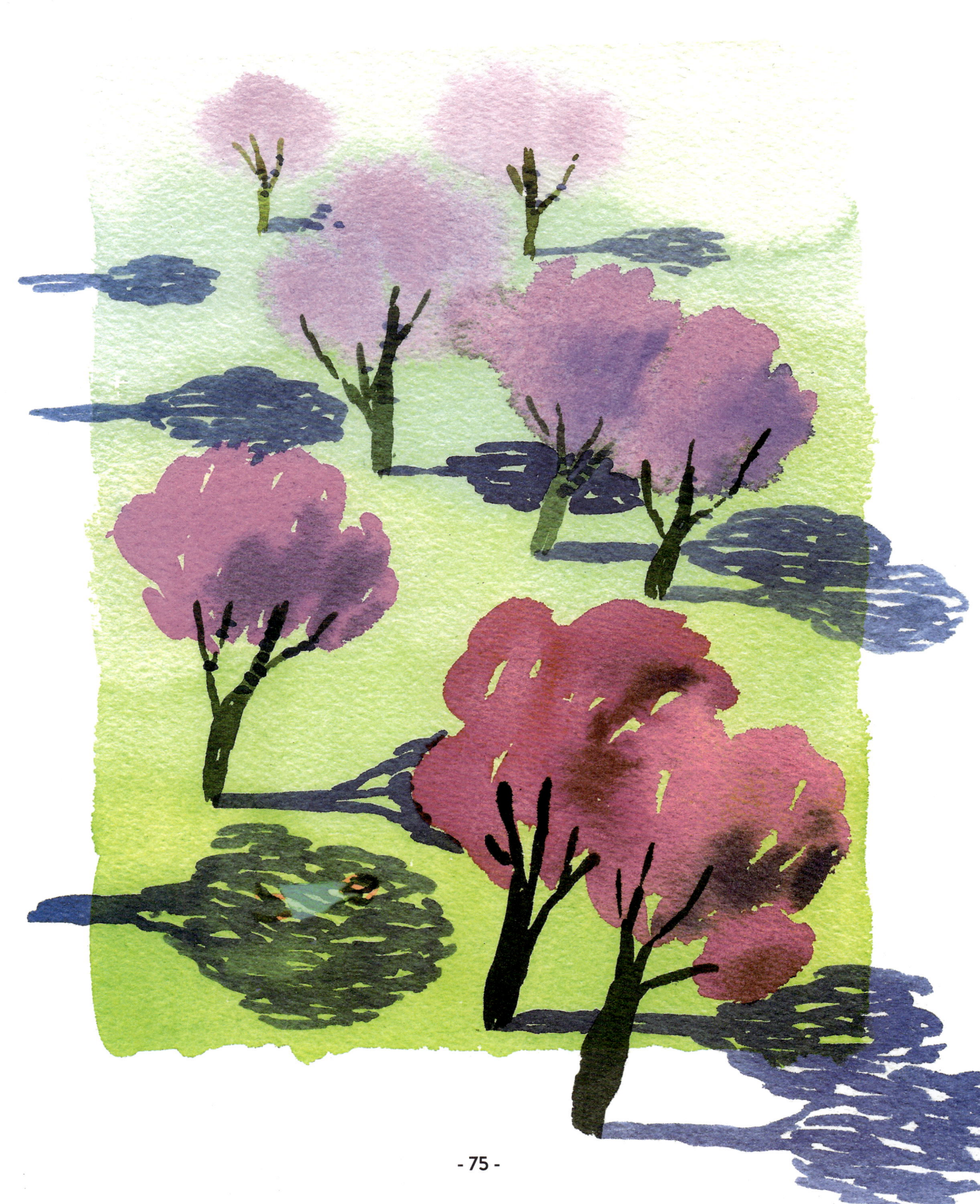

Week 24
Where Is the Light Coming From?

Here is an important lesson to bring your watercolors to life with light and shadow. This tree is flat. Draw a shadow in blue to give shape to its volume; that's the shaded part of the tree. Add a shadow projected to the ground so that the tree doesn't float in an undefined blank space. Magic! The tree has now transformed from a flat spot of color to something with volume—something that's anchored to the ground.

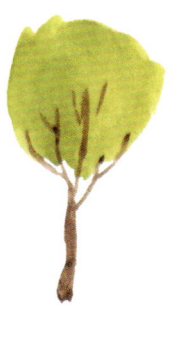
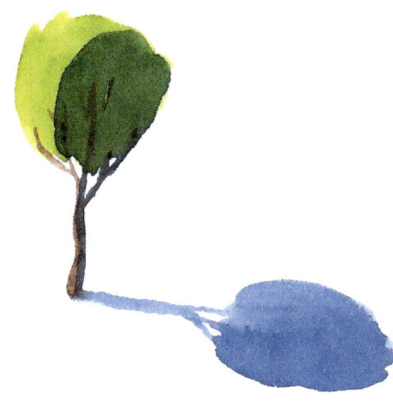

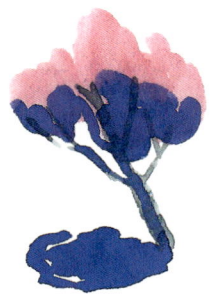
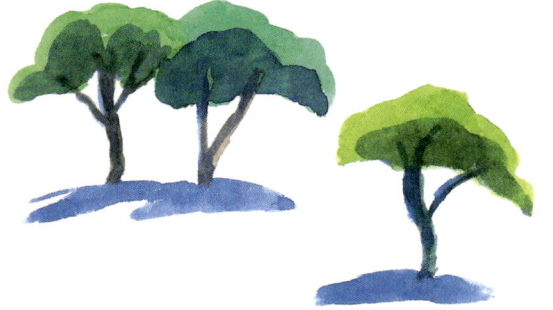
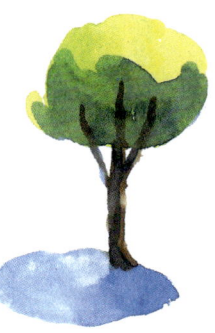

And now, the essential question: Where is the light coming from? Here, the sun is high, so the shadow projected to the ground is just under the tree. The sun is above the tree, so the shaded part of the tree is toward you. The sun lights up the top of the tree, so the shaded part of the tree is in the lower part of the foliage.

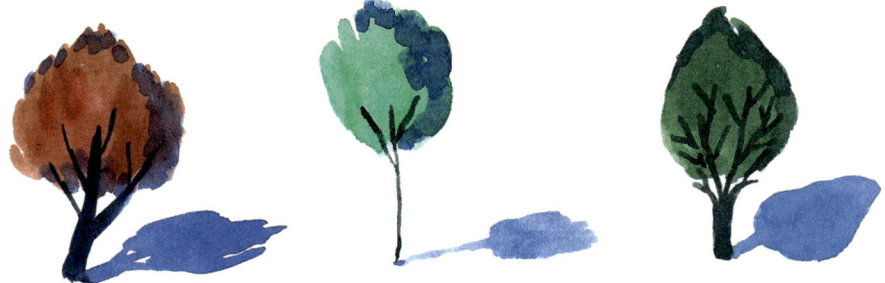

Here, the sun is behind you, slightly to your left, so it illuminates almost all of the face of the trees. The shaded part of the tree is behind, and you can barely see it. The sun is lower in the sky, so the projected shadow stretches out on the ground.

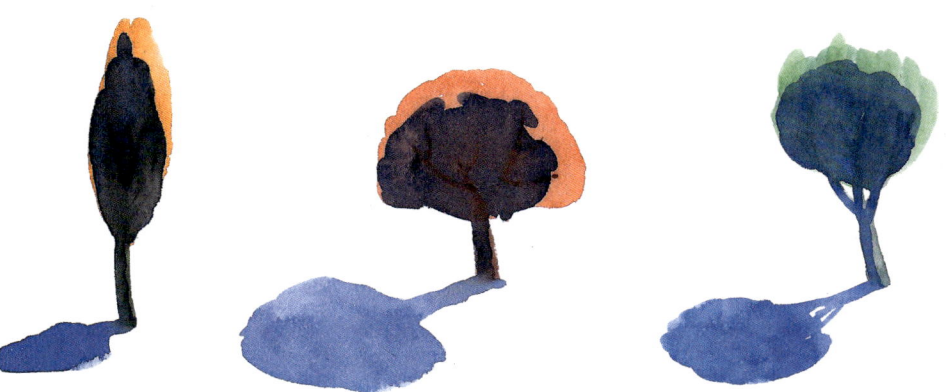

If the shadows are soft, with pale blue, it's winter! The light is diffuse and soft. The shadows have less contrast.

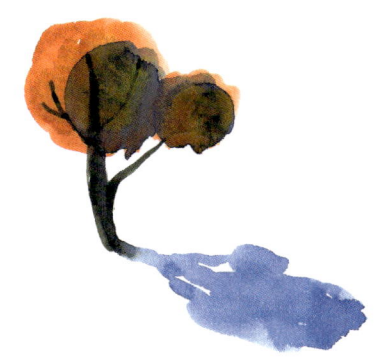 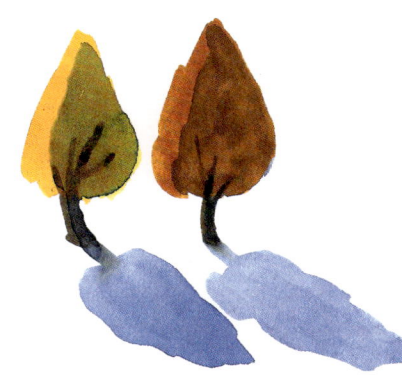

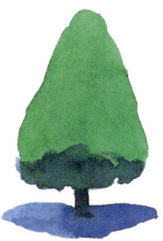 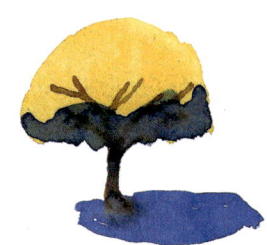

When the shadows are very pronounced, with dark blue, it is summer! The luminosity is strong, so the shadows have a lot of contrast.

When the sun is very low, as in the early morning or late afternoon, the shadows lengthen. They become immense.

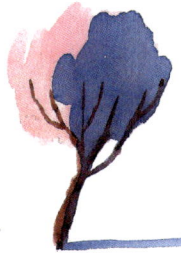 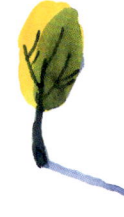

Week 25
Shaping the Volumes with Blue

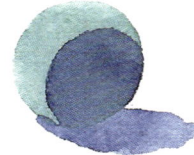  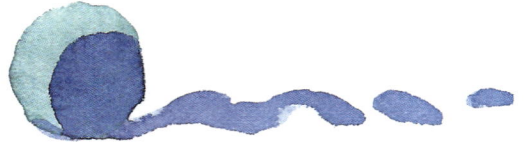

Take a look at this snowball. Its shaded part and its projected shadow indicate that it is round and is resting on the ground.

If the sun is low in the sky, its shadow extends and lengthens, as discussed in Week 24.

If the ground is not flat, its projected shadow follows the irregularities of the ground, as it often does in a snowy landscape.

Snow is a good exercise for understanding this week's challenge. In the snow, you can see how the blue shapes the volumes.

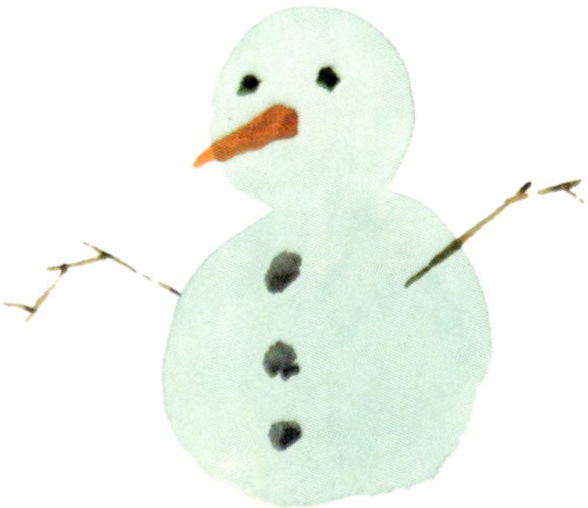

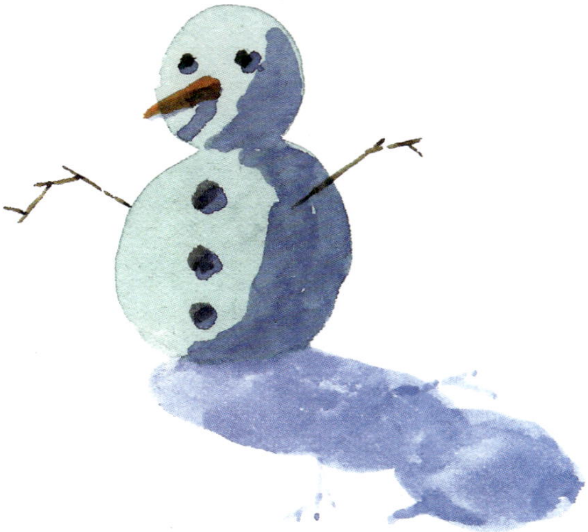

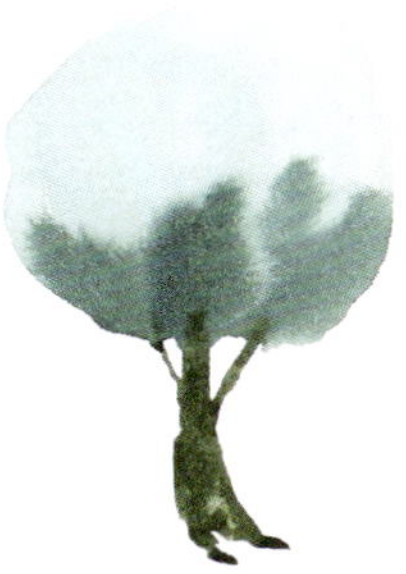

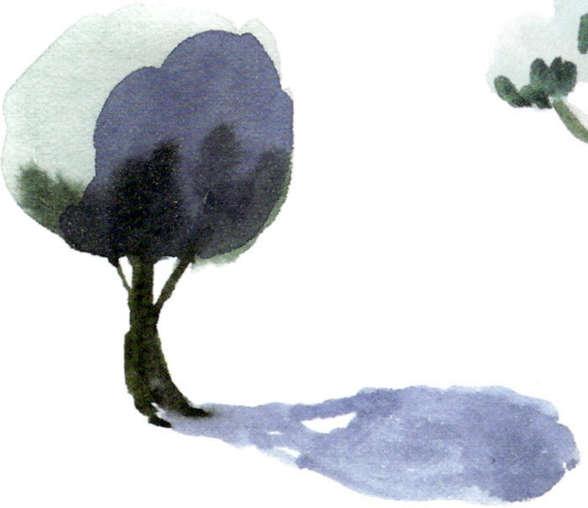

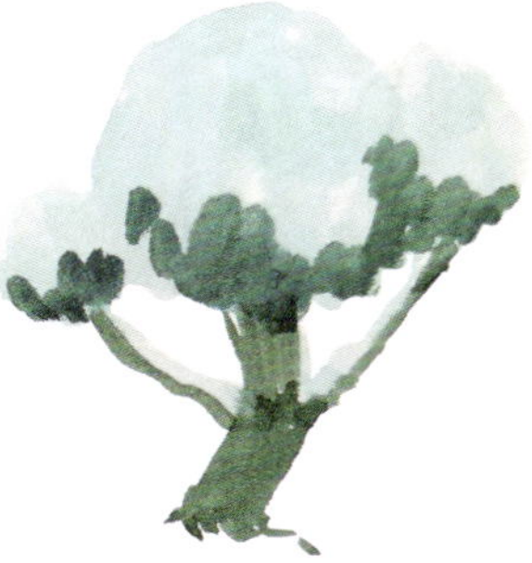

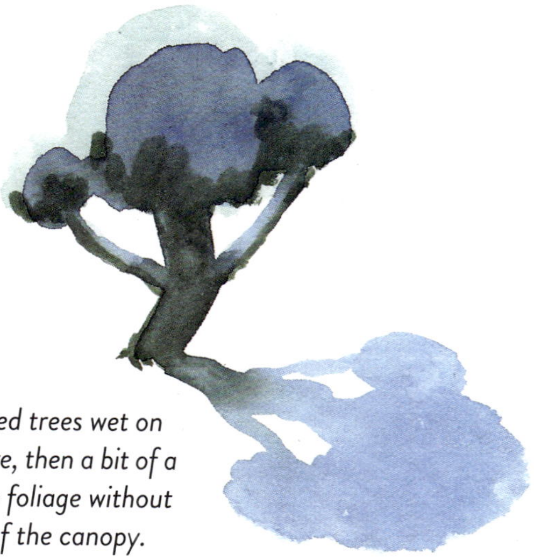

Paint these snow-covered trees wet on wet: the snow everywhere, then a bit of a darker paint mix for the foliage without snow in the lower part of the canopy.

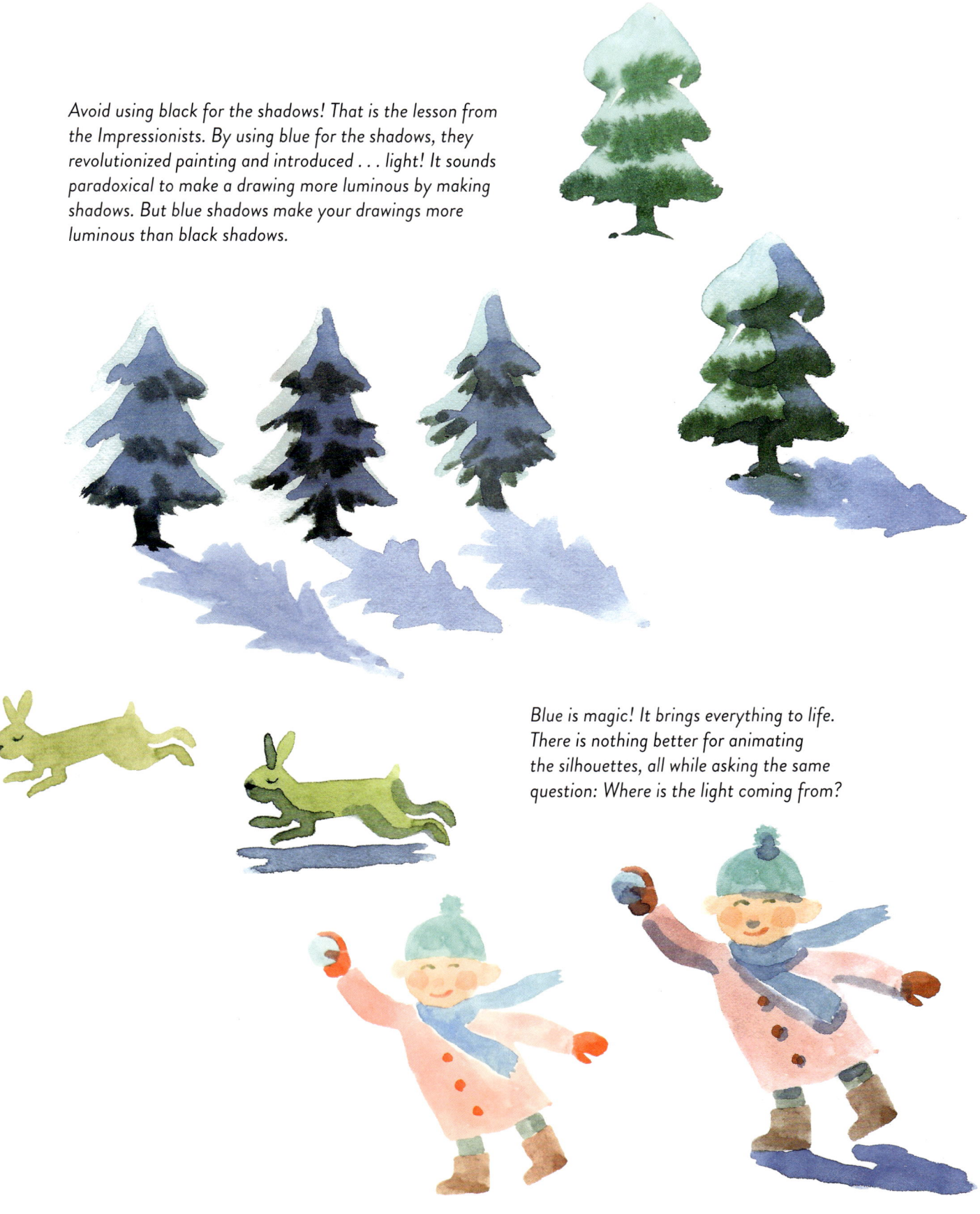

Avoid using black for the shadows! That is the lesson from the Impressionists. By using blue for the shadows, they revolutionized painting and introduced . . . light! It sounds paradoxical to make a drawing more luminous by making shadows. But blue shadows make your drawings more luminous than black shadows.

Blue is magic! It brings everything to life. There is nothing better for animating the silhouettes, all while asking the same question: Where is the light coming from?

For More Practice

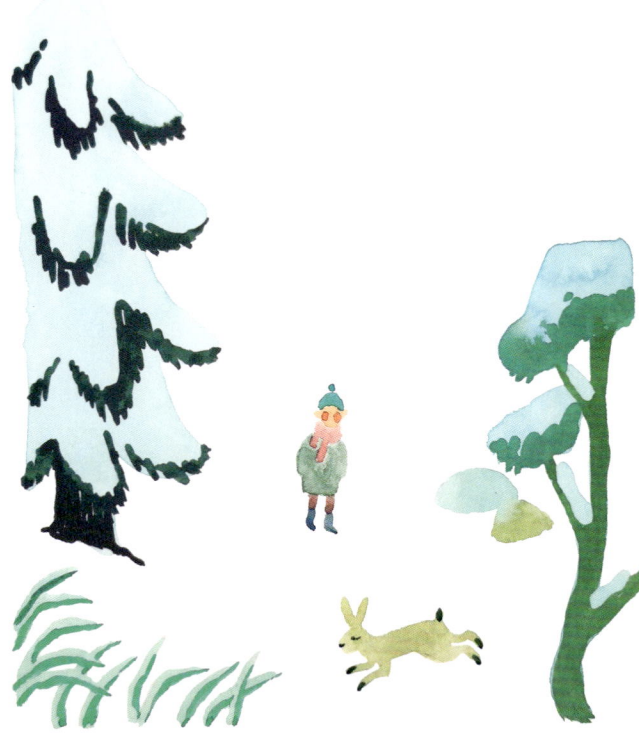

What is better than a snowy winter walk to see life through blue-colored glasses? Start with a few trees—a fir tree, an imaginary tree, two rocks, some plants in the foreground, and a fearless snowshoe hare. And the heroine, all wrapped up in a warm coat!

Now it's time for the shadows. With a brush soaked in blue, give volume to all the elements of the scene and trace their shadows. Then fill in the background with a pale blue wash. After it dries, go over it with a deep blue wash, bringing out the distant silhouettes of three fir trees.

Give volume to the distant fir trees with a bluish paint mix. Vary the blues for the shadows by adding more or less turquoise. A snowy landscape has a beautiful variety of blues in the shadows.

There it is! All that is left to do is warm yourself up with a steaming cup of hot chocolate!

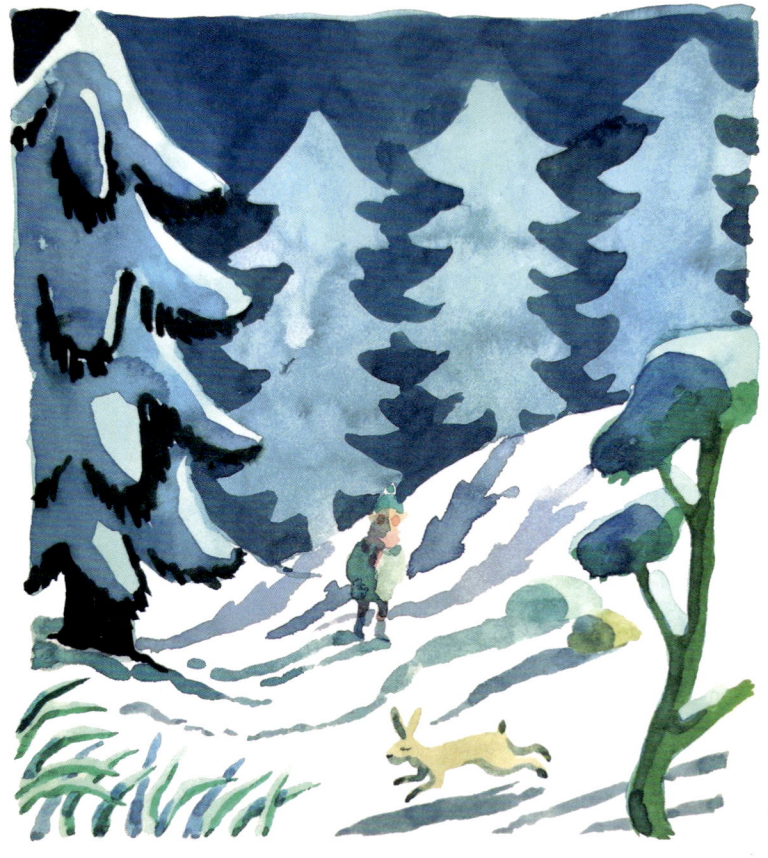

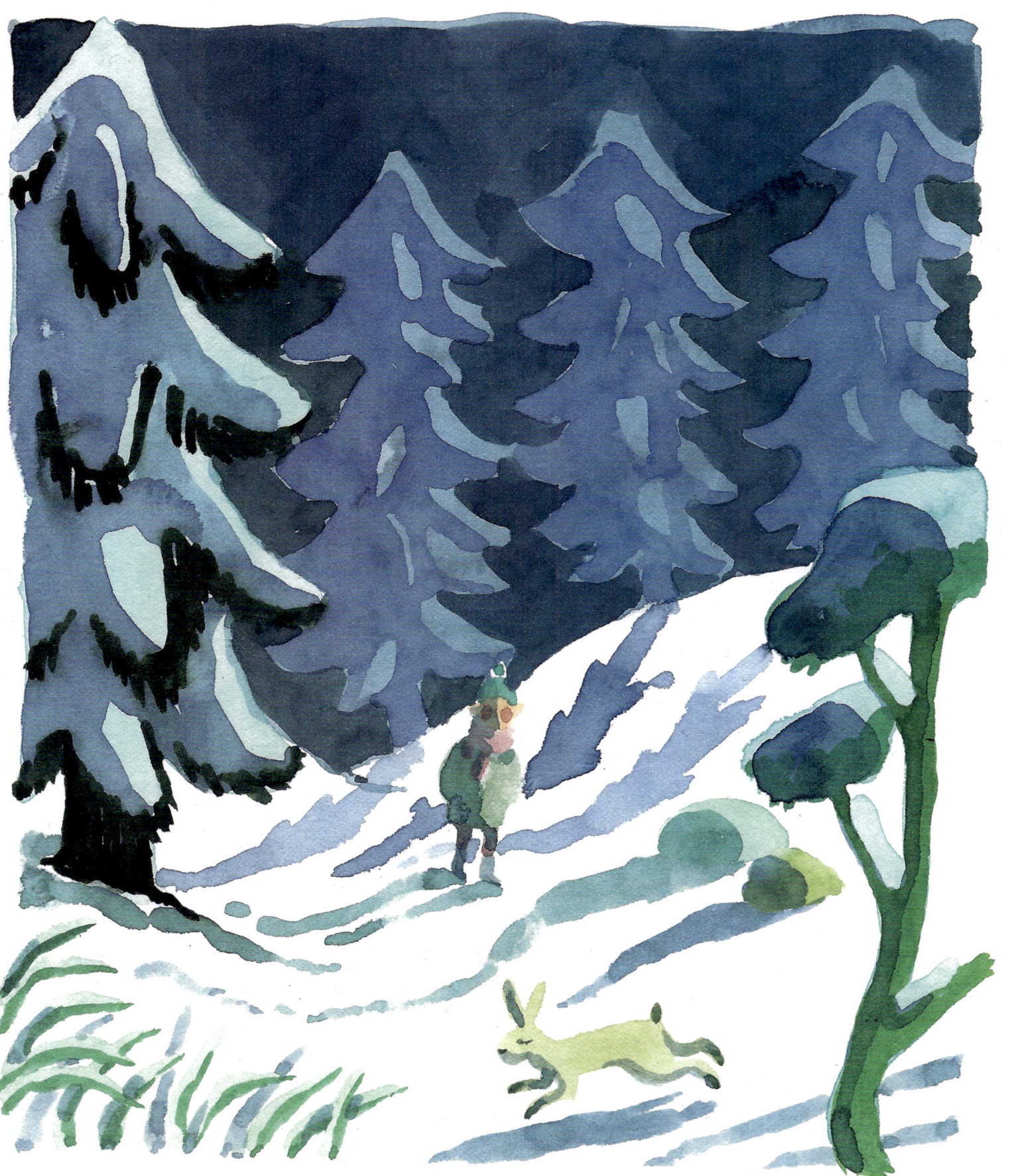

Week 26
Lightening a Color

Colors are organized in a color wheel. The primary colors—yellow, magenta, and cyan—are distributed on each side of this wheel.

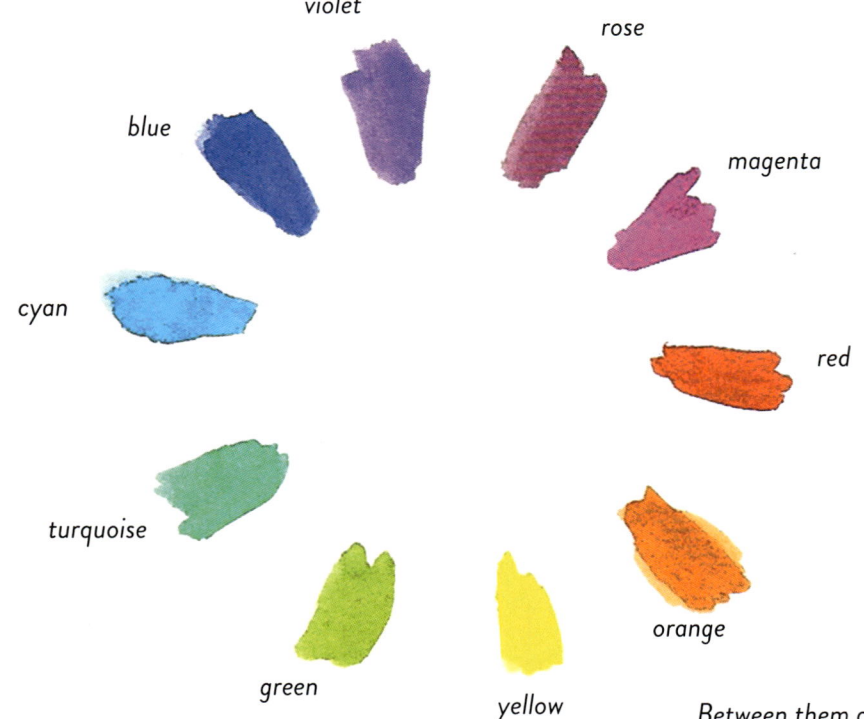

violet

rose

blue

magenta

cyan

red

turquoise

orange

green

yellow

Between them are the secondary colors: the oranges and reds, a mixture of yellow and magenta; the greens, a mixture of yellow and cyan; and the violets and blues, a mixture of magenta and cyan.

These colors are more or less dark. To saturate a color, load your brush with lots of pigments and a little water, yielding a very colored paint mix. To lighten a shade, dilute this paint mix with more and more water.

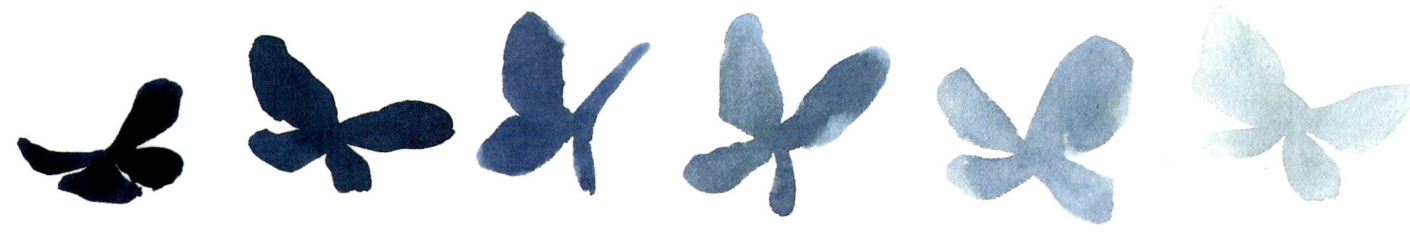

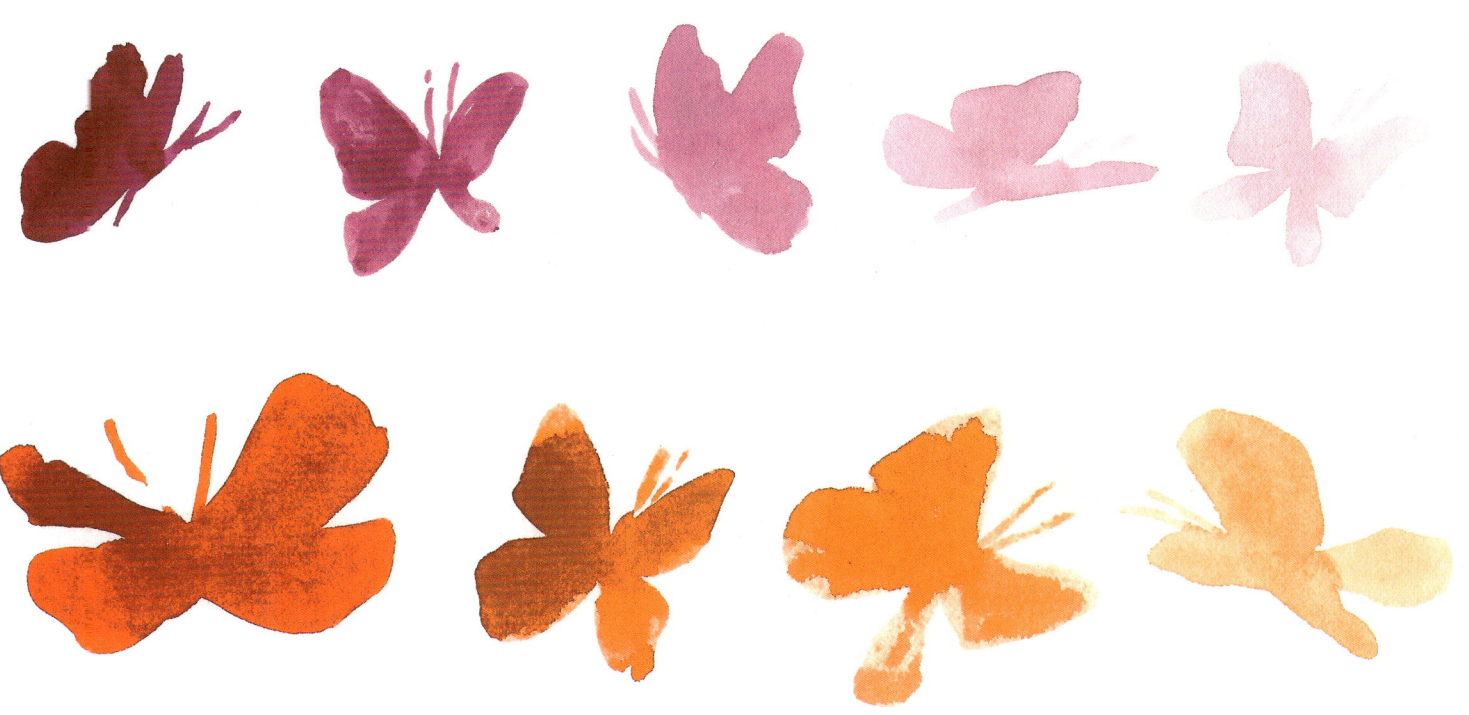

Practice lightening the colors with rows of butterflies in flight.

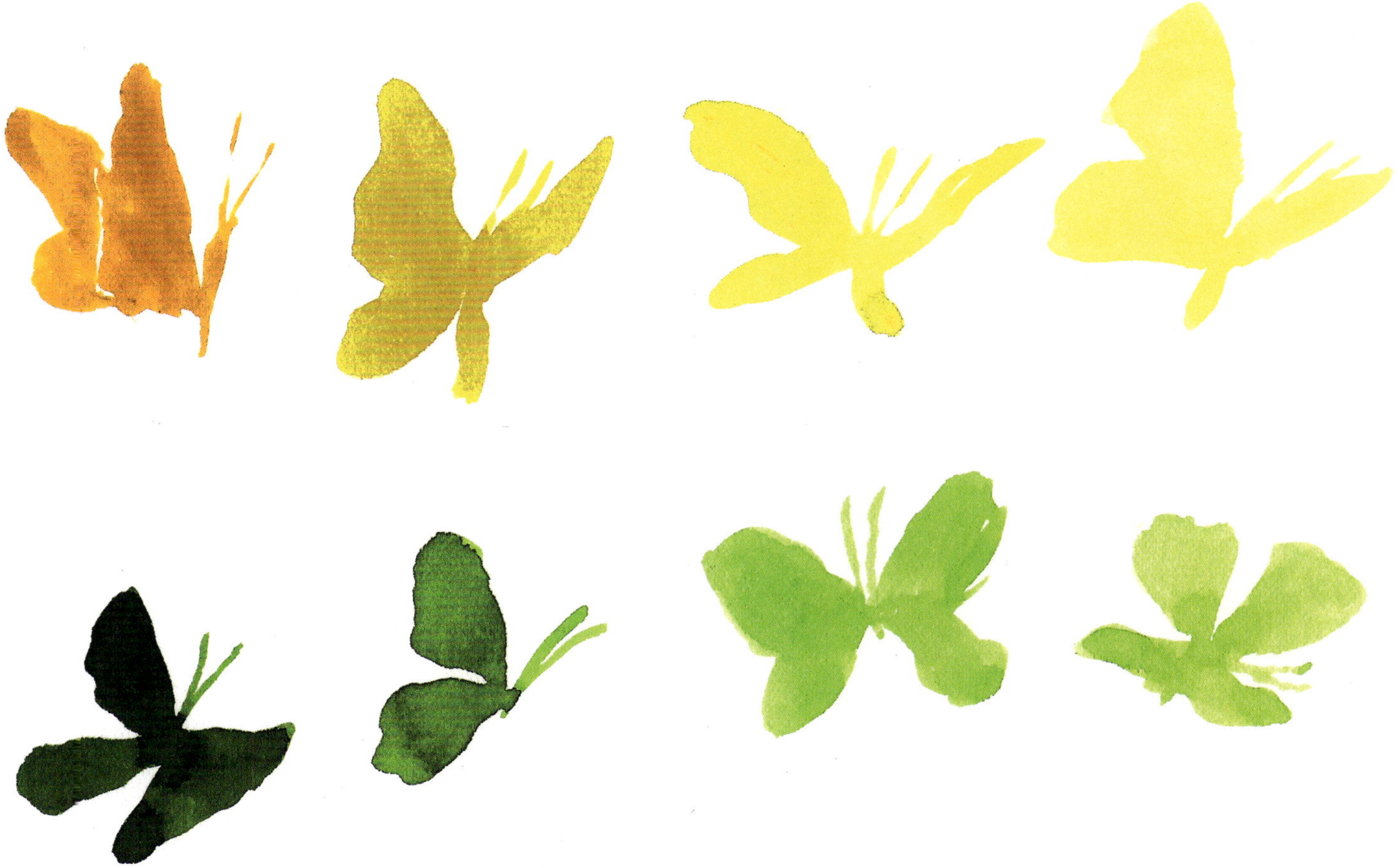

Week 27
Warm and Cool Colors

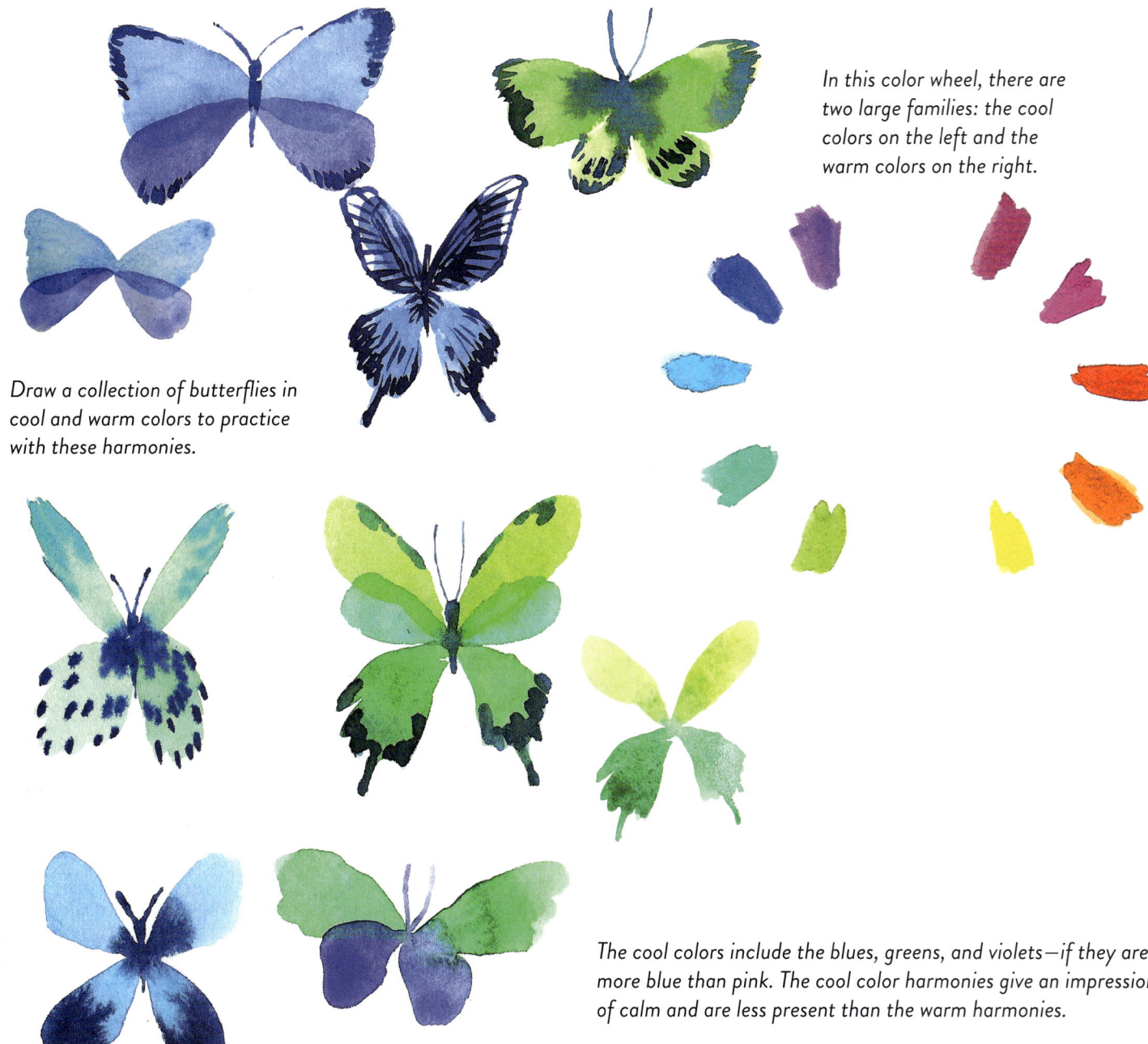

In this color wheel, there are two large families: the cool colors on the left and the warm colors on the right.

Draw a collection of butterflies in cool and warm colors to practice with these harmonies.

The cool colors include the blues, greens, and violets—if they are more blue than pink. The cool color harmonies give an impression of calm and are less present than the warm harmonies.

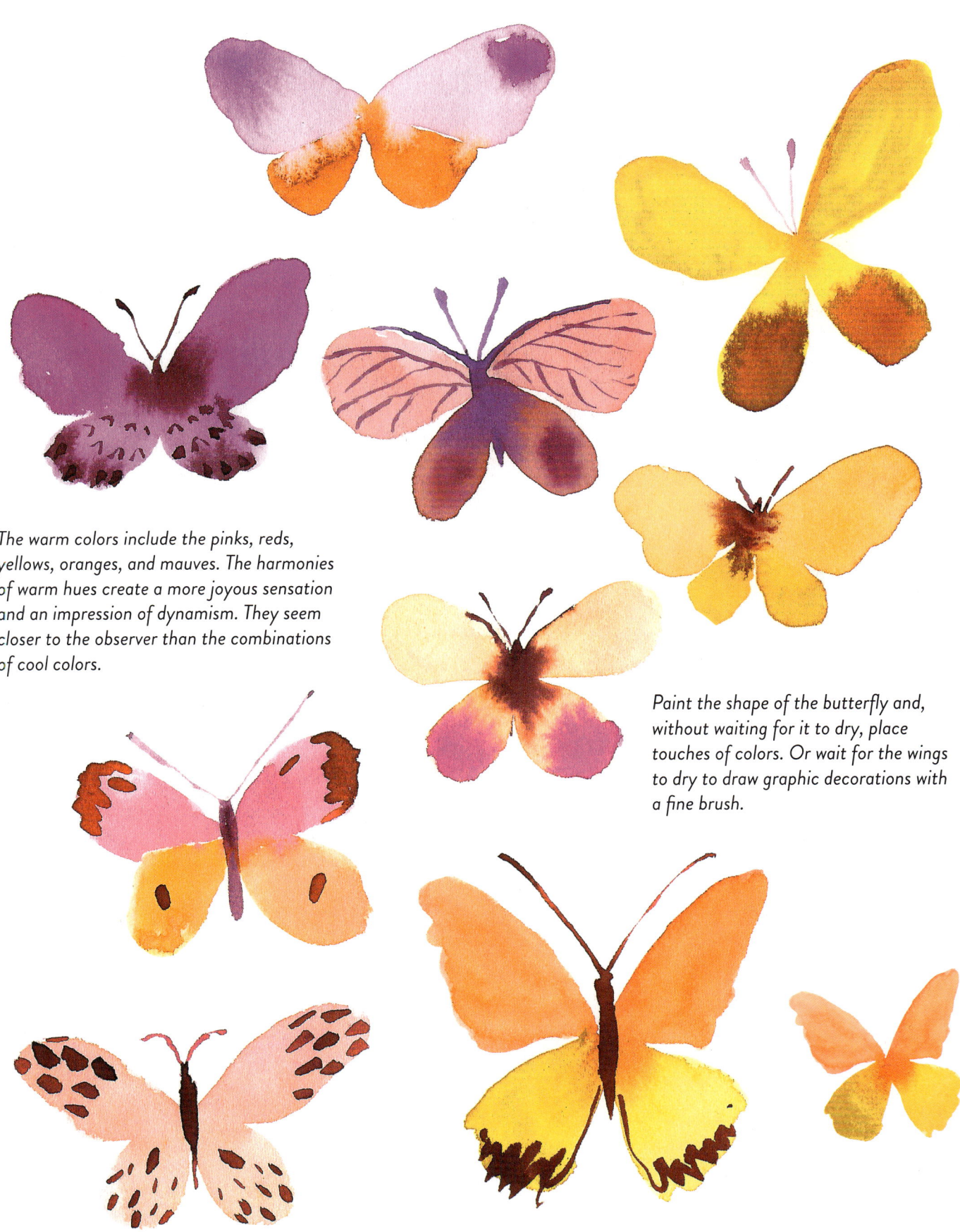

The warm colors include the pinks, reds, yellows, oranges, and mauves. The harmonies of warm hues create a more joyous sensation and an impression of dynamism. They seem closer to the observer than the combinations of cool colors.

Paint the shape of the butterfly and, without waiting for it to dry, place touches of colors. Or wait for the wings to dry to draw graphic decorations with a fine brush.

For More Practice

To practice with warm and cool colors, imagine a scene in contrasted color. On wet paper, start by placing a luminous yellow ray and a bluish paint mix.

Draw a surge of butterflies. The closer the butterflies are to you, the larger and more pigmented they are. The more distant the butterflies are, the smaller and lighter they are.

Painted on the background, a young woman enjoys the ray of sunshine in her butterfly greenhouse. Feel the warmth of the ray of light—all the presence of the warm and cool atmospheres is there!

Add some shadows to the blue to give shape to the chair and the young woman!

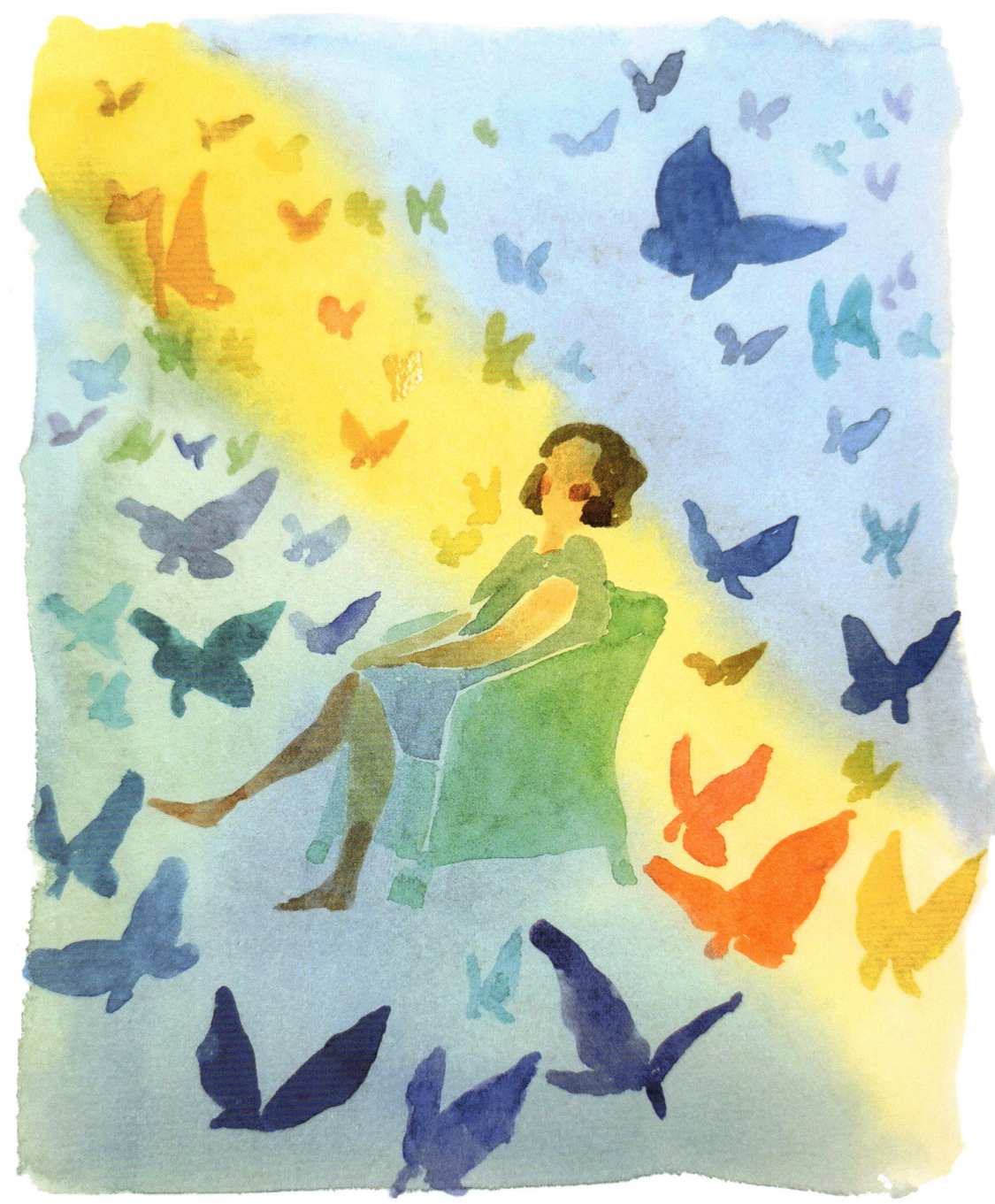

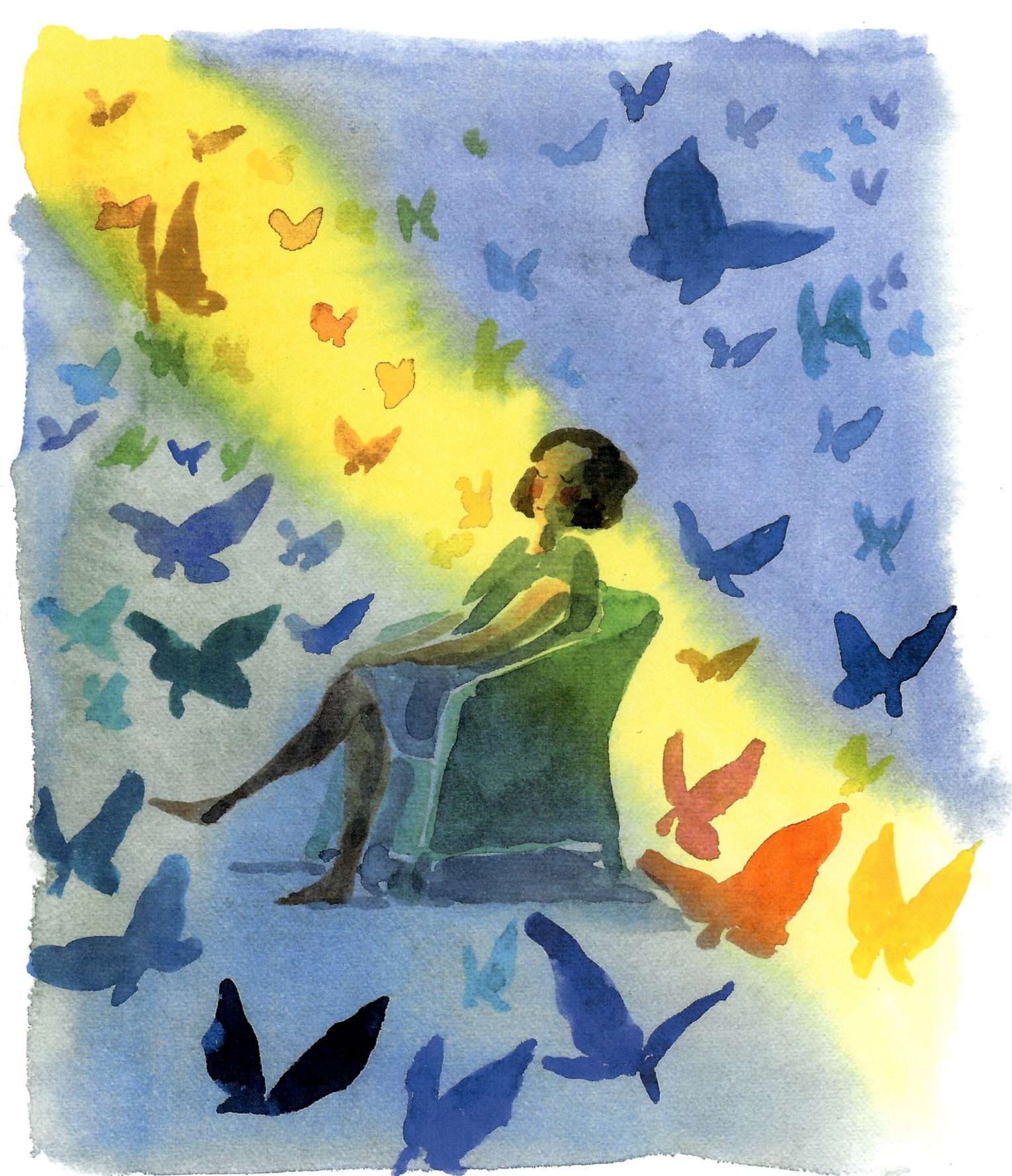

Week 28

Camaïeux: Painting with Monochromes or Adjacent Colors

If you choose colors that are next to each other on the color wheel, you can create camaïeux of adjacent colors, without clashes.

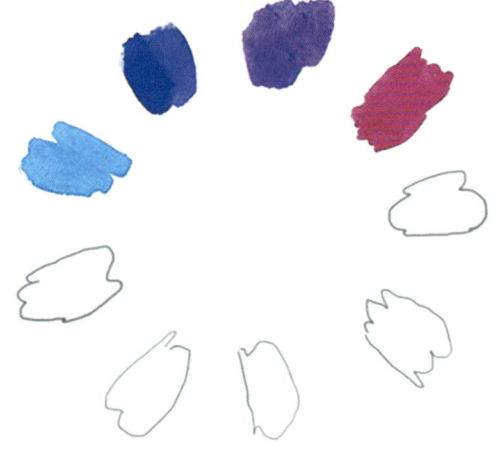

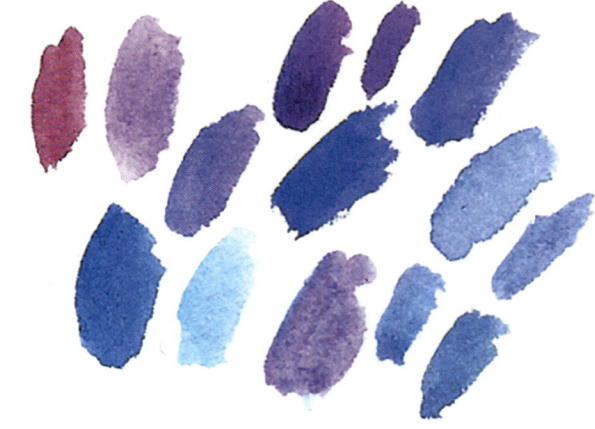

To obtain a camaïeu, "pull" a color toward its neighbors on the left and right of the color wheel. The blue is tinged with cyan on one side and violet on the other. Here is a camaïeu in blue.

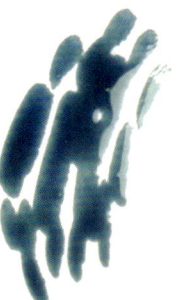

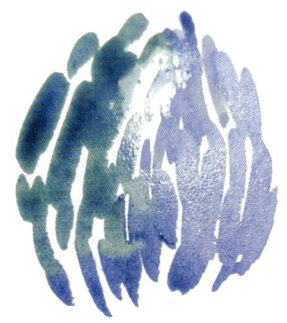

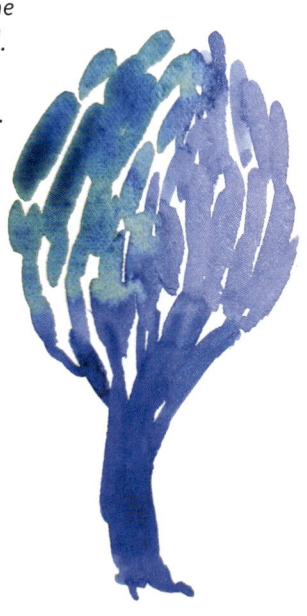

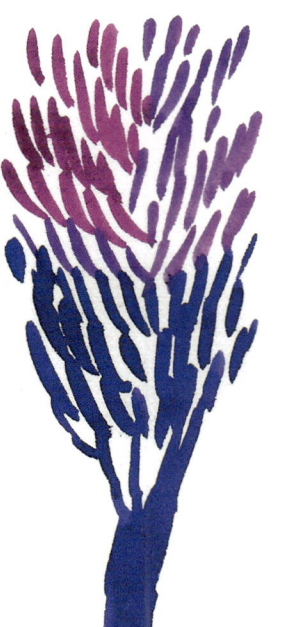

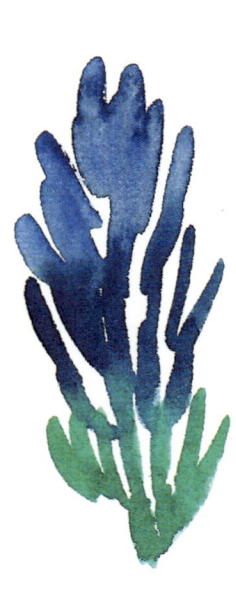

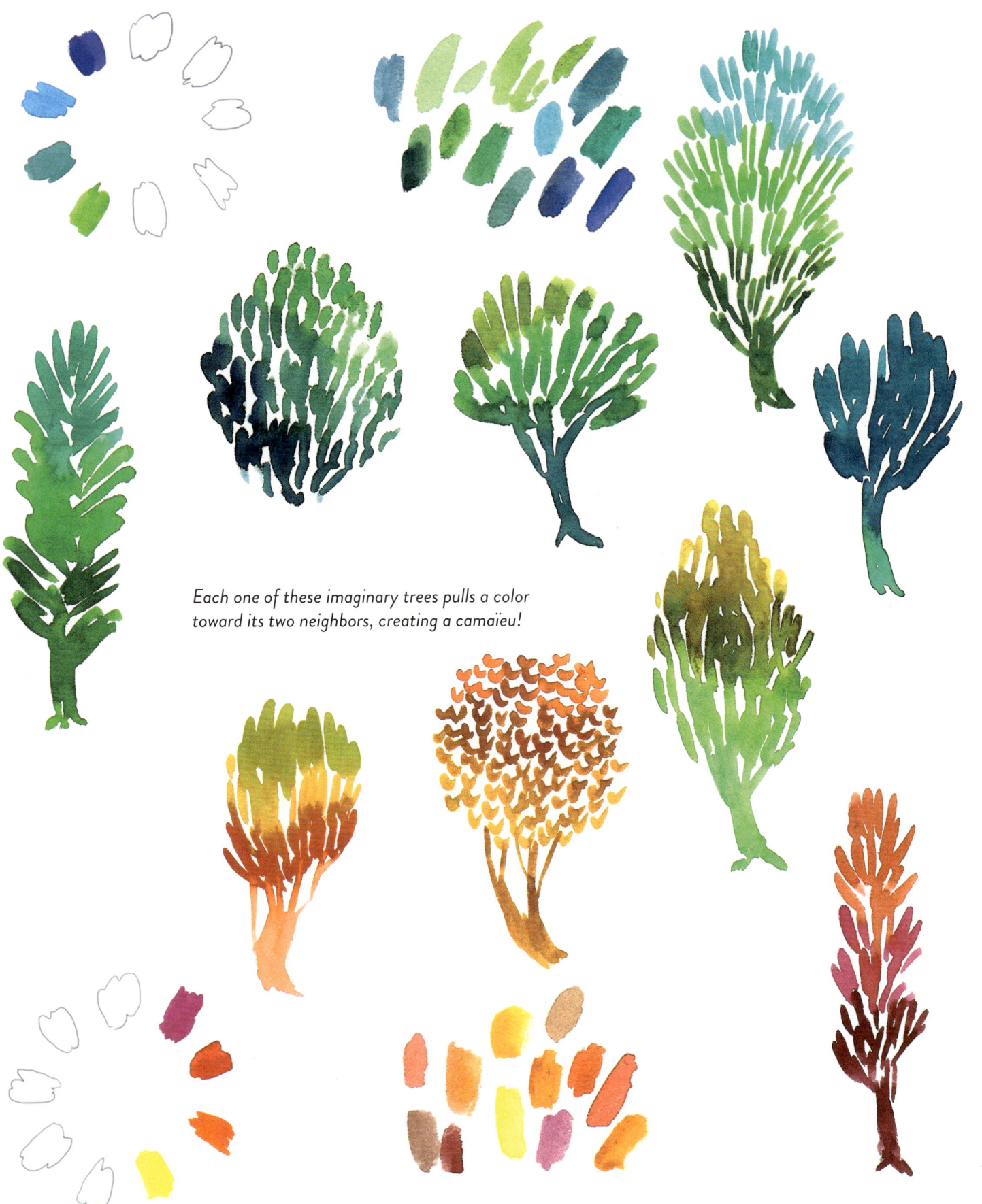

Each one of these imaginary trees pulls a color
toward its two neighbors, creating a camaïeu!

Week 29
Complementary Colors

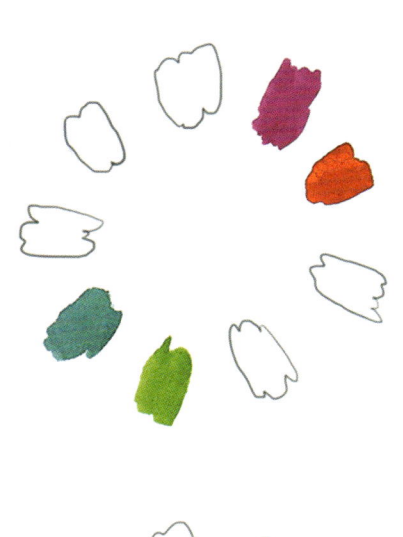

On opposite sides of the color wheel, the complementary colors form the most striking contrast.

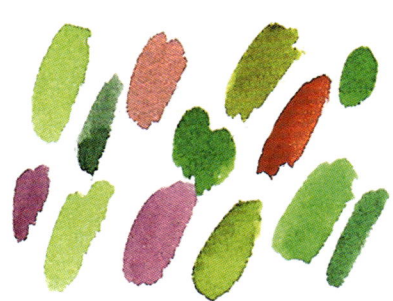

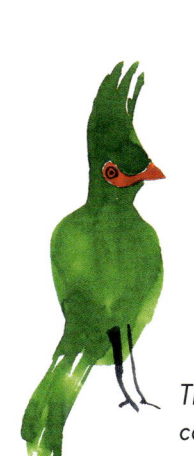

The reds and pinks contrast marvelously with the greens.

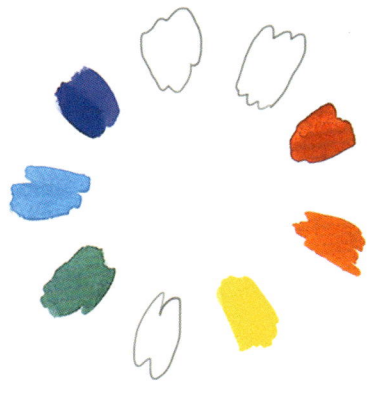

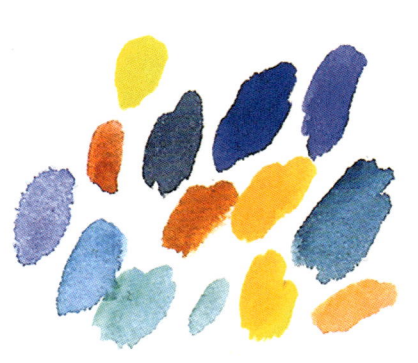

Blues and oranges make the most contrast.

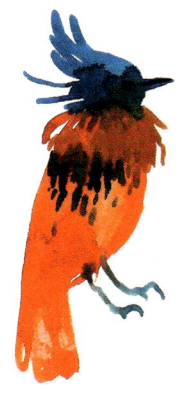

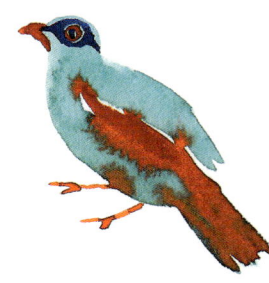

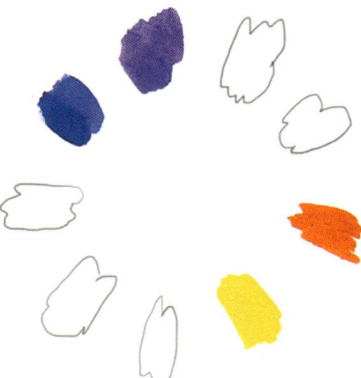

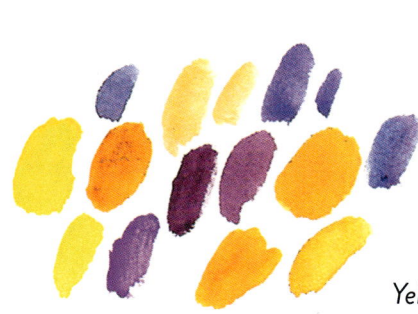

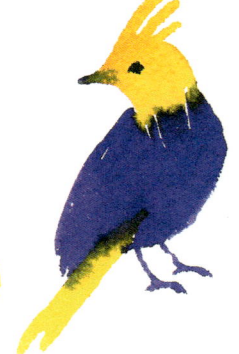

Yellows and violets play up their differences.

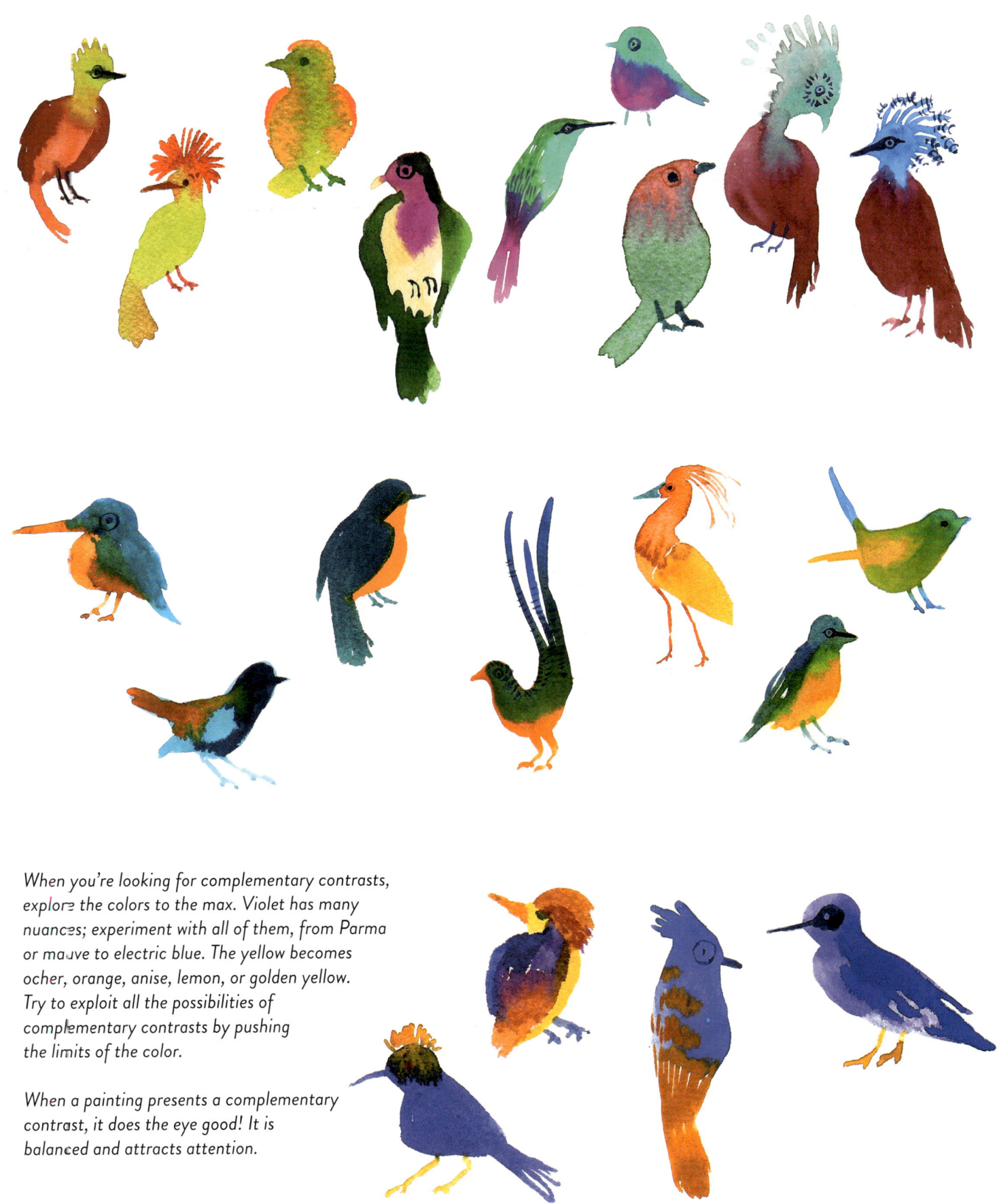

When you're looking for complementary contrasts, explore the colors to the max. Violet has many nuances; experiment with all of them, from Parma or mauve to electric blue. The yellow becomes ocher, orange, anise, lemon, or golden yellow. Try to exploit all the possibilities of complementary contrasts by pushing the limits of the color.

When a painting presents a complementary contrast, it does the eye good! It is balanced and attracts attention.

For More Practice

Play around with the camaïeux and the complementary colors! The birds are in a camaïeu of red, pink, and orange. A camaïeu in green and turquoise dresses the foliage of the tree.

The birds stand out sharply from the scene thanks to the complementary contrast of the pink-red with the green of the leaves.

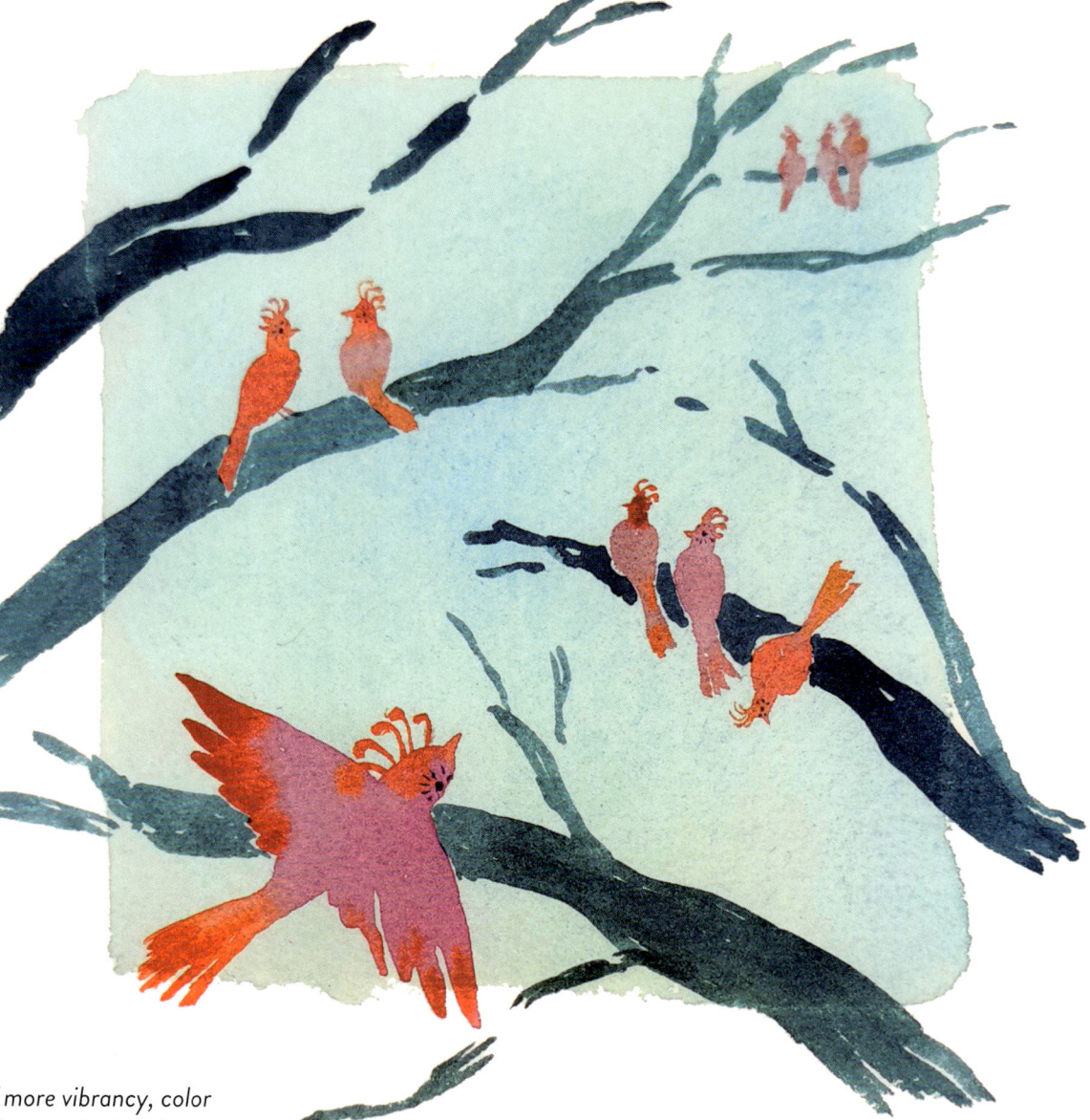

Paint the background in sky blue. Once that is dry, draw the firebirds and then the branches with a soft brush. Draw the birds in the distance in pale pink, without giving them much detail.

To give the impression of more vibrancy, color outside the blue frame when you're drawing the branches and leaves.

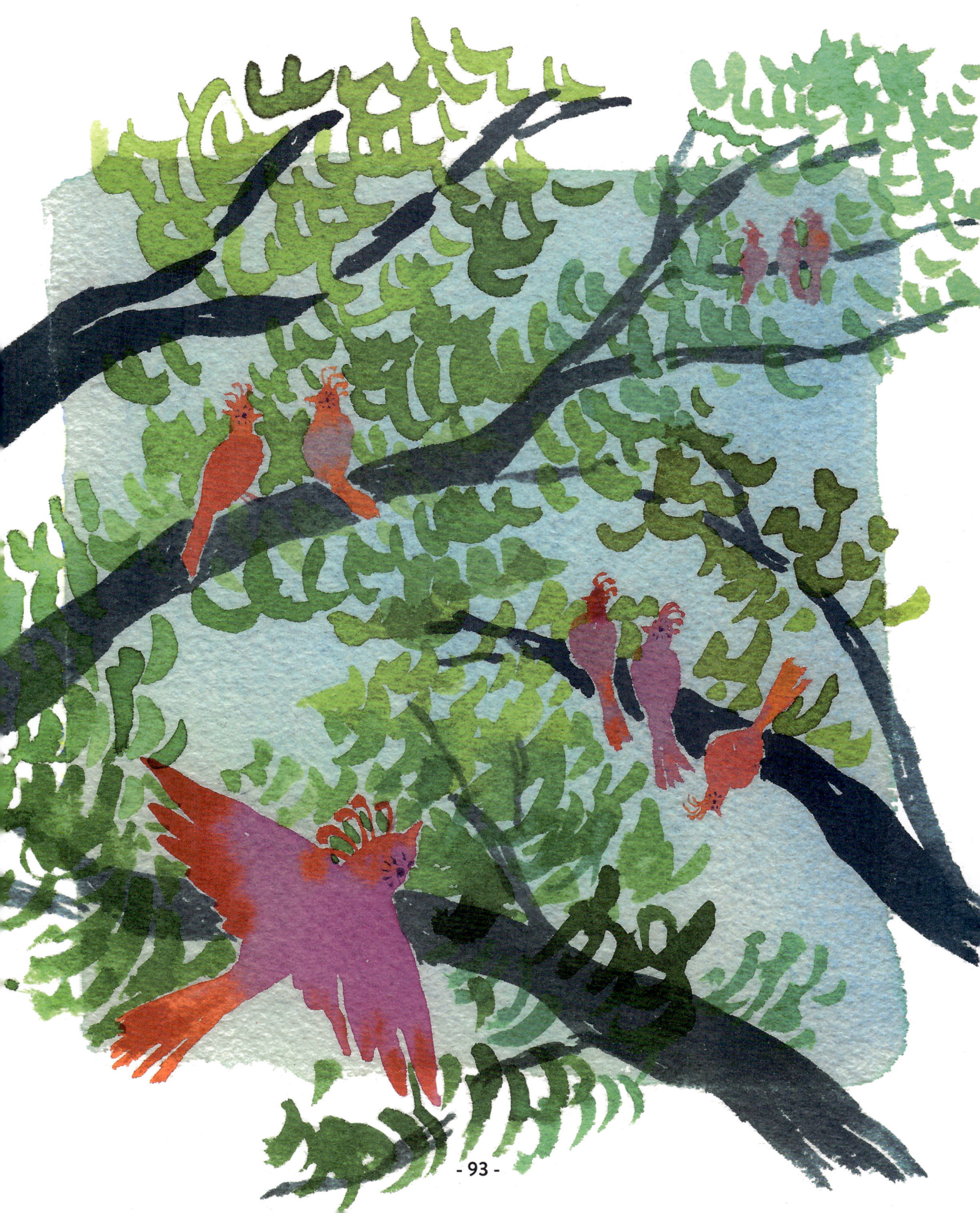

Week 30
Desaturating a Color with Its Complement

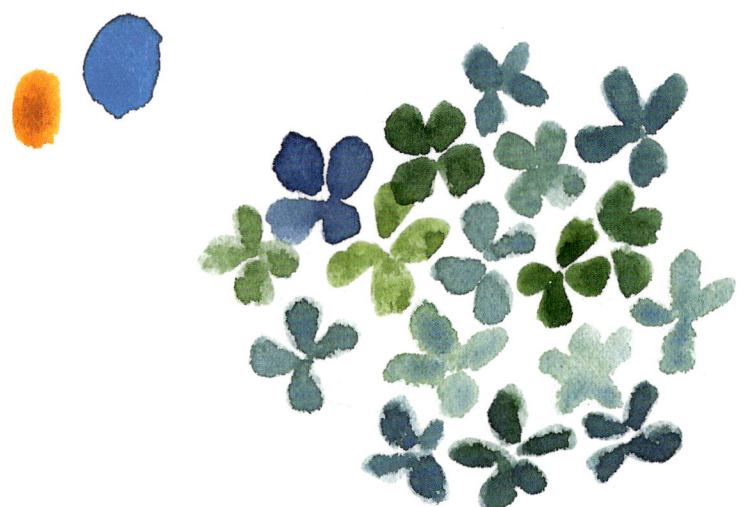

When you're traveling, all you need is a minimal watercolor box with very few colors. Sometimes these few colors are very bold and lack subtlety. To make a color more delicate, add a drop of its complementary color.

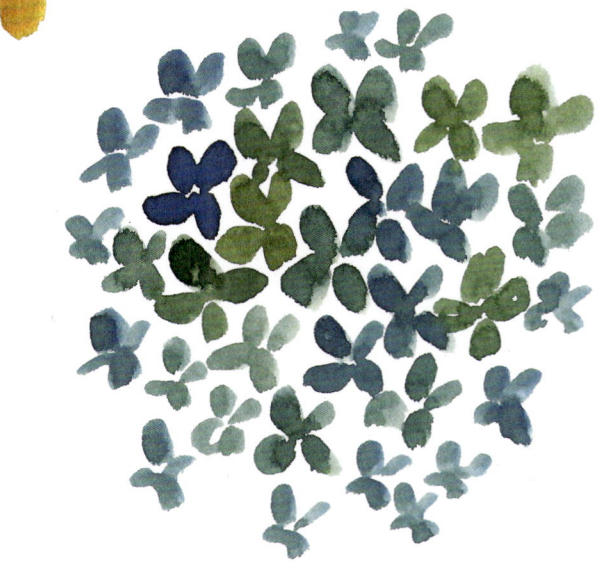

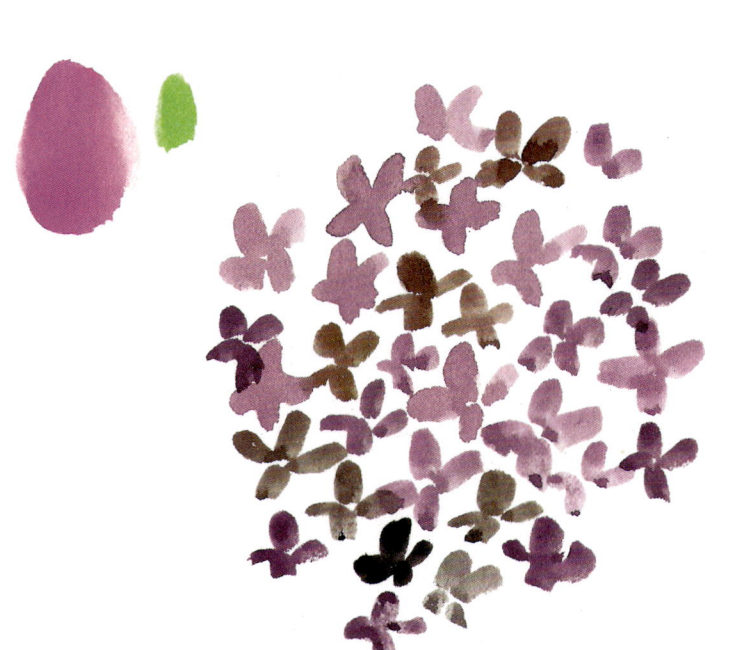

The effect is magic! "Cut" a magenta with a drop of green to obtain a more interesting color. Depending on the quantity of green added, you can produce a desaturated and nuanced spectrum. It is particularly striking for this page of wilted or dried flowers, which need colors that are slightly faded.

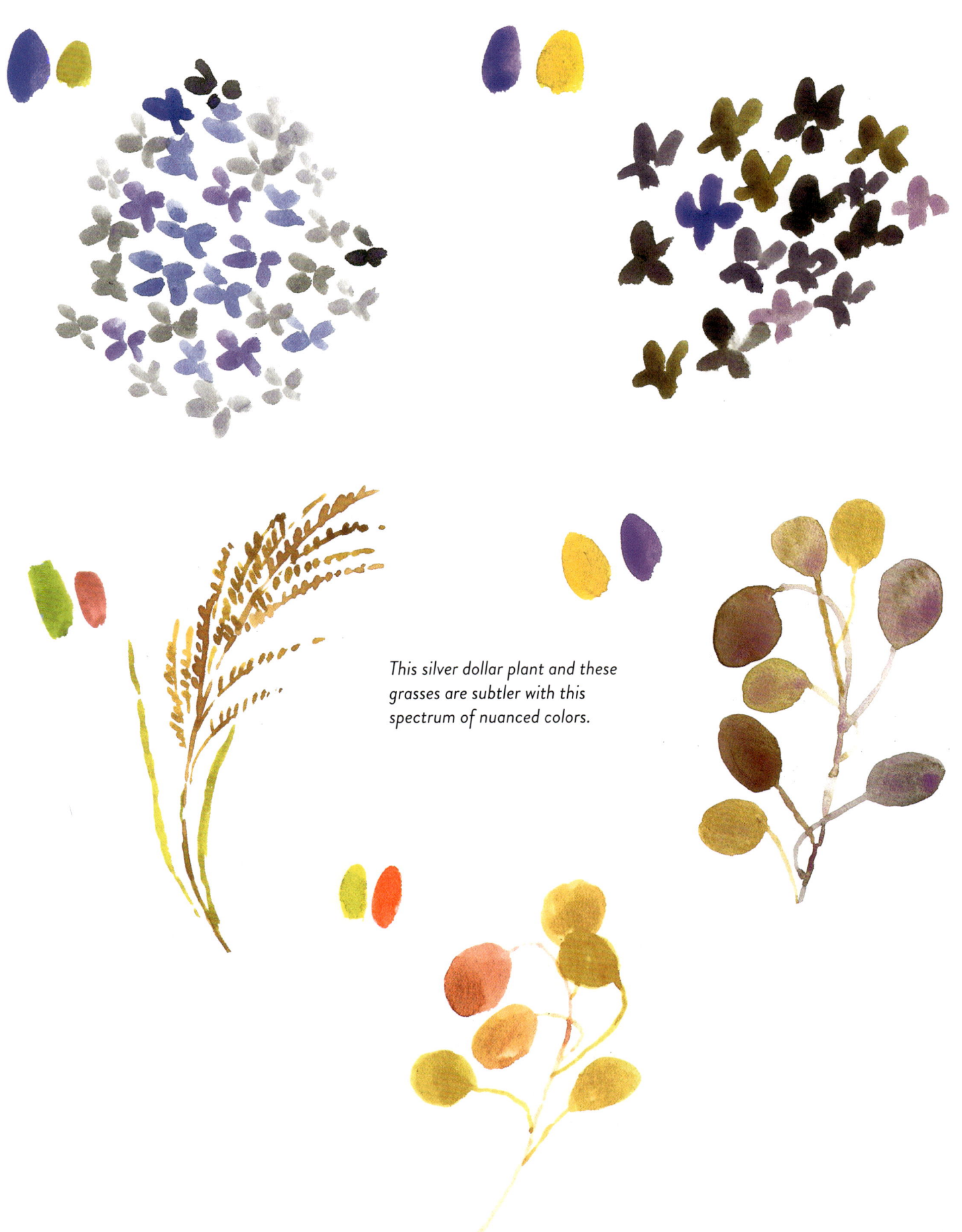

This silver dollar plant and these grasses are subtler with this spectrum of nuanced colors.

Week 31
Shading a Volume with Its Complement

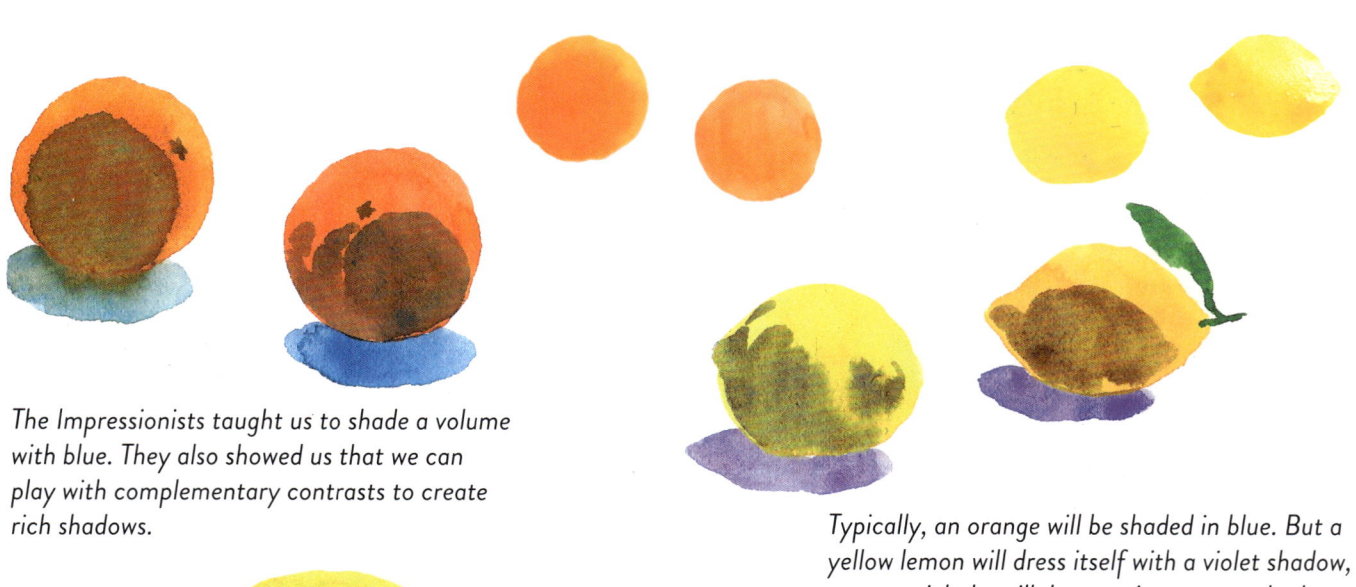

The Impressionists taught us to shade a volume with blue. They also showed us that we can play with complementary contrasts to create rich shadows.

Typically, an orange will be shaded in blue. But a yellow lemon will dress itself with a violet shadow, a green artichoke will dress up in a mauve shadow, and so on for the shading of the object itself.

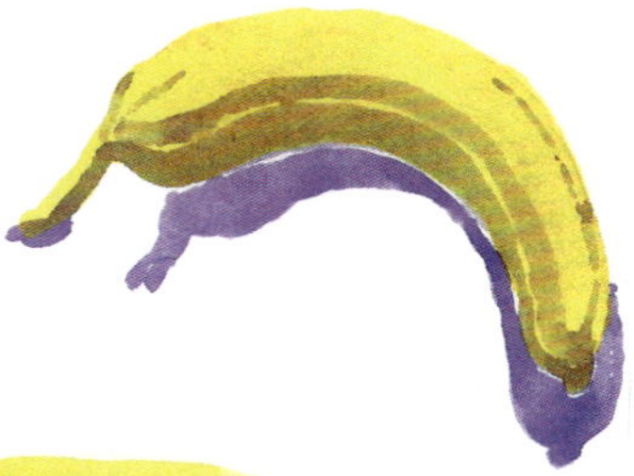

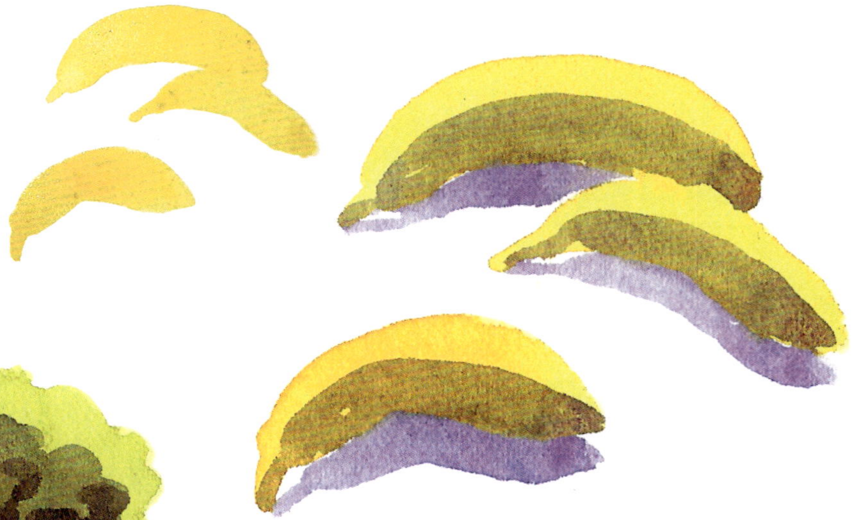

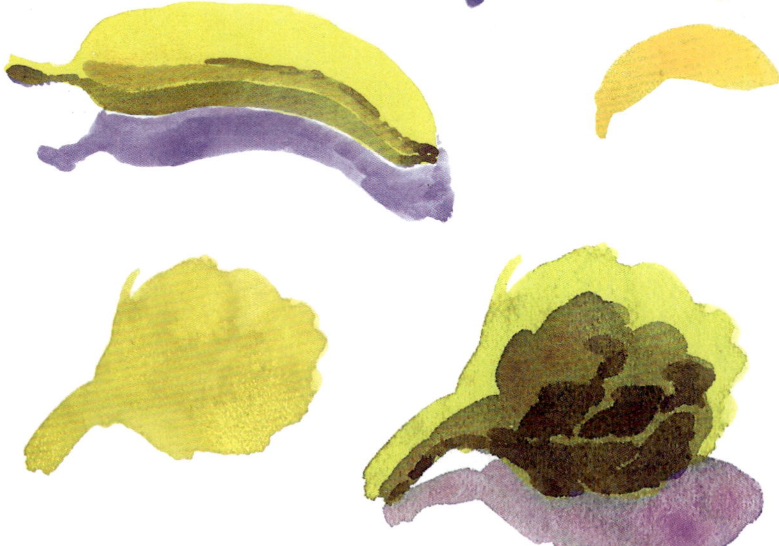

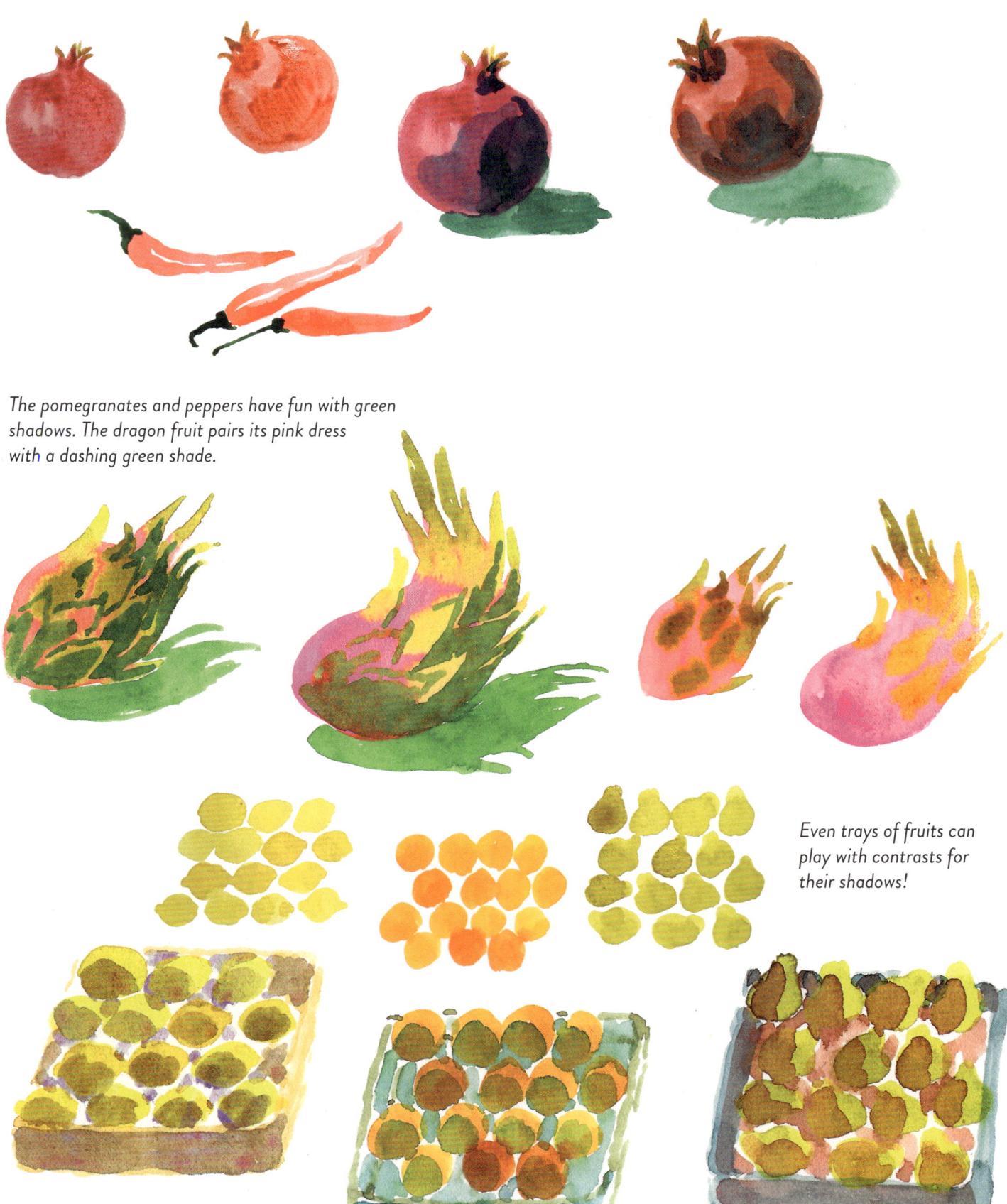

The pomegranates and peppers have fun with green shadows. The dragon fruit pairs its pink dress with a dashing green shade.

Even trays of fruits can play with contrasts for their shadows!

The produce stand is so beautiful. The fruits and vegetables have contrasting shadows. These bouquets of hydrangeas are so delicate, with their nuanced shades.

This is a lovely exercise for complementary contrasts, in all their forms.

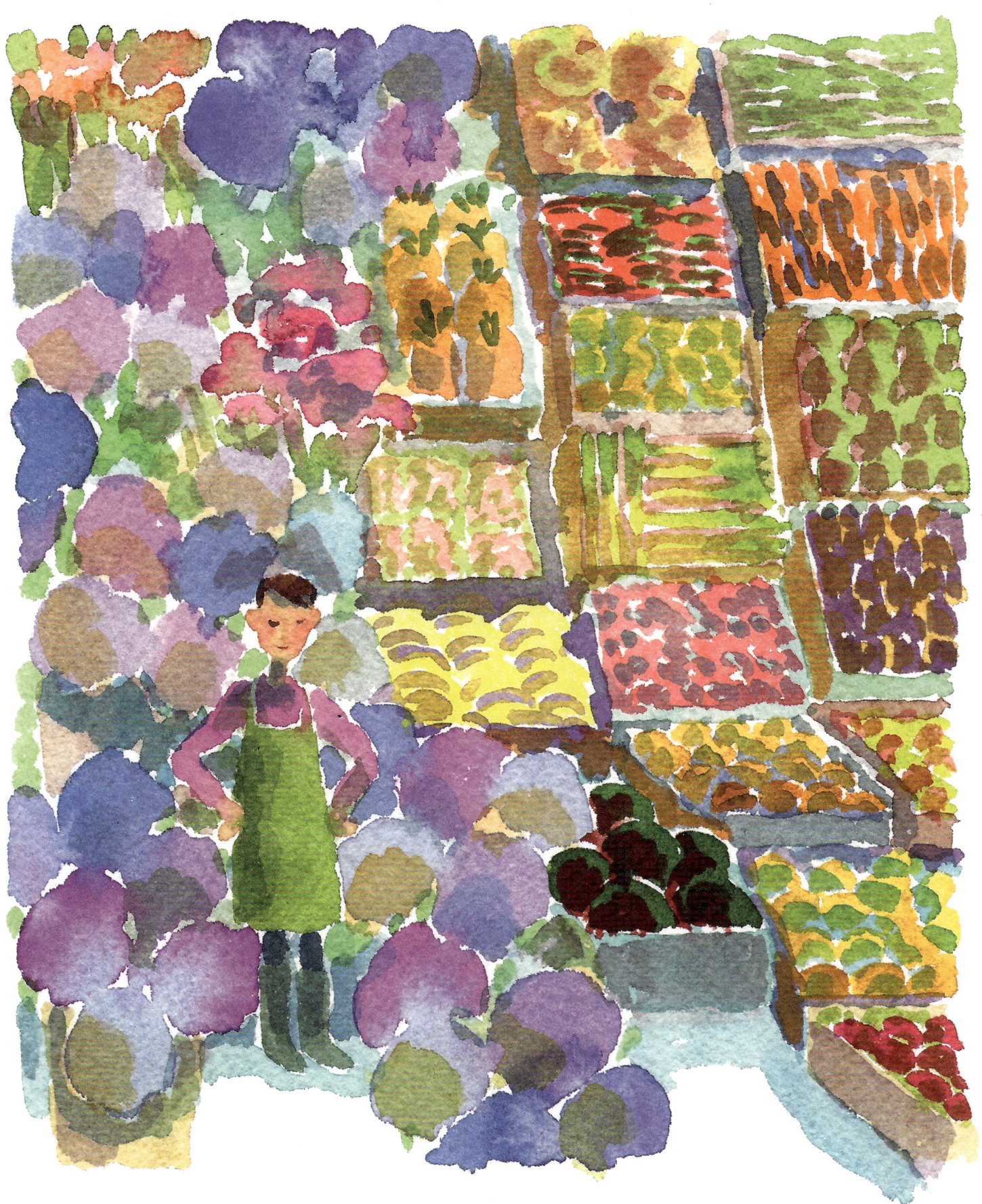

Week 32
The Colorful Grays

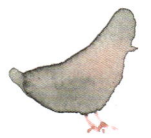

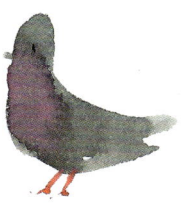

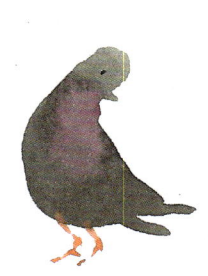

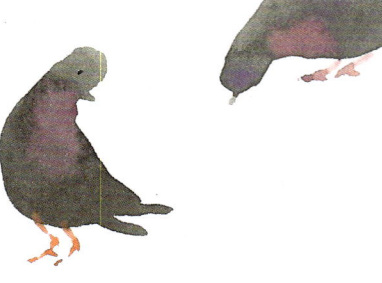

Gray doesn't get a lot of love. But gray has a delicate soul— and nuances to make the rest of the color spectrum pale with envy! All you need to do is really look, and honor it, by mixing all the colors.

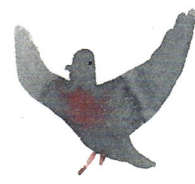

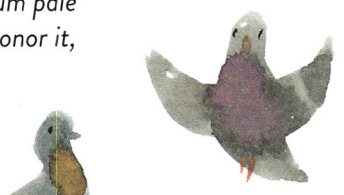

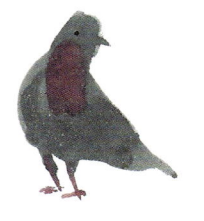

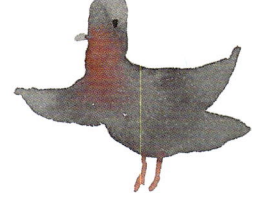

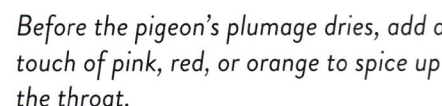

Before the pigeon's plumage dries, add a touch of pink, red, or orange to spice up the throat.

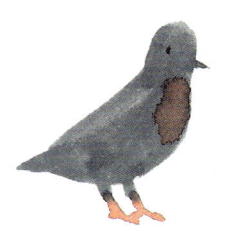

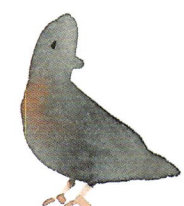

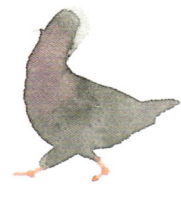

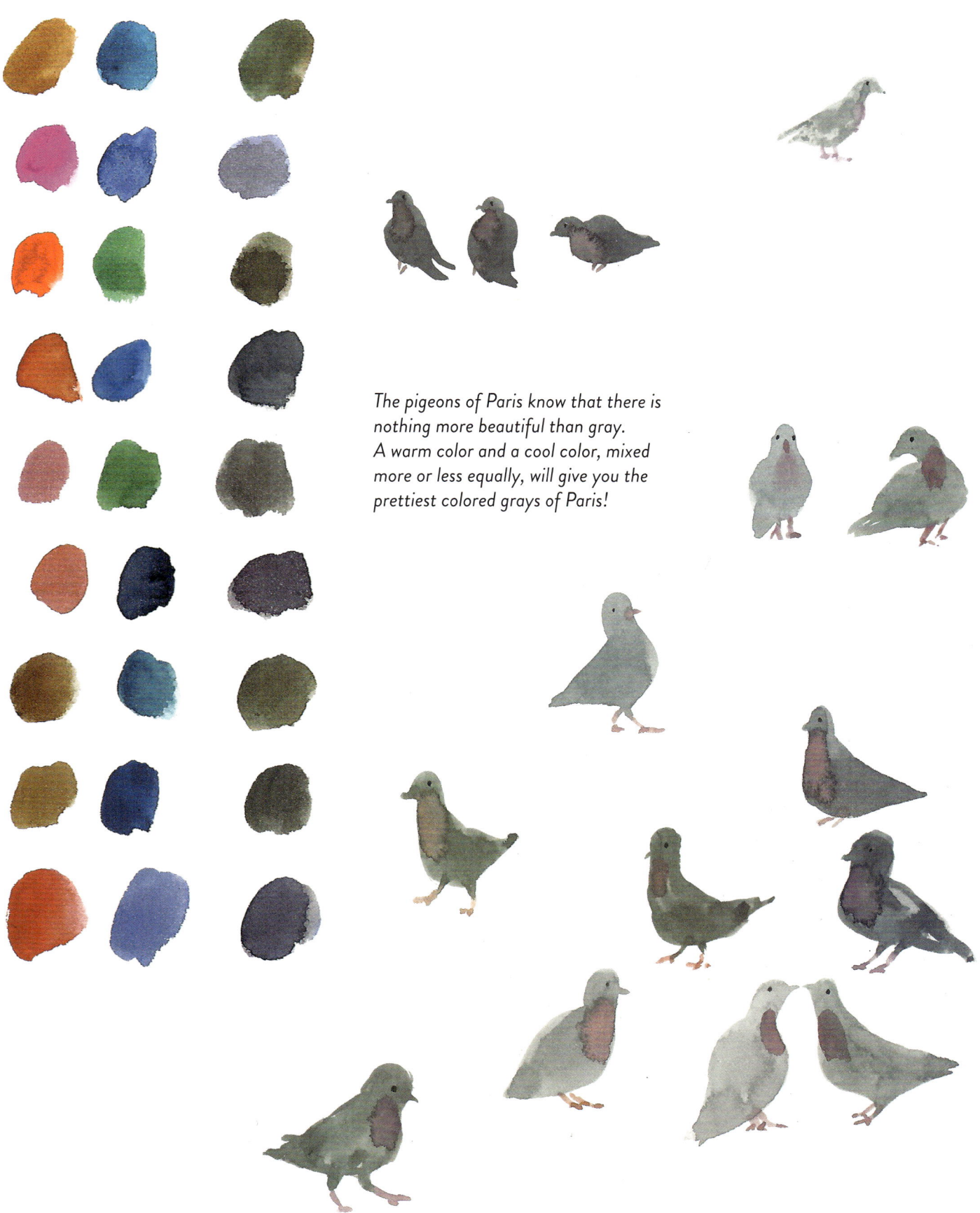

The pigeons of Paris know that there is nothing more beautiful than gray.
A warm color and a cool color, mixed more or less equally, will give you the prettiest colored grays of Paris!

Week 33
The Colorful Blacks

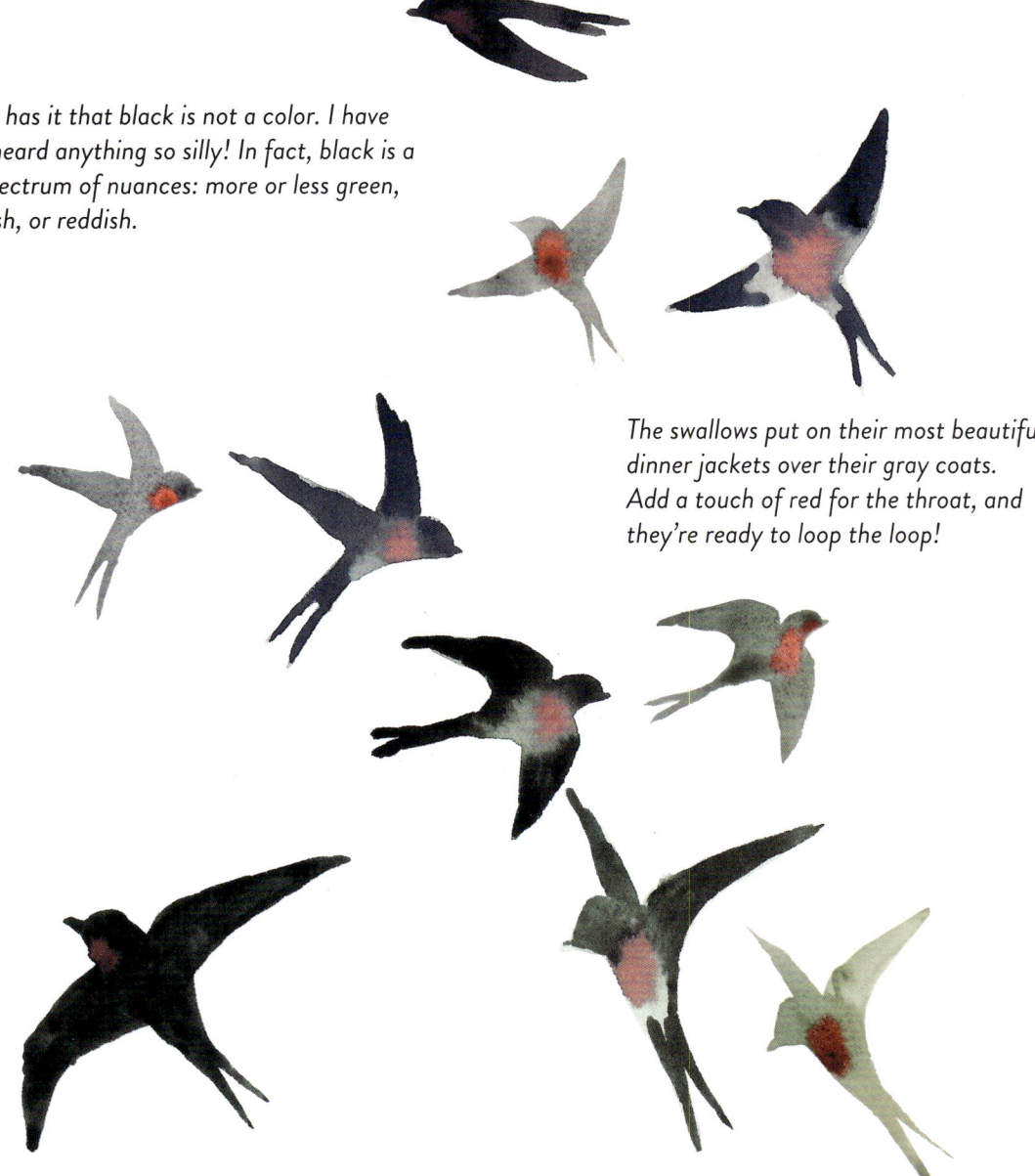

Rumor has it that black is not a color. I have never heard anything so silly! In fact, black is a vast spectrum of nuances: more or less green, or bluish, or reddish.

The swallows put on their most beautiful dinner jackets over their gray coats. Add a touch of red for the throat, and they're ready to loop the loop!

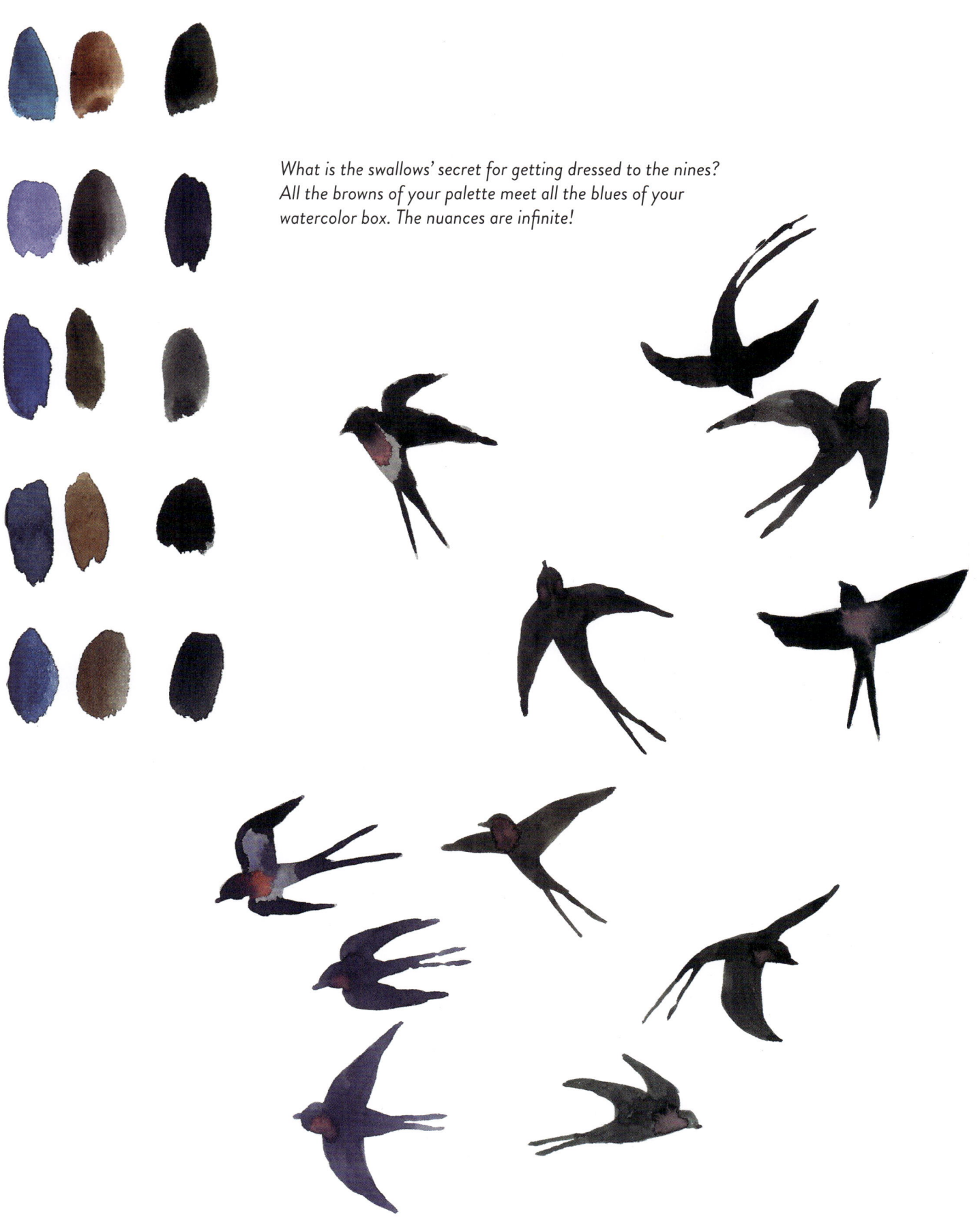

What is the swallows' secret for getting dressed to the nines?
All the browns of your palette meet all the blues of your
watercolor box. The nuances are infinite!

For More Practice

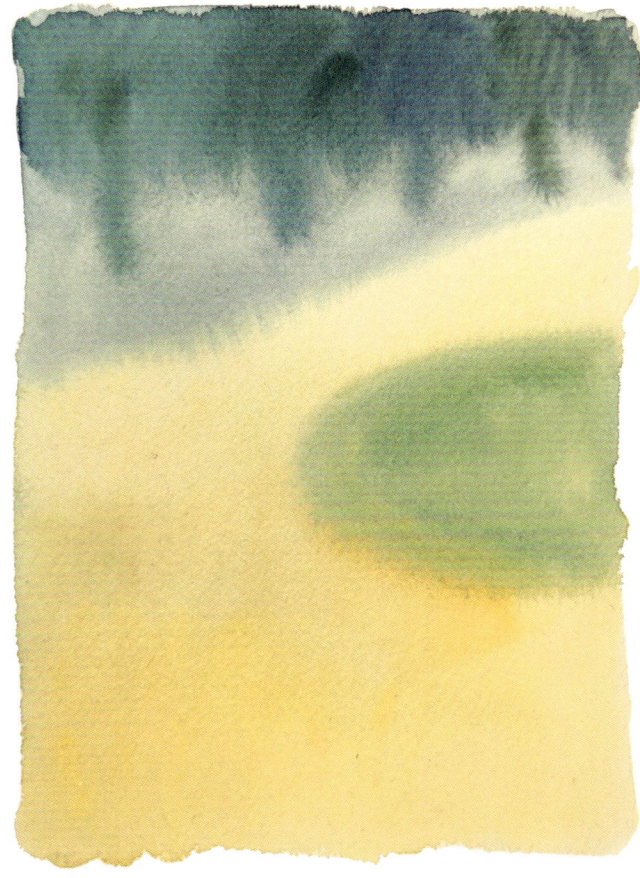

Do you want to take a rest at the Royal Palace? Paint, in wet on wet, the chalky ocher of the ground, a verdigris for the fountain, and some bluish trees for shade.

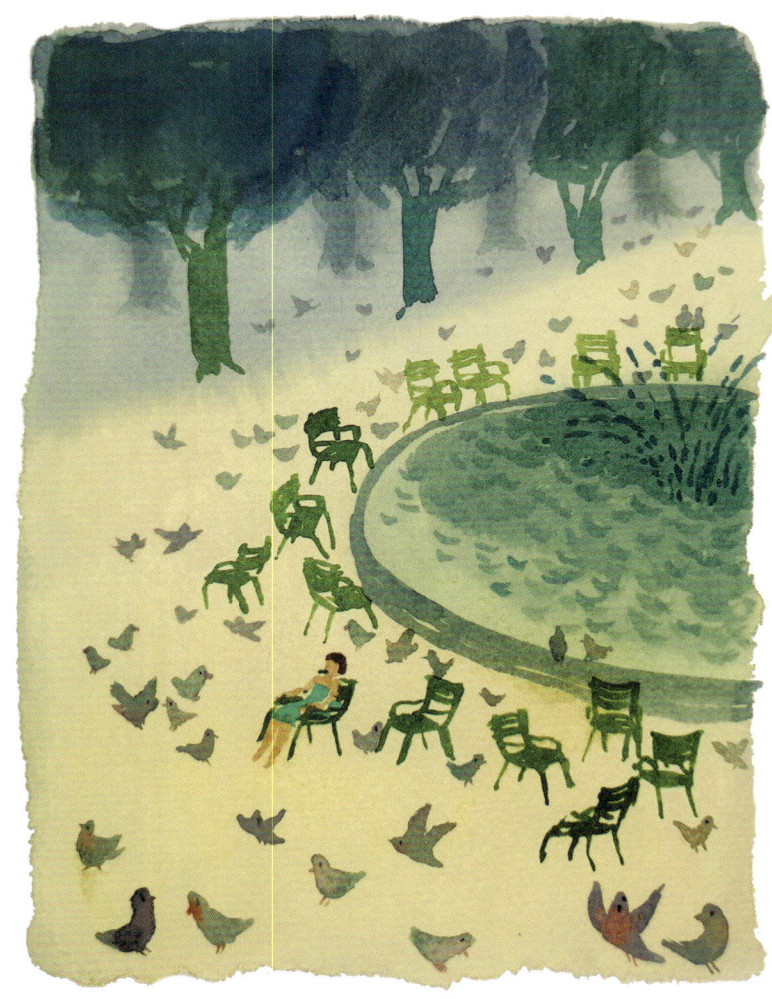

Draw a few green park chairs for reading in the sunshine, making them paler the farther away they are. Add more well-defined trees for the scenery and many pigeons in a thousand nuances of colored gray. As with the chairs, the more distant they are, the paler and less well-defined they are.

Add some bluish shadows and swallows in colorful blacks, and the sunbathing can begin.

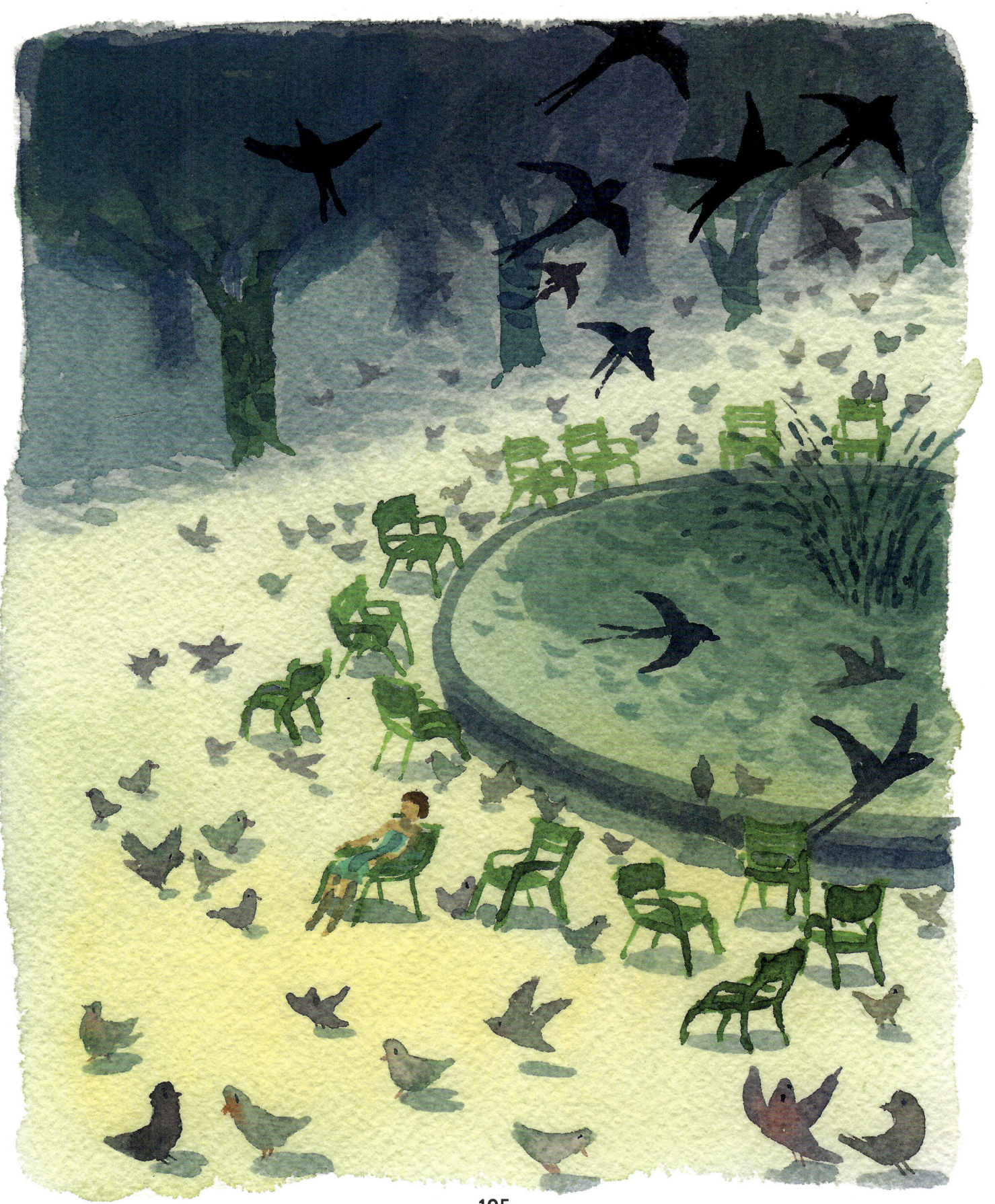

Week 34
Shaping the Line with the Brush

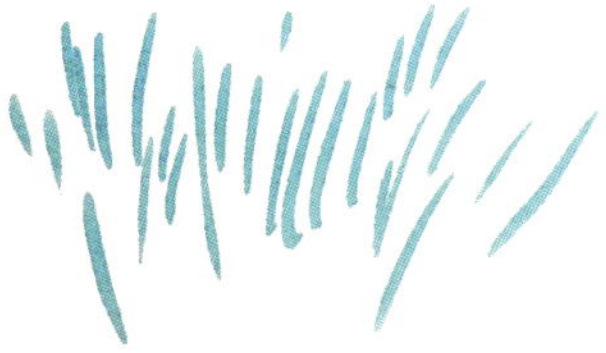

Draw these wild grasses with a fine brush, with a supple and light motion.

The brush is a precious tool. Adjust the line for each object you paint. Find the brush and the motion that are best adapted to the nature of the object you're painting.

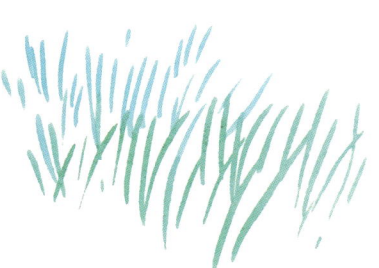

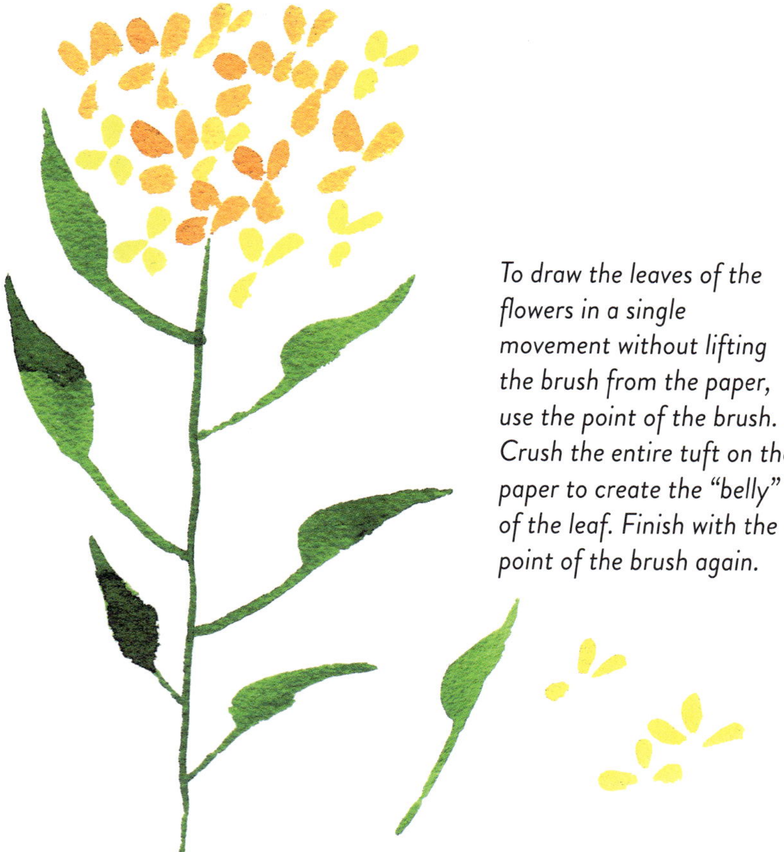

To draw the leaves of the flowers in a single movement without lifting the brush from the paper, use the point of the brush. Crush the entire tuft on the paper to create the "belly" of the leaf. Finish with the point of the brush again.

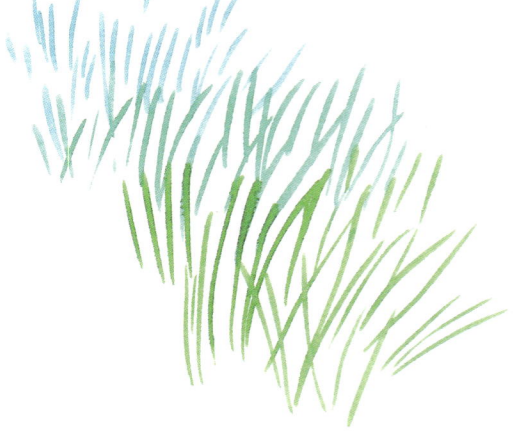

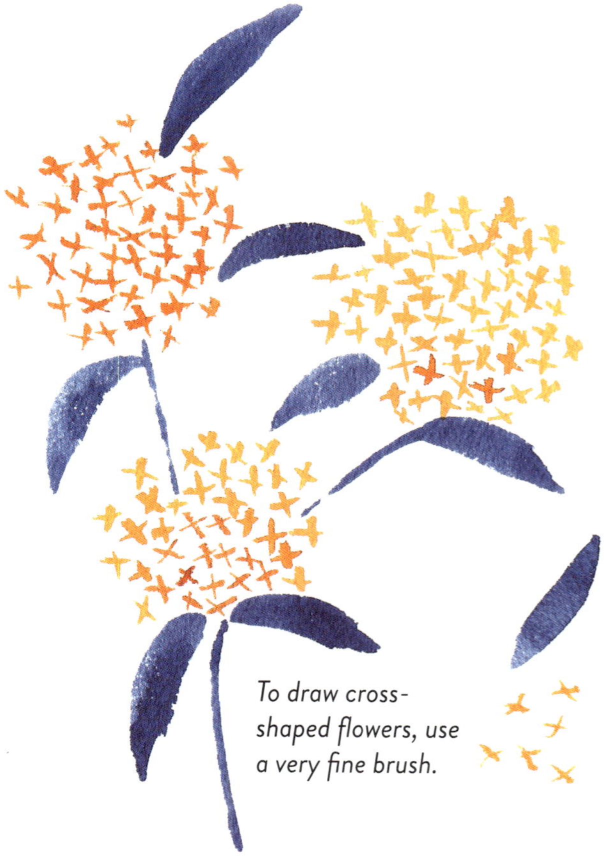

To draw cross-shaped flowers, use a very fine brush.

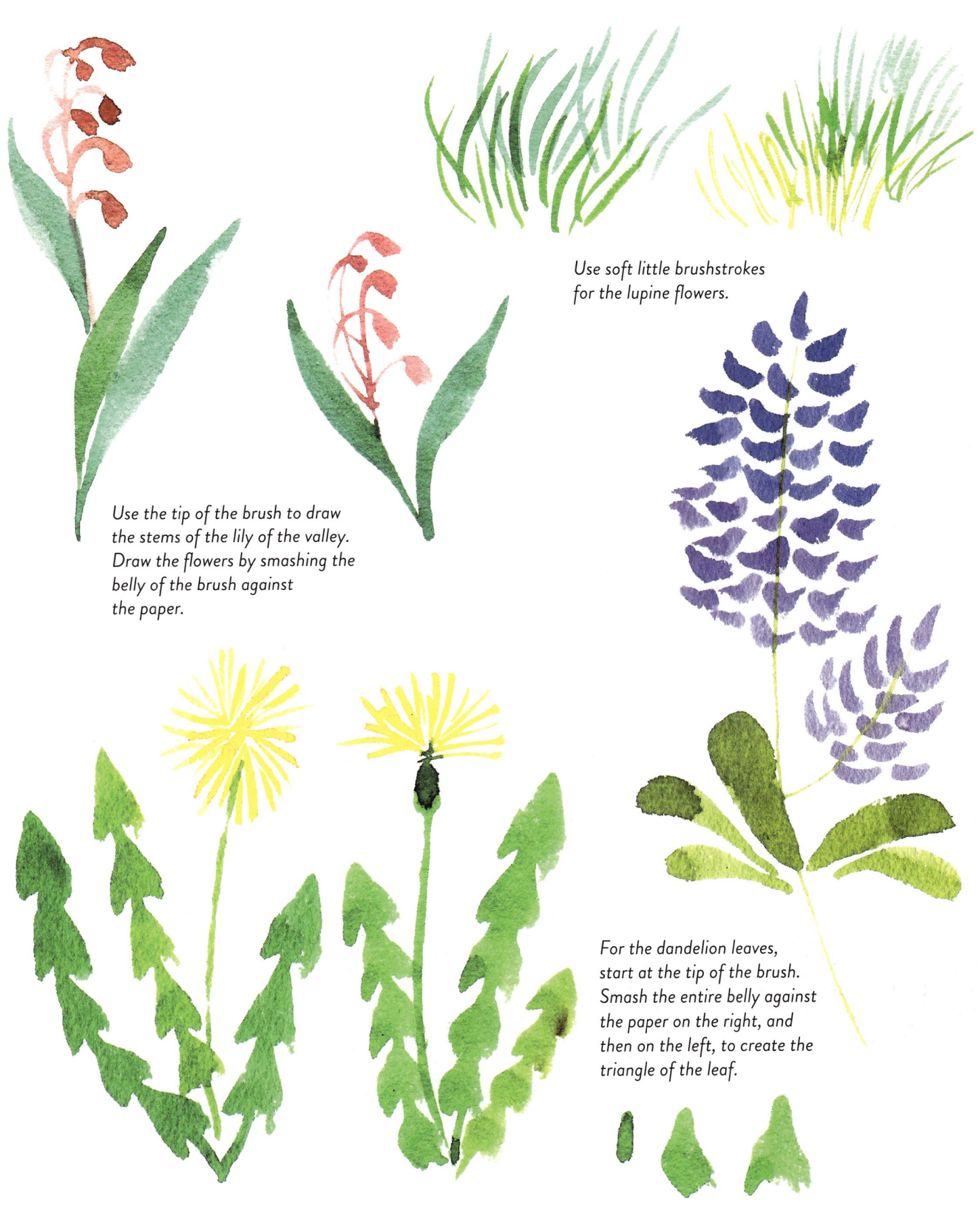

Use soft little brushstrokes for the lupine flowers.

Use the tip of the brush to draw the stems of the lily of the valley. Draw the flowers by smashing the belly of the brush against the paper.

For the dandelion leaves, start at the tip of the brush. Smash the entire belly against the paper on the right, and then on the left, to create the triangle of the leaf.

Week 35
Drawing Animals by Shaping the Line

As with the leaves last week, shape the line of the brush. Use the very fine tip, flatten the belly, pull the line, and push the color until you create the final shape—however complex it may be.

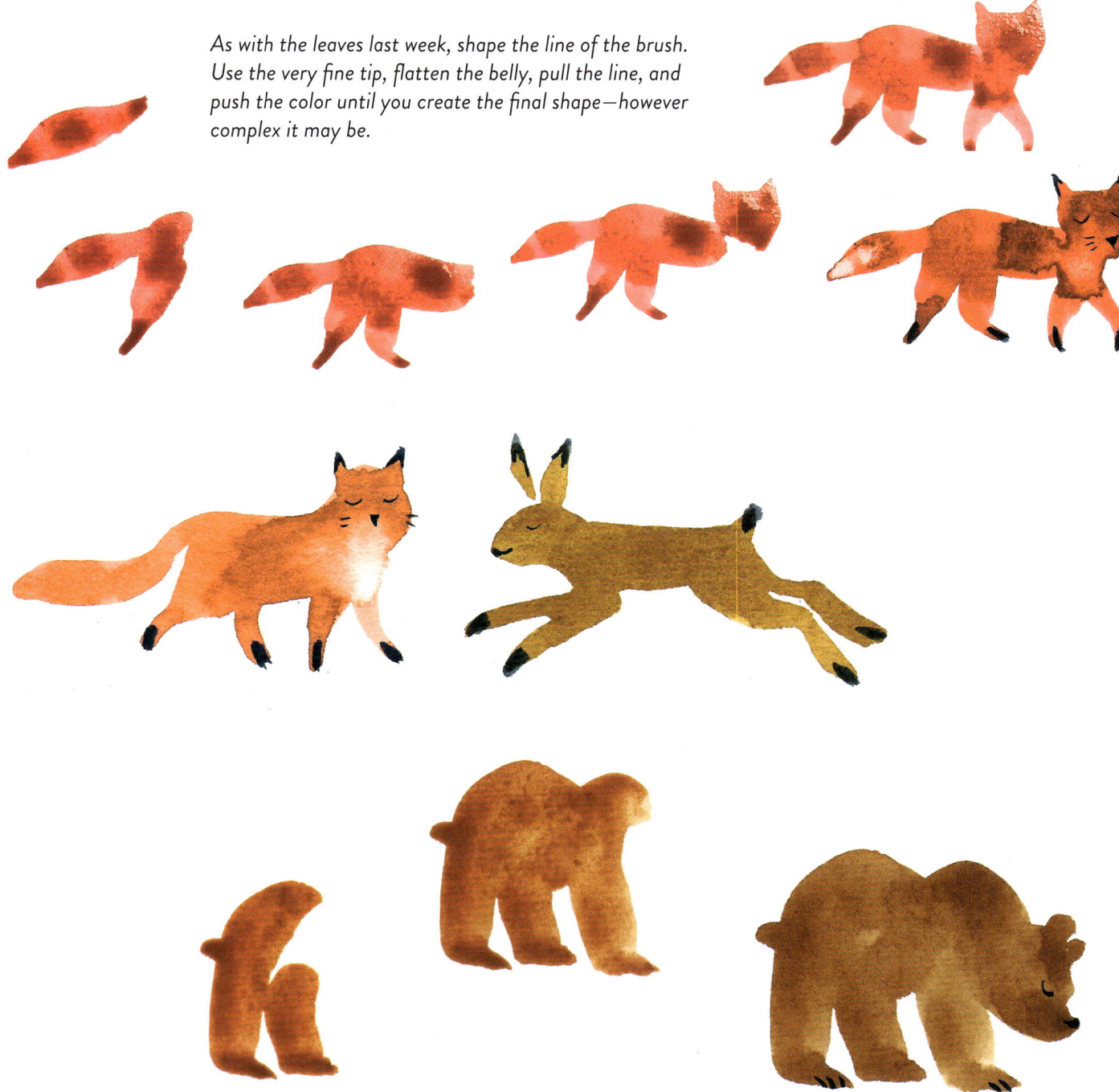

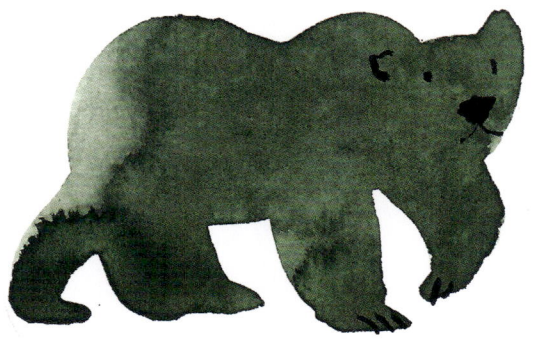

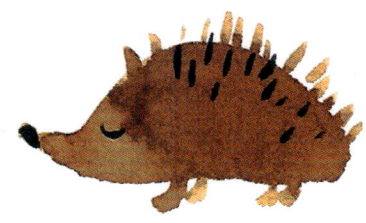

These wild animals are terrific examples of modulation using a round brush with a fine tip, of average size. Once the body is dry, use a very fine brush to trace the details.

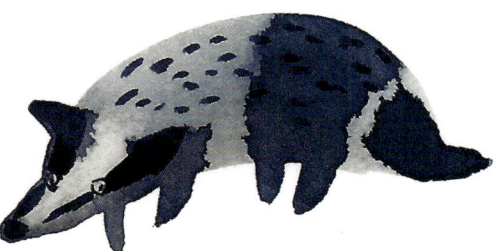

When you draw the shapes in watercolor, don't color them at all. Instead, imagine them as a calligraphy of ideograms. That lends a lot of dynamism to the shapes and makes them more graphic.

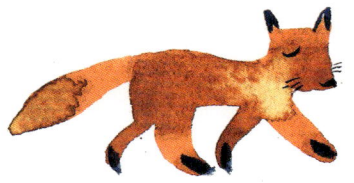

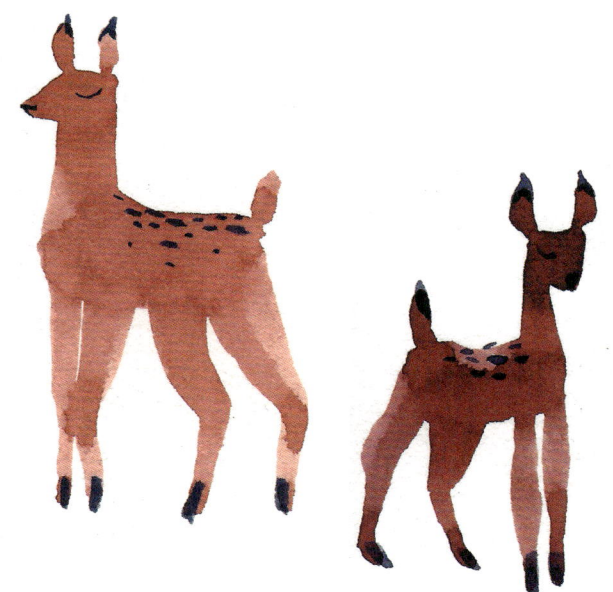

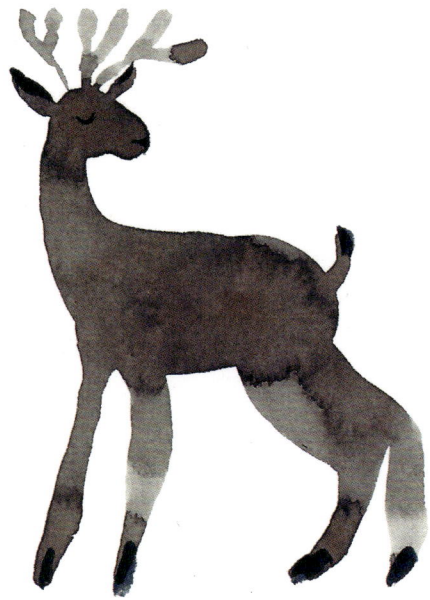

For More Practice

A vegetable garden is good practice for modulations of brushstrokes.

Draw the large masses of blue, green, and ocher in wet on wet in the abundant garden.

With a few supple brushstrokes, place the vegetable plants in the flower beds, a greenhouse in the distance, and some wild animals visiting the gardener, who is absorbed in his work.

The very graphic flowers in the foreground bring a viewer into the image. With a little watering and the addition of a few shadows, the vegetable garden bubbles with life!

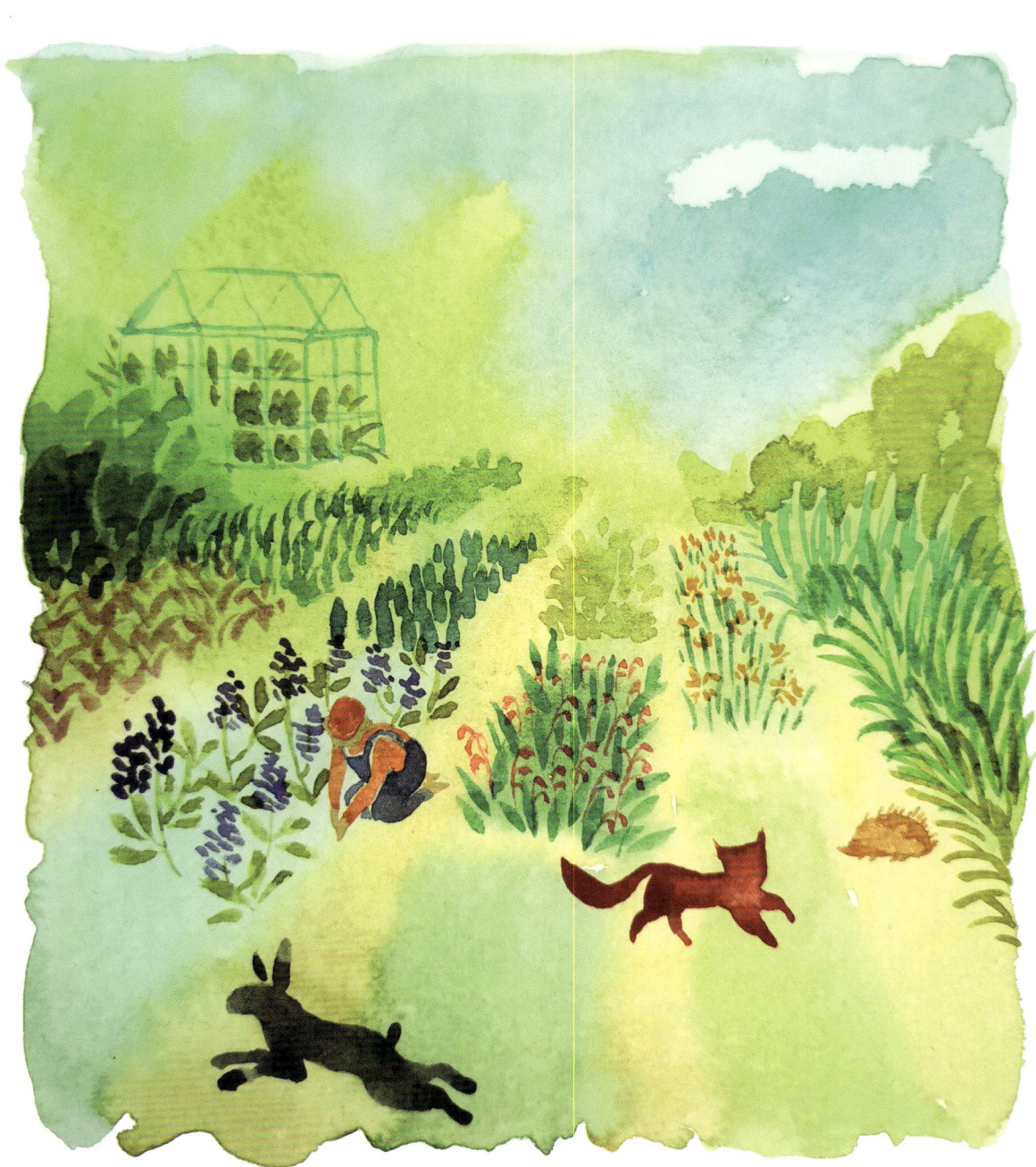

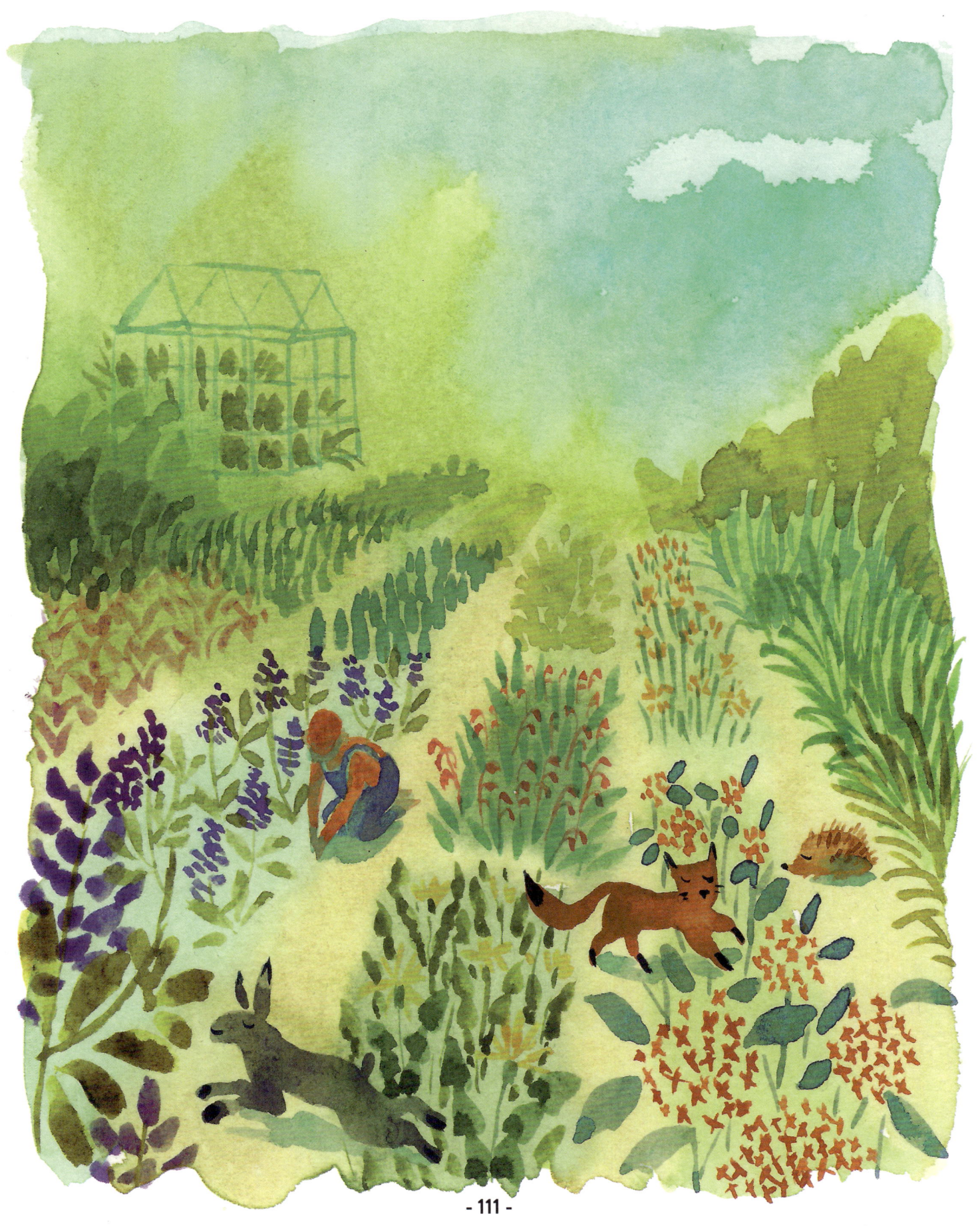

Week 36

The Expressivity of Movement

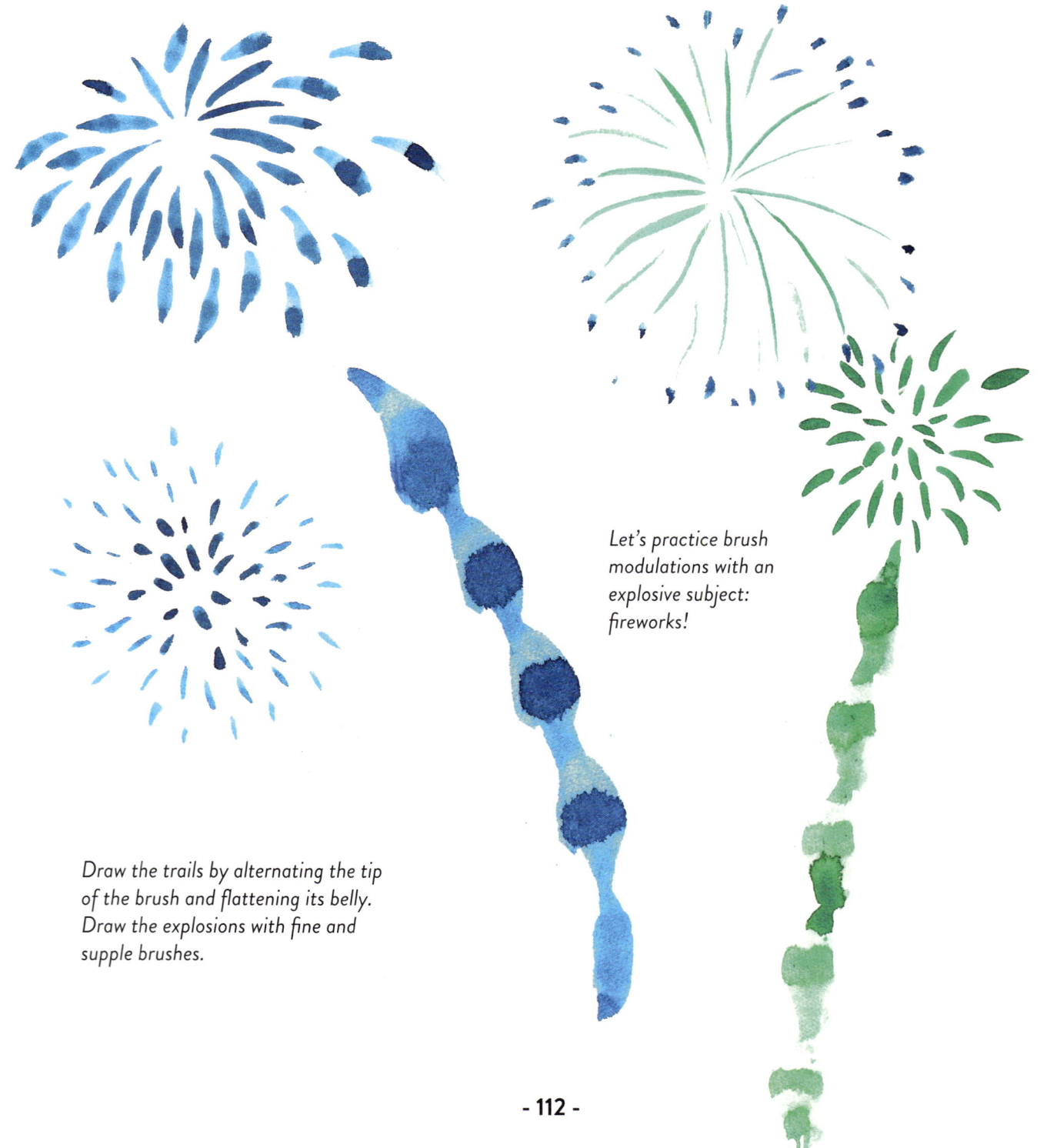

Let's practice brush modulations with an explosive subject: fireworks!

Draw the trails by alternating the tip of the brush and flattening its belly. Draw the explosions with fine and supple brushes.

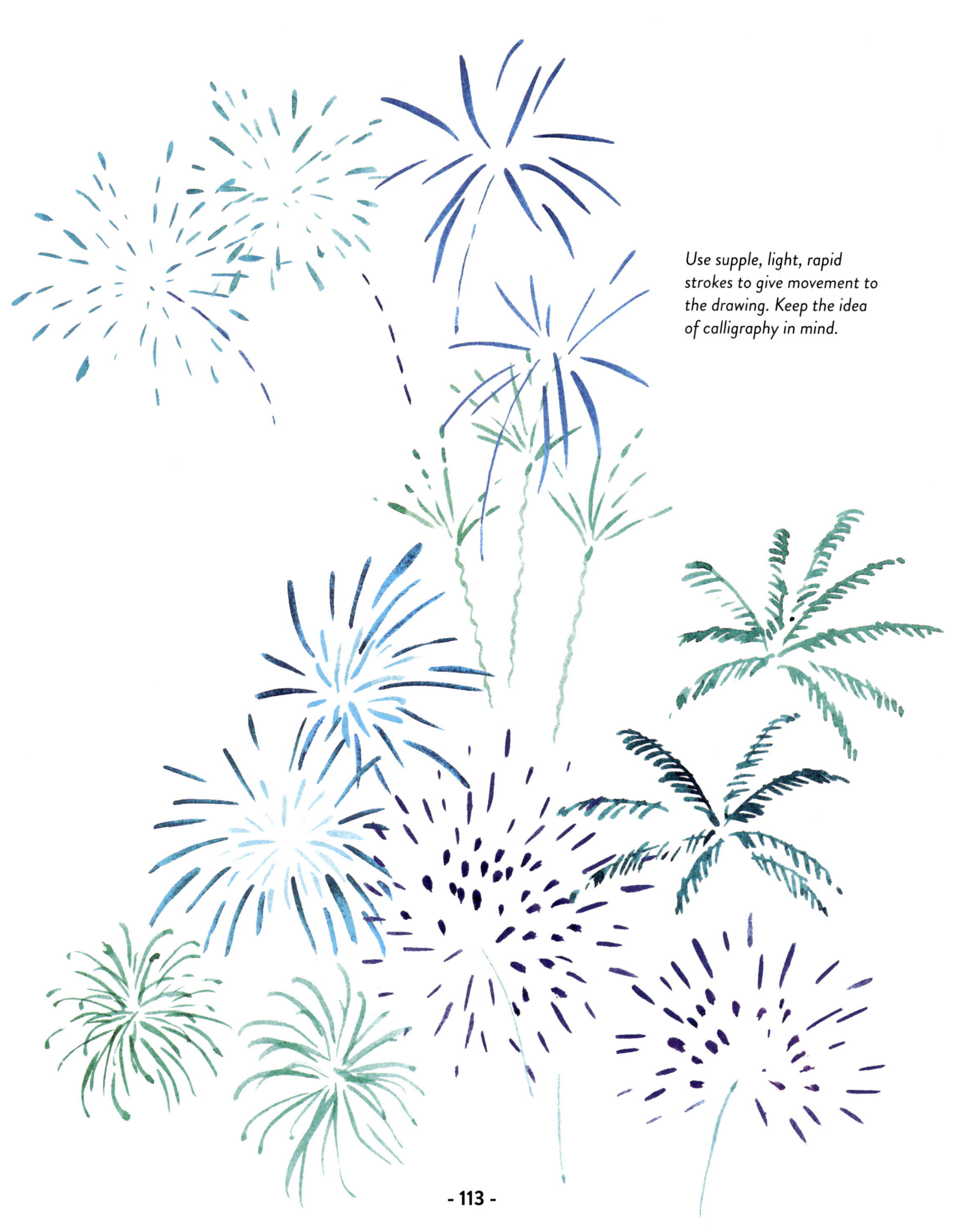

Use supple, light, rapid strokes to give movement to the drawing. Keep the idea of calligraphy in mind.

Week 37
The Virtues of the Flat Brush

For each script and graphic design, use the appropriate brush. To draw fireworks, use fine and supple brushes. For buildings and architectural features, use flat brushes to stick to the rigidity and angles of the subject.

Use a small flat brush to draw a skyline at the horizon.

Use a medium-sized flat brush for the closer roofs.

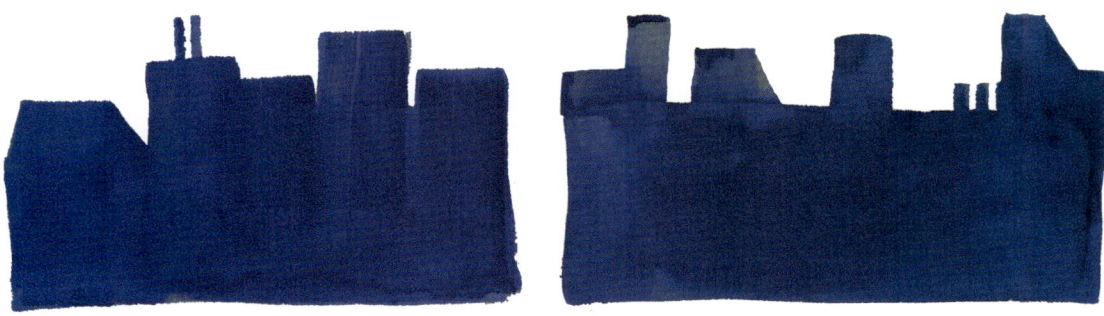

Use a large flat brush for the closest buildings. Draw each rectangle with a single stroke of the brush and the roofs in two brushstrokes. Add the chimneys last.

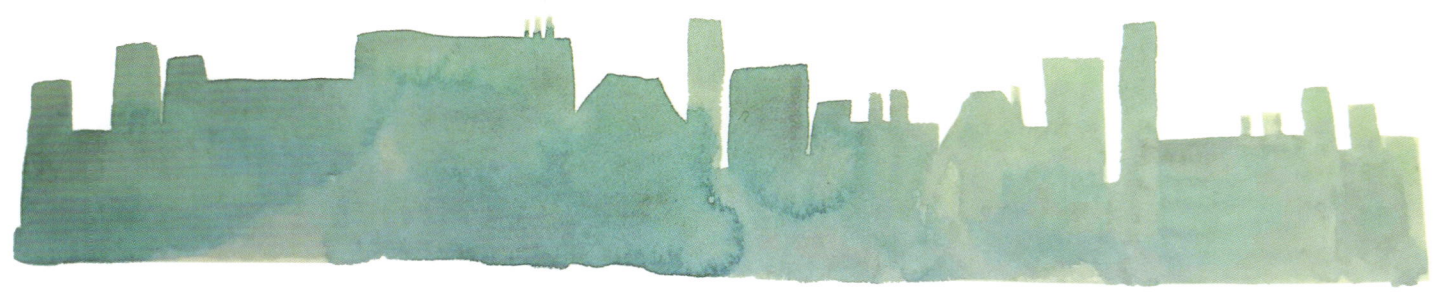

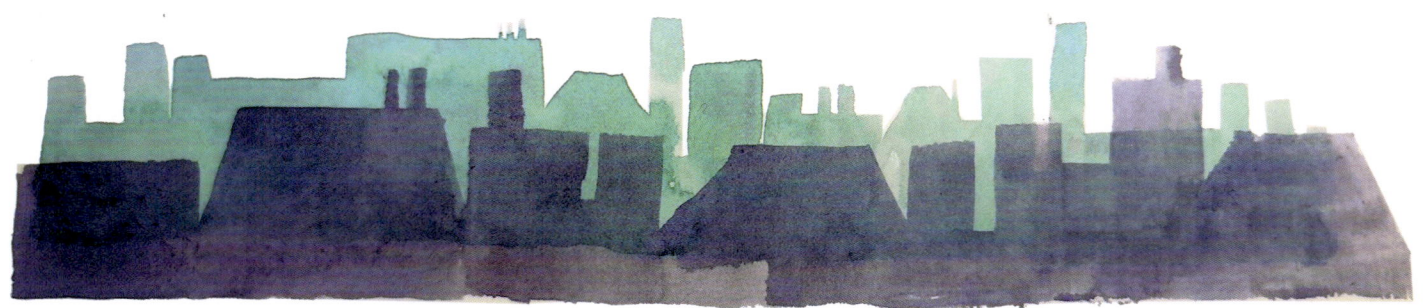

Overlap the layers to create a horizon of roofs:
pale cyan for the background, violet for
the intermediate one, and dark blue for the
foreground. Vary the size of the flat brushes.

For More Practice

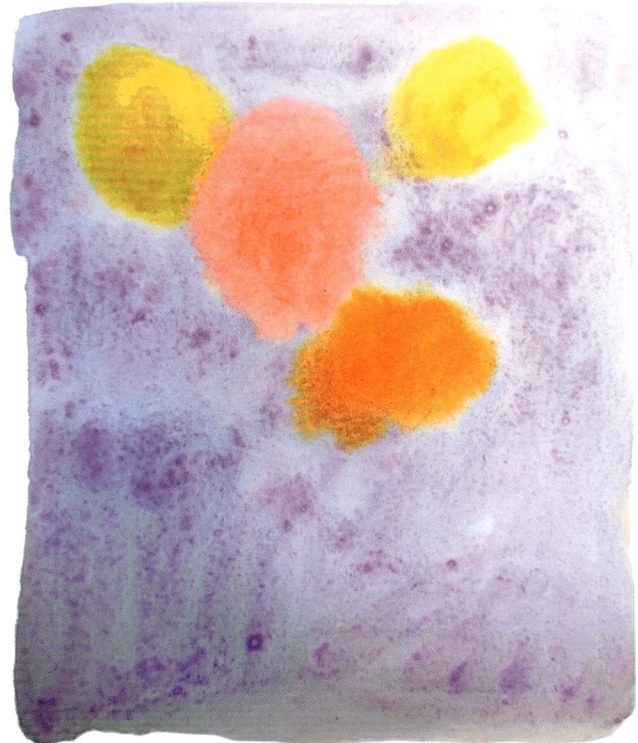

A beautiful summer evening for watching fireworks above the city starts with the colors in large quantities. Paint the violet sky and the luminous pyrotechnic explosions on wet paper.

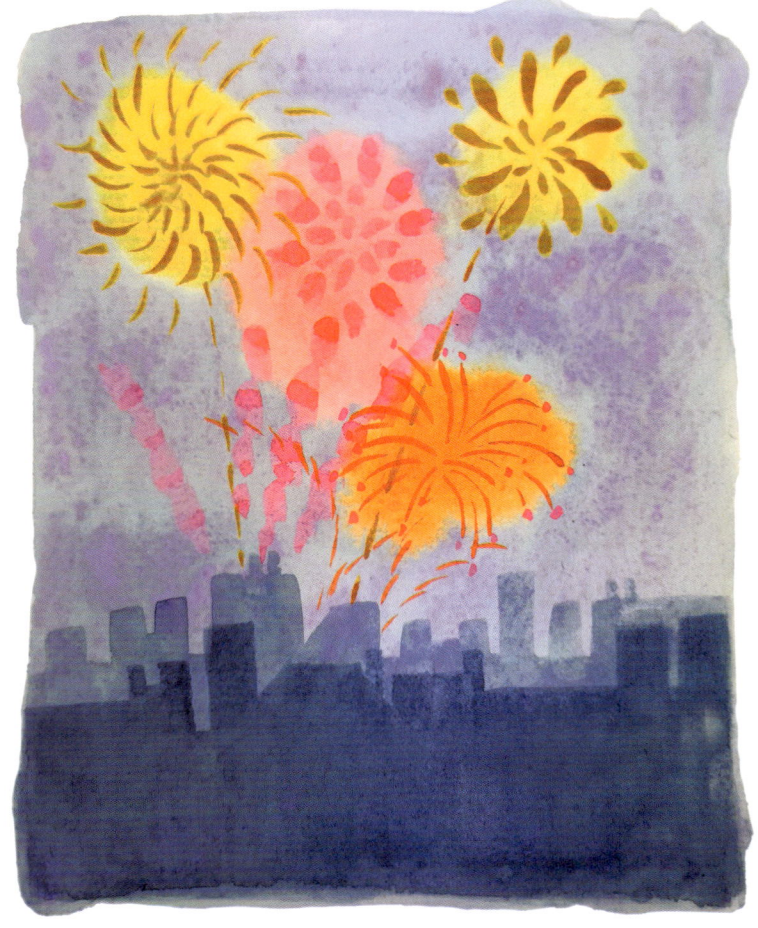

Once the background is dry, draw some bursts of fireworks with a brush, paying attention to the suppleness and expressivity of the movement.

Place the roofs, spreading them across the scene, in front of the silhouette of a spectator on the tin roof, like a puppet in a shadow theater.

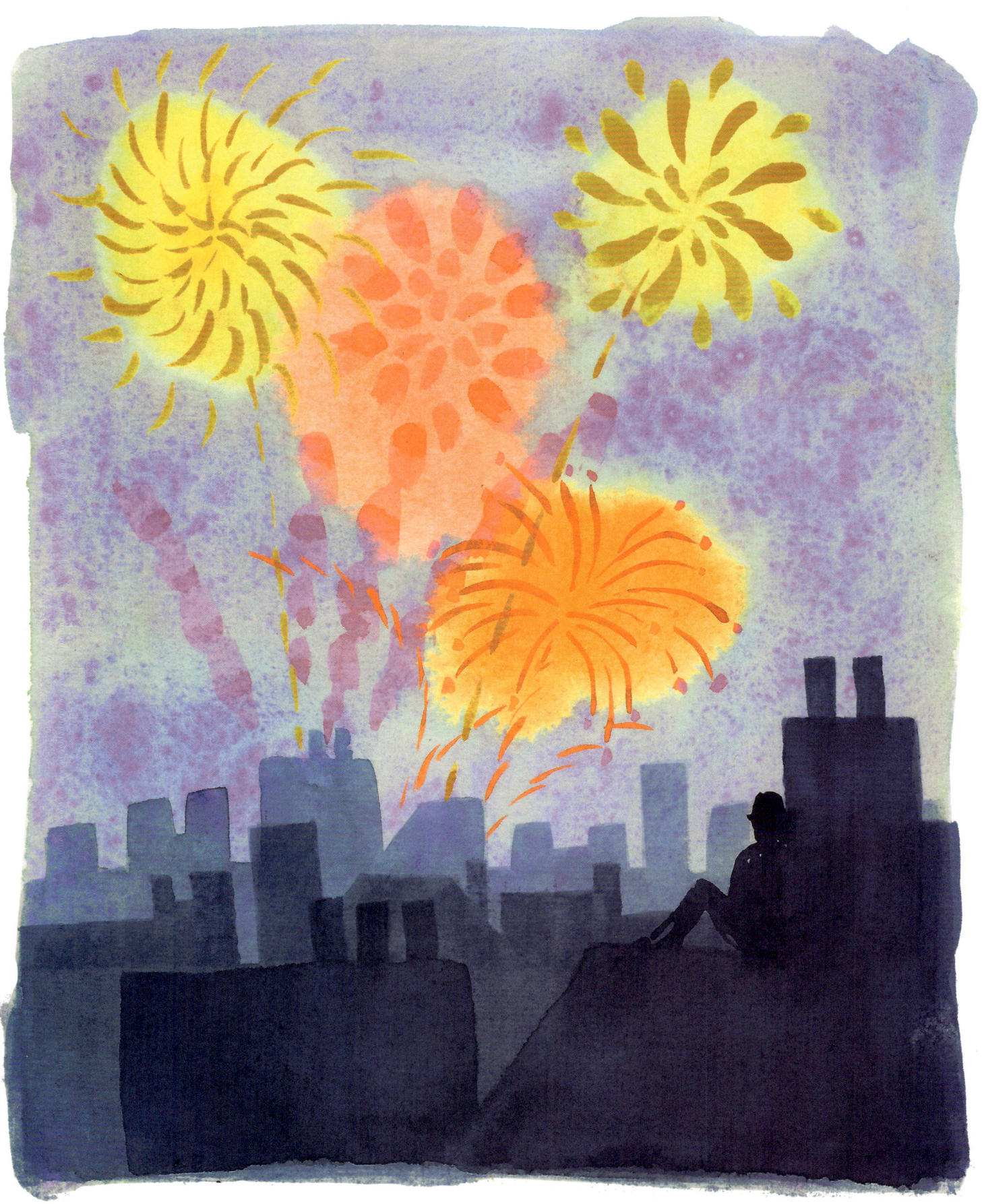

Week 38

Using a Dry Brush

There is nothing more fun than using a dry brush to draw the branches of fennel, sprigs of lavender, or garlic flowers!

For this technique, use an old, cheap brush. Load the brush with a little water and a small quantity of paint mix. "Wipe" the brush on the paper palette so that the bristles are dry enough to separate from each other. Warning: This could ruin a precious brush.

Express the material nature of some flowers and their textured foliage. Give a graphic and gestural impulse to your brush to make the flowers flourish!

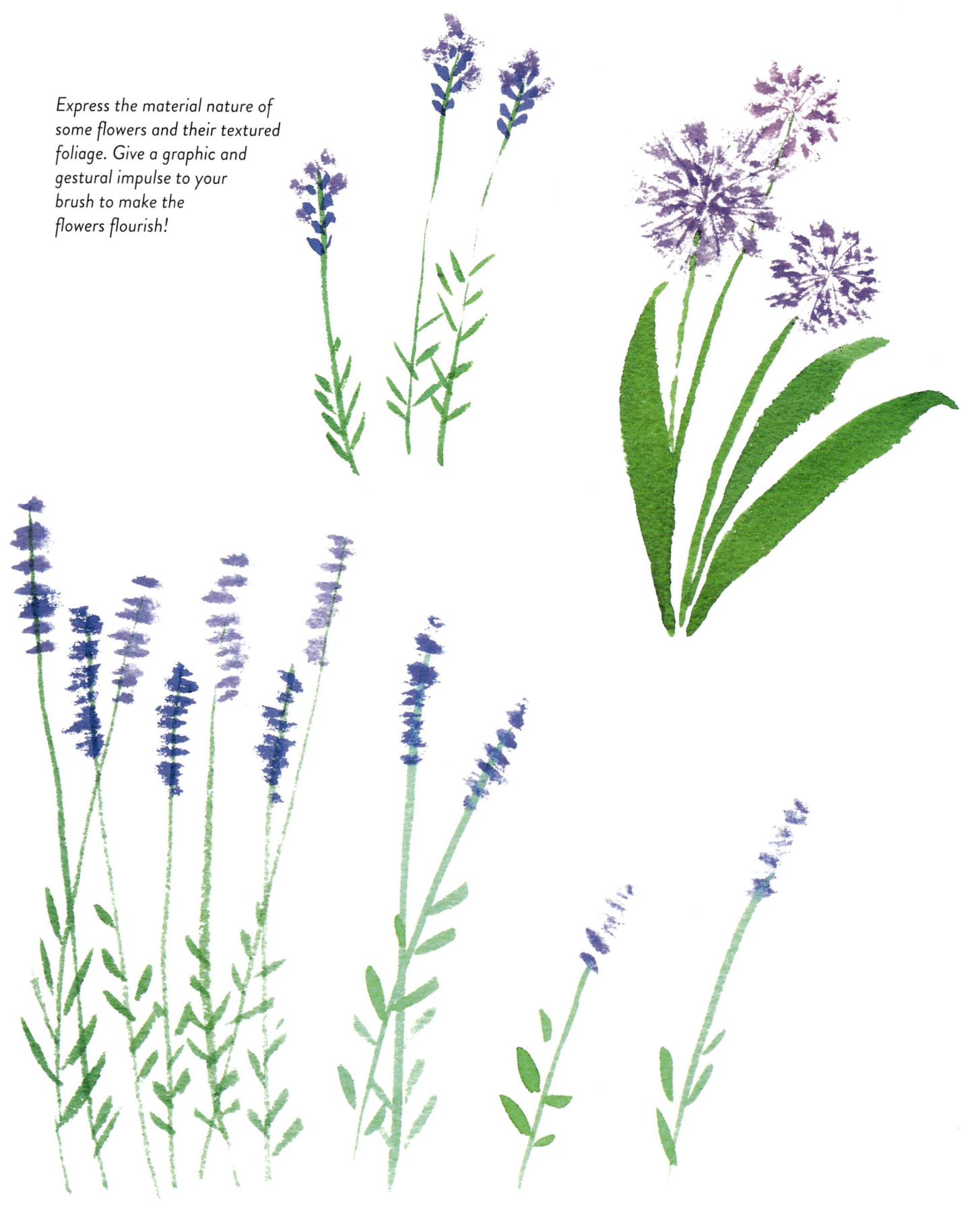

Week 39
Spattering and Splashes

Use an old toothbrush for spattering. Make a very diluted paint mix with lots of water. Soak the brush in the paint mix, and soak up lots of paint. Rub the brush with your finger, directing the spatters toward the paper. With practice, you can obtain an effect that is light and very fine, or more pronounced and dense, and more or less directed in its shape.

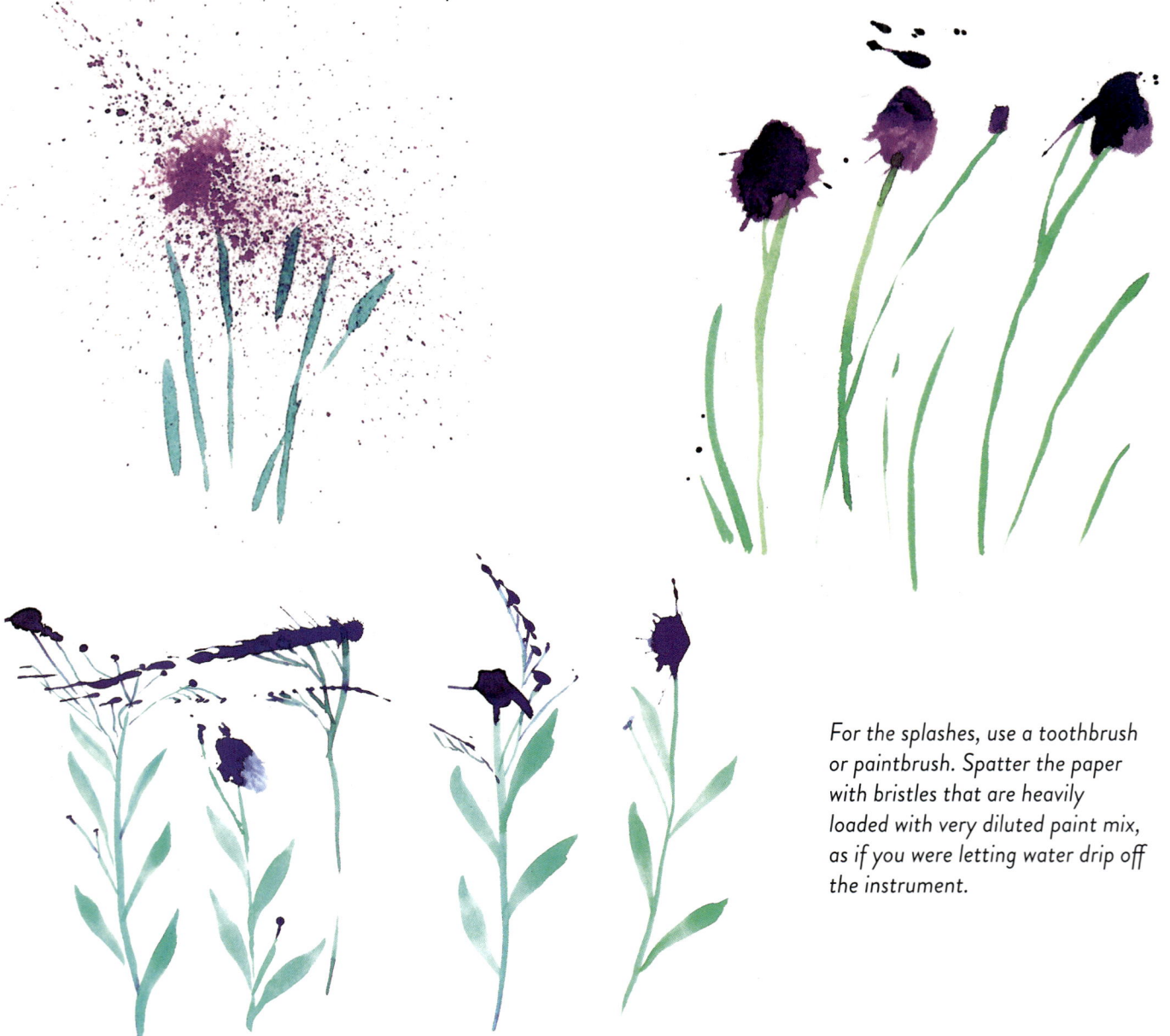

For the splashes, use a toothbrush or paintbrush. Spatter the paper with bristles that are heavily loaded with very diluted paint mix, as if you were letting water drip off the instrument.

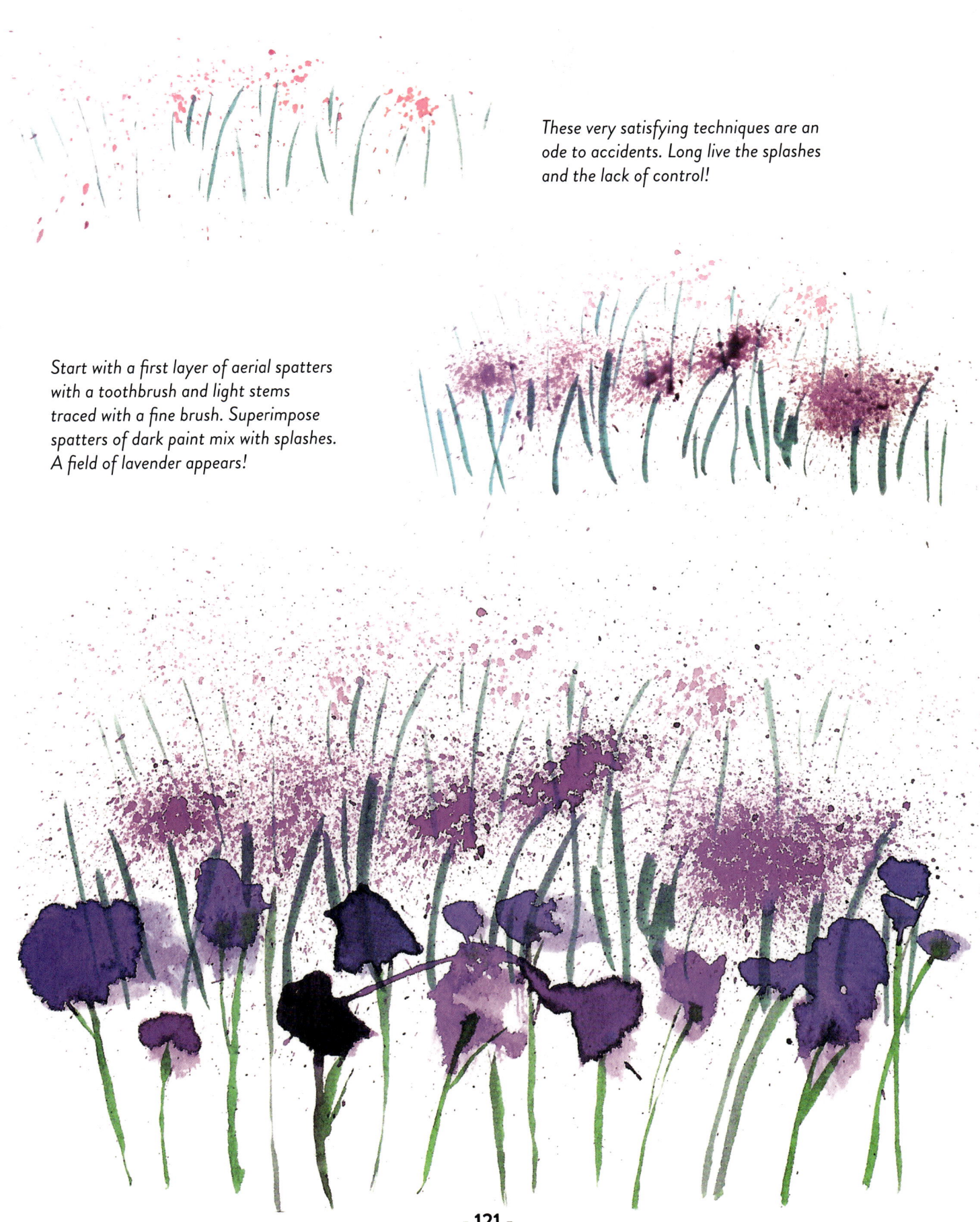

These very satisfying techniques are an ode to accidents. Long live the splashes and the lack of control!

Start with a first layer of aerial spatters with a toothbrush and light stems traced with a fine brush. Superimpose spatters of dark paint mix with splashes. A field of lavender appears!

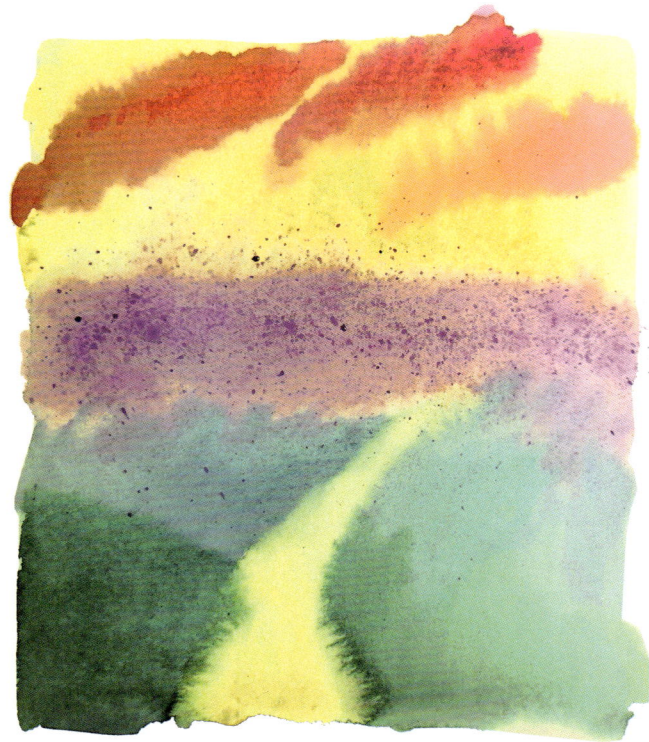

For this stroll through a field of lavender, paint the large masses of color in pale yellow, Parma violet, and blue green on wet paper. Without waiting for these colors to dry, sketch some colorful clouds.

When the background is dry, lightly spatter the background of the lavender field.

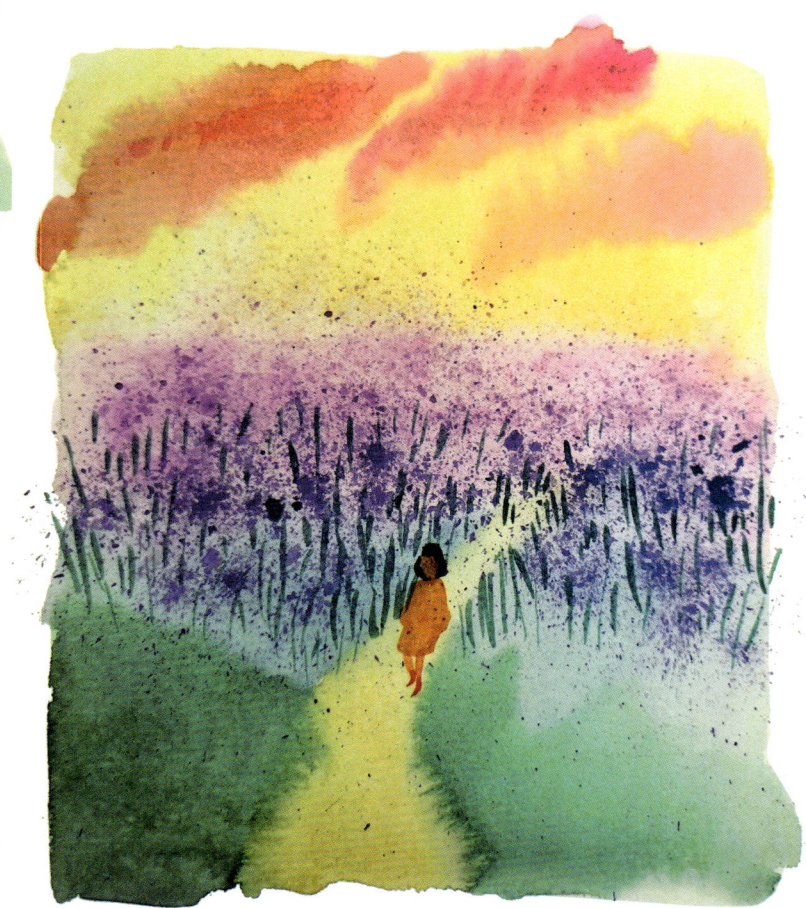

Using a toothbrush loaded with a dark violet paint mix, superimpose a second layer of thicker spattering. Draw some supple stems. A walker appears in a dress that contrasts with the violet field.

In the foreground, let loose! A joyous attack of blue and dark violet splashes enlivens the perspective. Some shadows on the figure complete the luminous atmosphere.

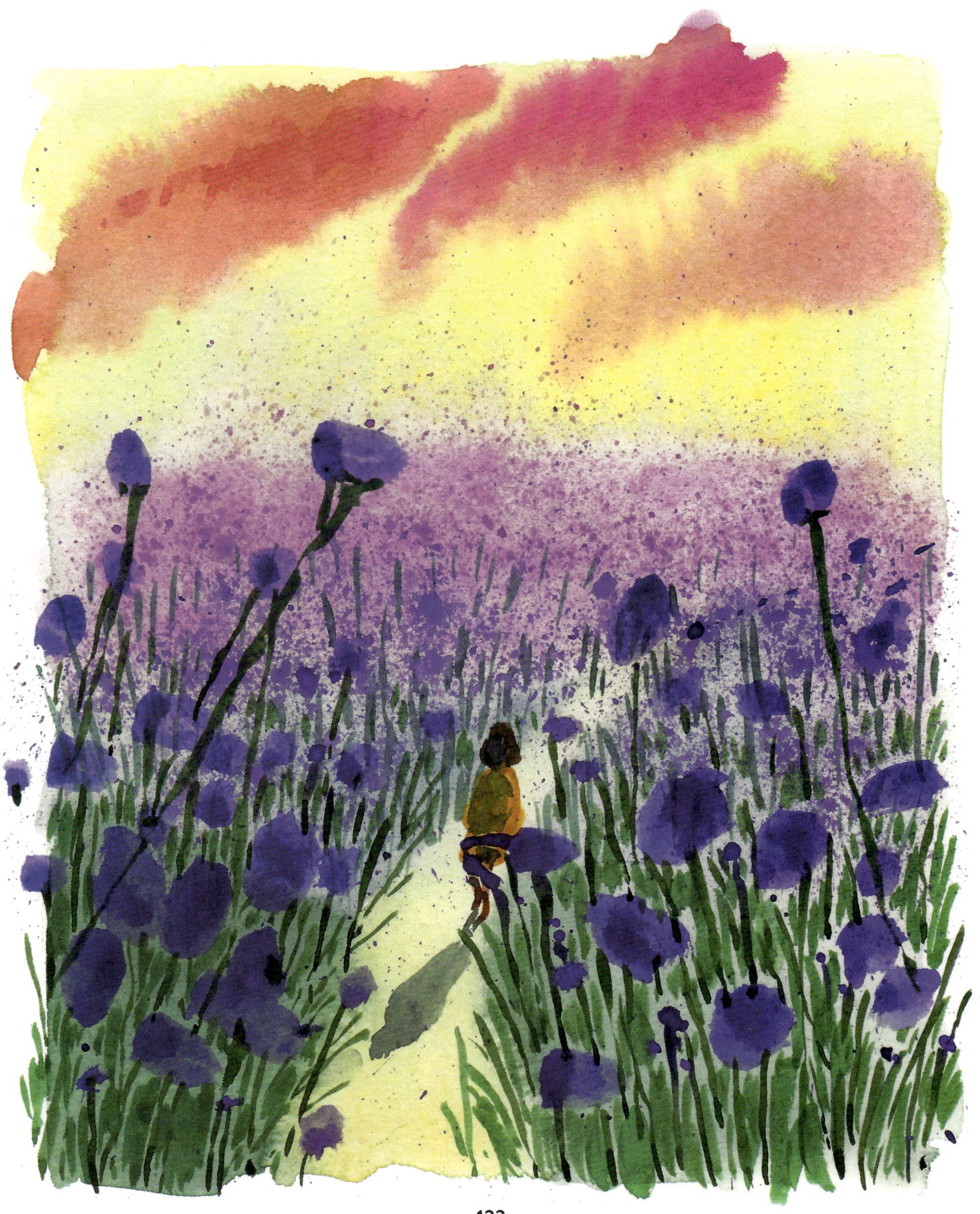

Week 40
Painting with Salt

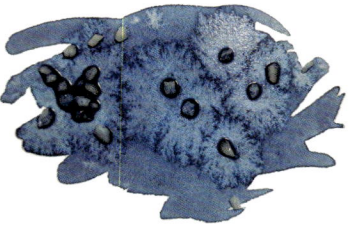
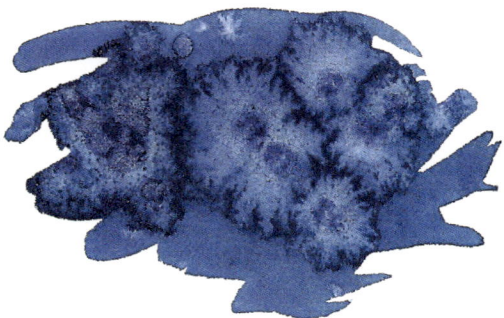

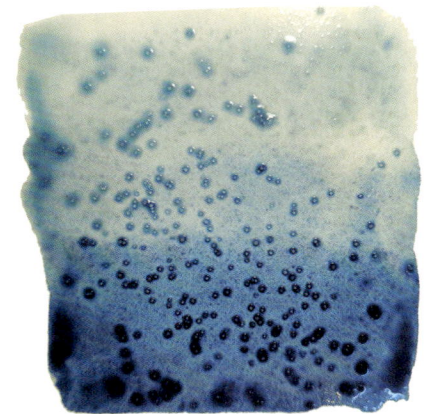

Crystals of salt push back wet pigments, creating random stars and halos. The salt that works best is fleur de sel from Guérande, France—a luxurious taste or a taste for luxury?

Sprinkle the fleur de sel on a paint mix. Don't touch anything else yet. Wait patiently for a long time for the stars to appear and dry, because the salt retains humidity well. Remove the leftover salt from the paper after the drying is complete.

On the left, make a gradation, and once the salted background is dry, draw the swimmer. On the right, draw the bather first, and then paint the background.

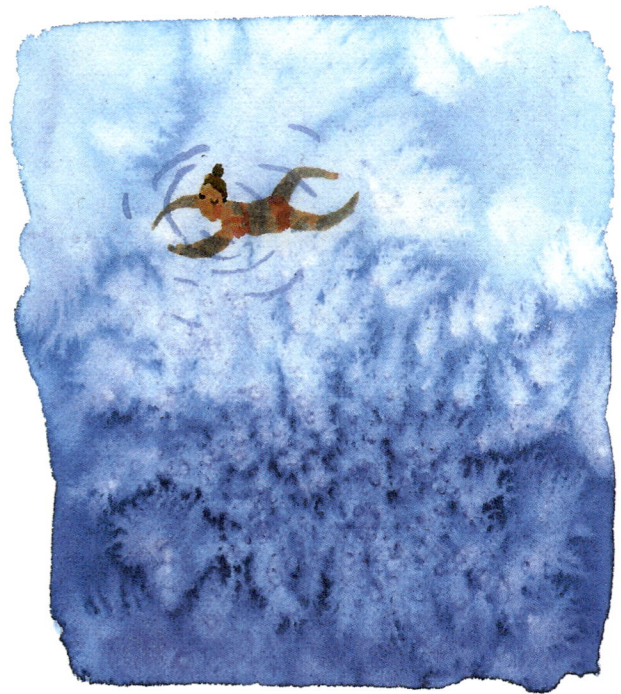
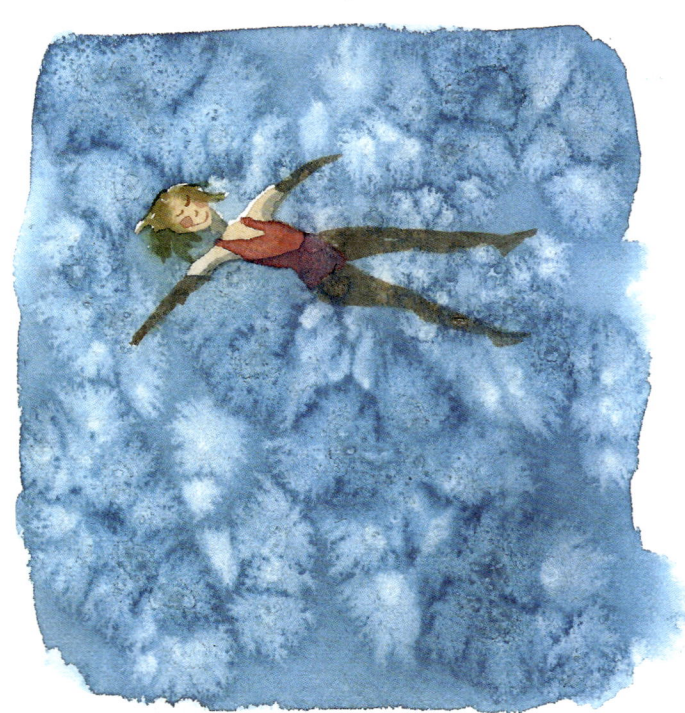

If you paint a blue background with nuances of violet and green, the salt creates the Northern Lights. For other landscapes, the salt crystals yield a great blizzard and polar cold!

This salt technique will come in handy if you want to paint "a dress the color of the weather"!

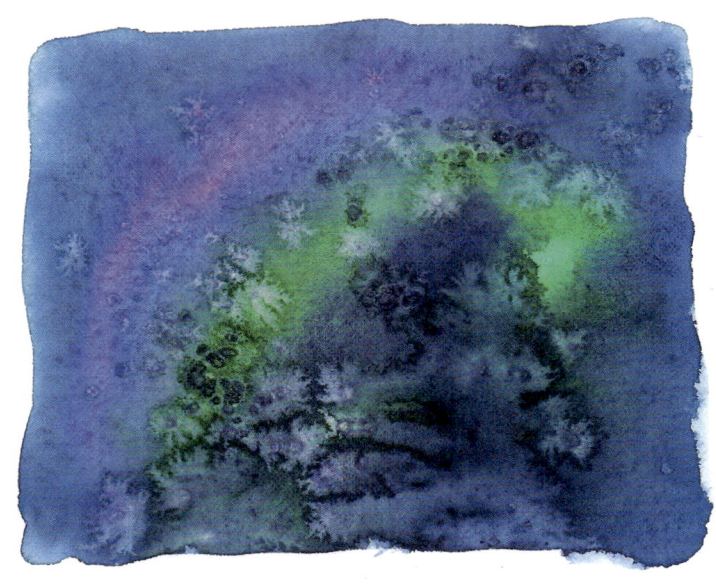

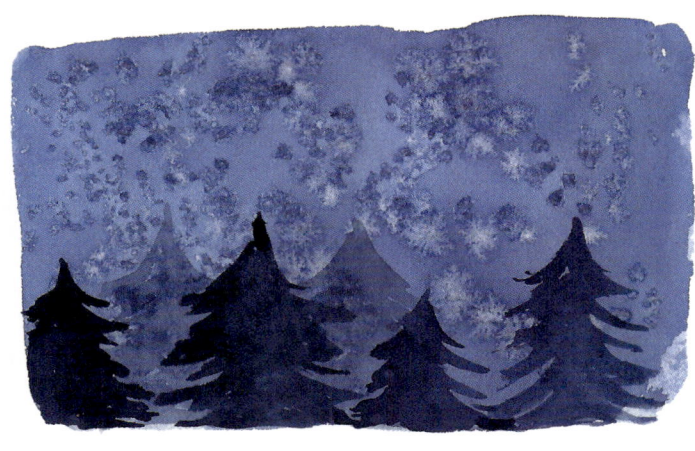

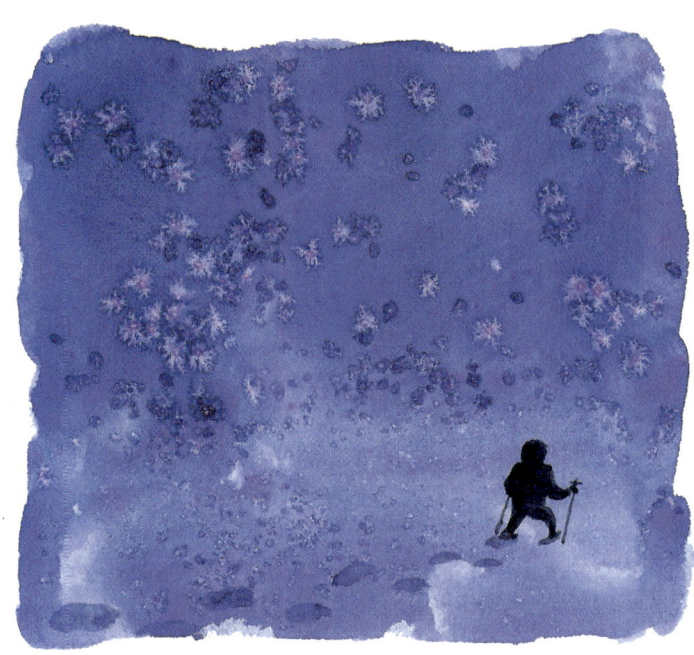

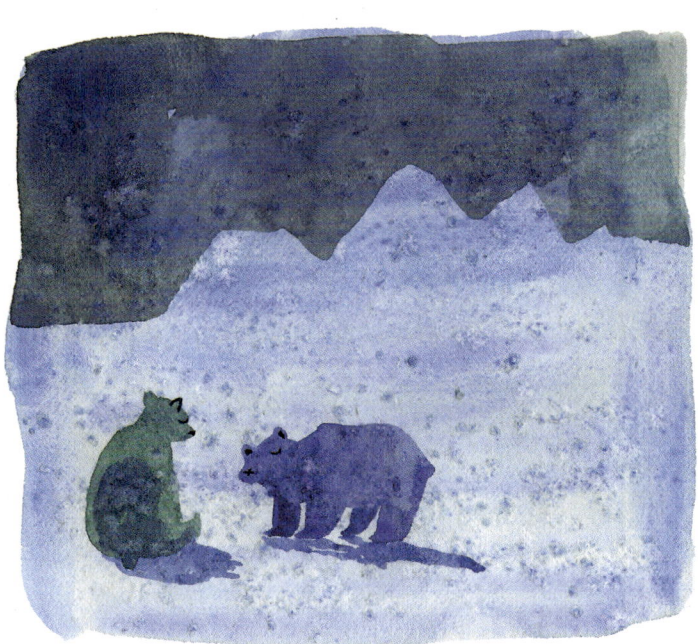

Week 41
Liquid Gum Resist

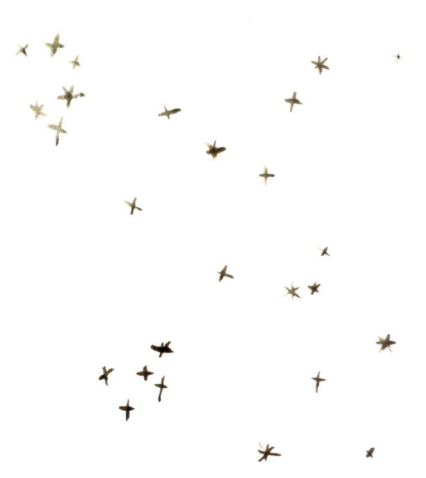 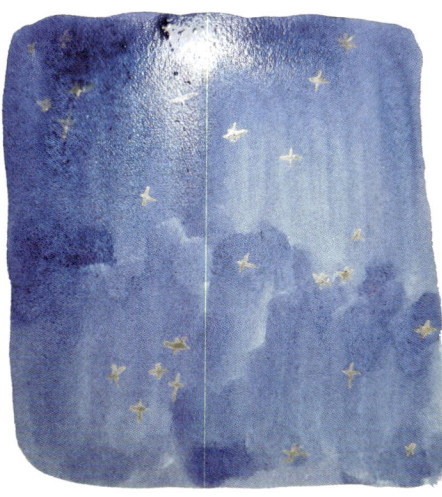 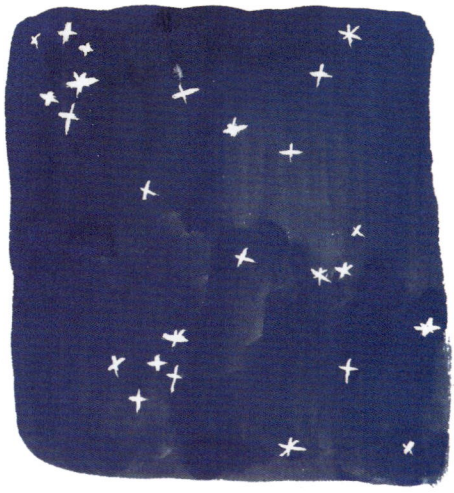

To apply this liquid gum—also known as gum arabic, drawing gum, and masking liquid—use a cheap brush, because the product damages the bristles. Clean the brush immediately; this liquid dries very fast, and afterward it is useless! Soak the tip of the brush in the liquid, and draw the stars. Wait five minutes for the drawing to dry. Then paint a background, painting right over the resist. Wait for the watercolor to be dry before rubbing off the masked zones with a rubber brick. The liquid gum comes off in pieces. Ta-da! The stars remain white.

The gum resist is a practical way to keep white zones white when painting large colored washes as a base. Use it to create effects of reflection, especially in water.

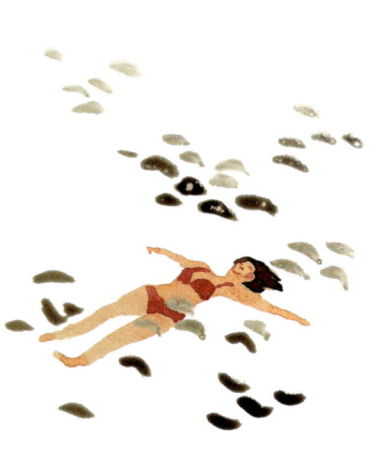 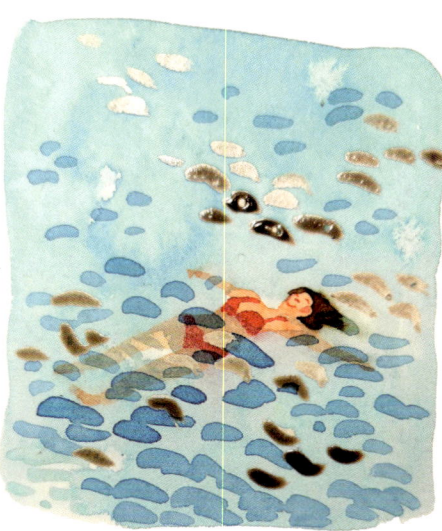 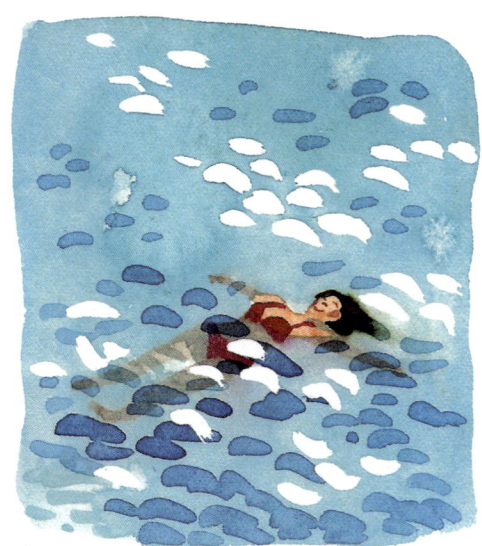

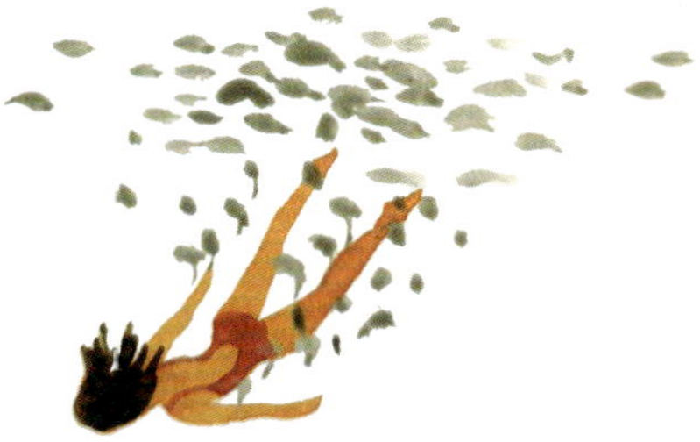

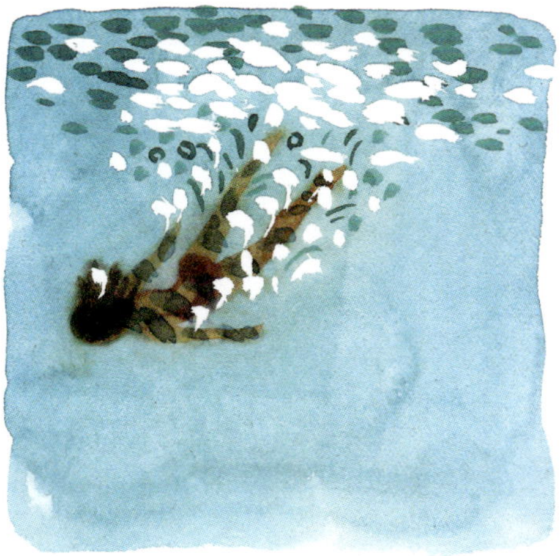

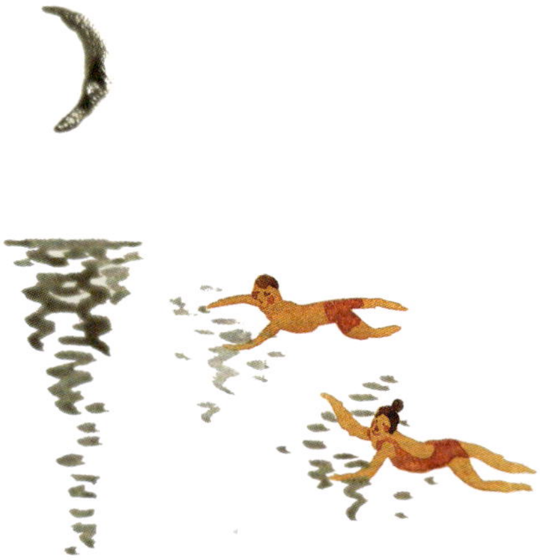

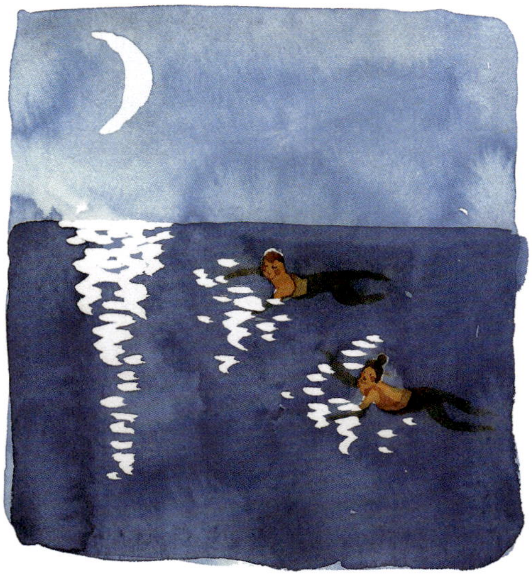

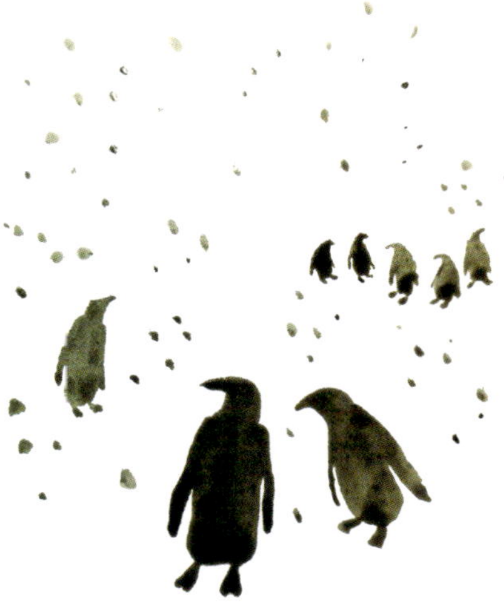

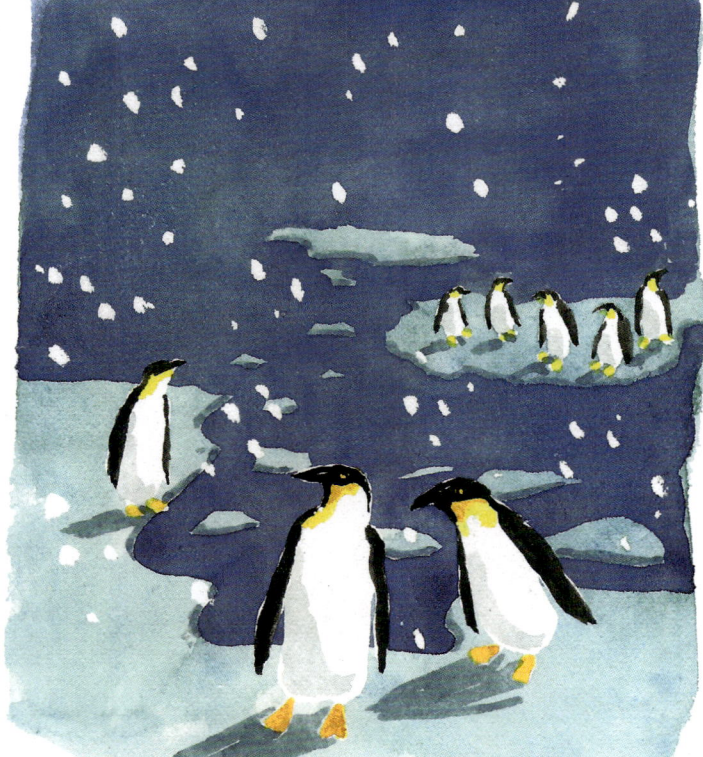

When painting a
background in a wash
over the liquid gum, a
few traces of watercolor
remain, as on the
penguins to the right.
These traces come off
well in the end; rub them
with the rubber brick.

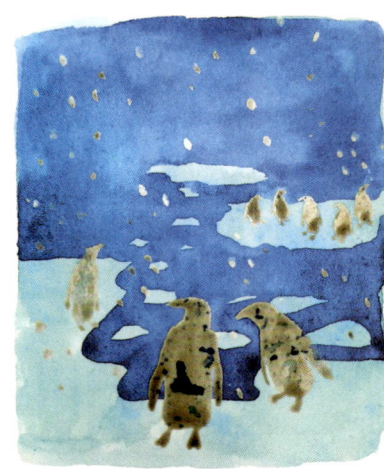

For More Practice

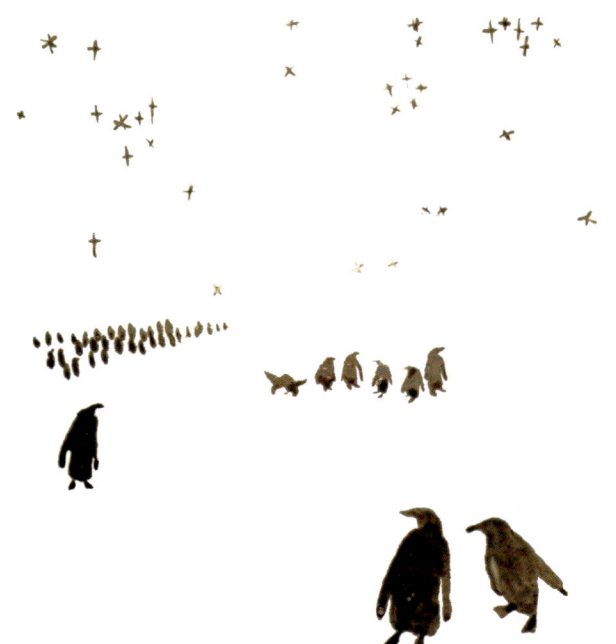

To draw this polar landscape, use the liquid gum to draw the penguins and some stars.

Once the liquid gum is dry, paint a large light blue wash all over the paper and a dark blue wash for the sky. Without waiting for the dark blue paint to dry, sprinkle it with salt to make some crystals grow.

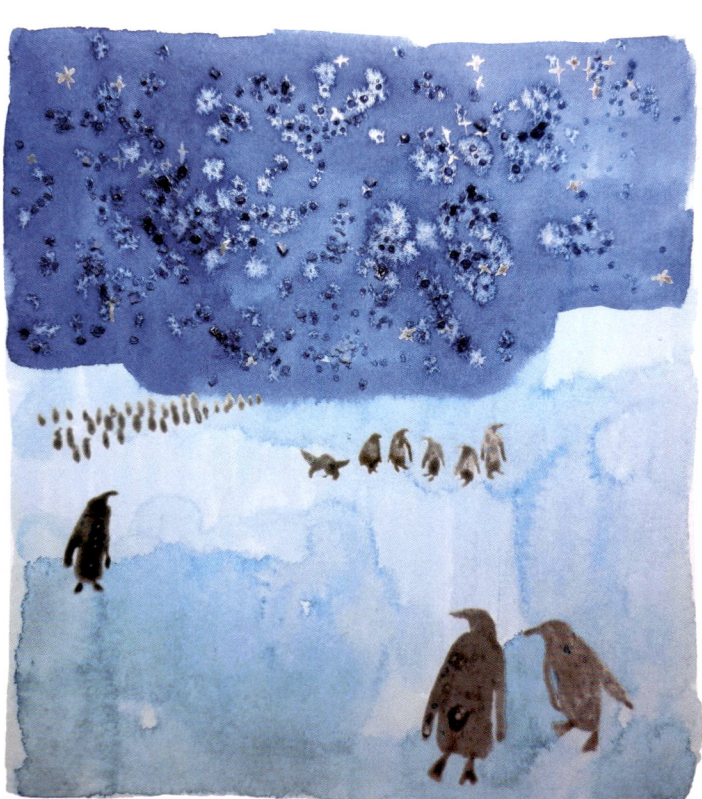

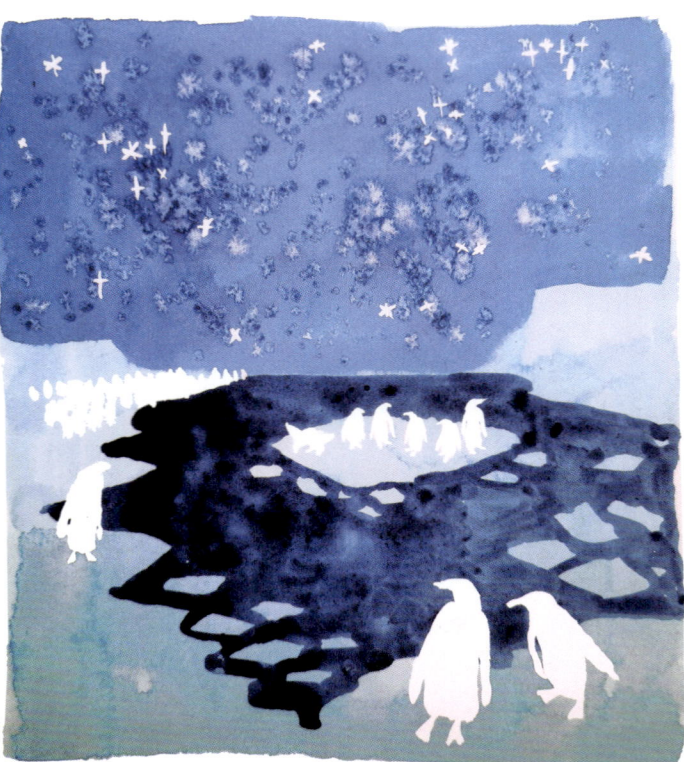

With a very dark blue, paint the ocean, quickly drawing a slender ice floe. Wait to rub off the liquid gum. The sky is starry, and the penguins are immaculate!

Dress the penguins in yellow and black. Shade them with a touch of blue, and then shade the thickness of the ice floe!

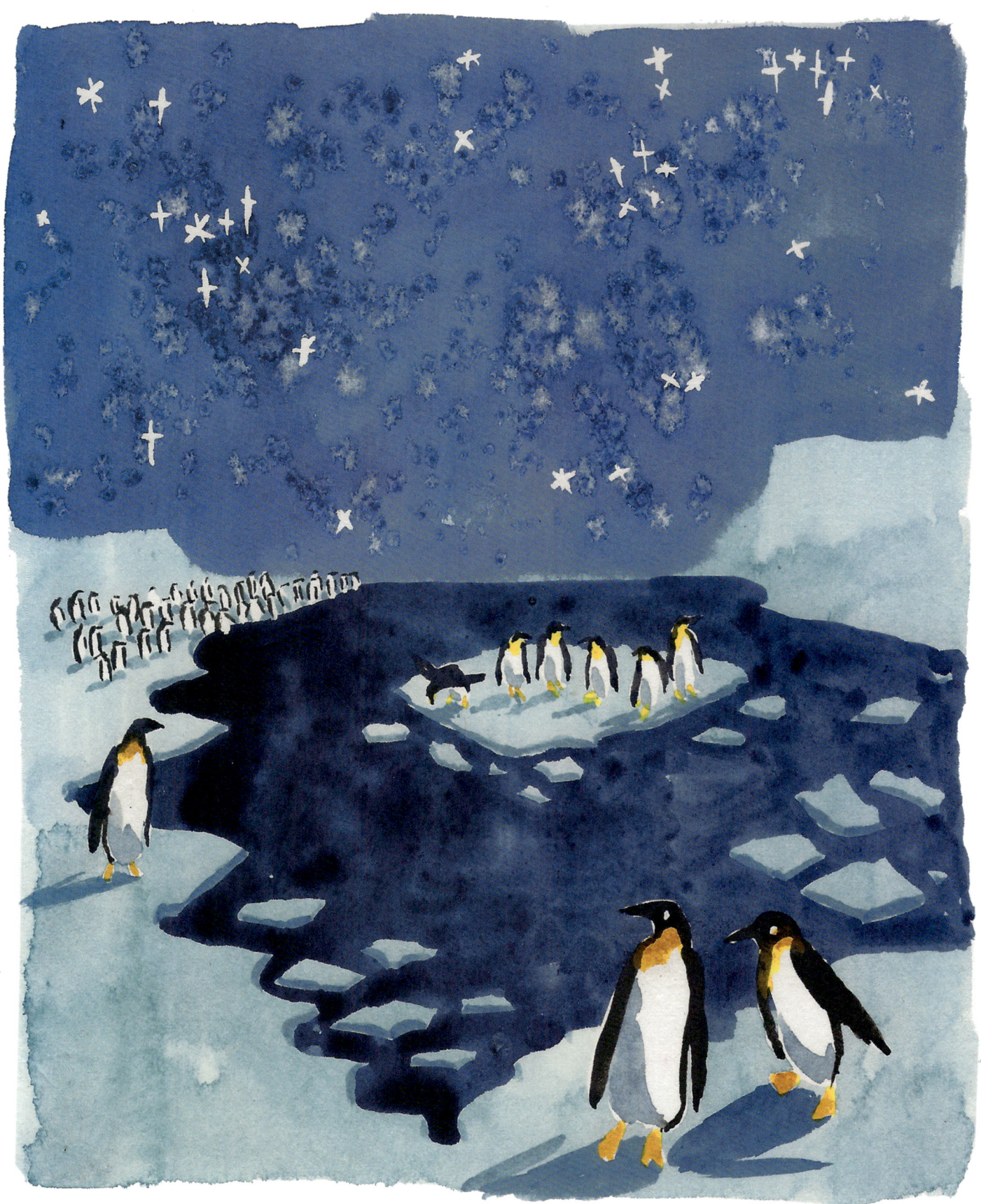

Week 42
Interpreting the Textures

You can never finish everything,
so don't even try to finish well!

To make a texture interesting,
add a few scales, preferably
on the part of the crocodile
that is closest to you.

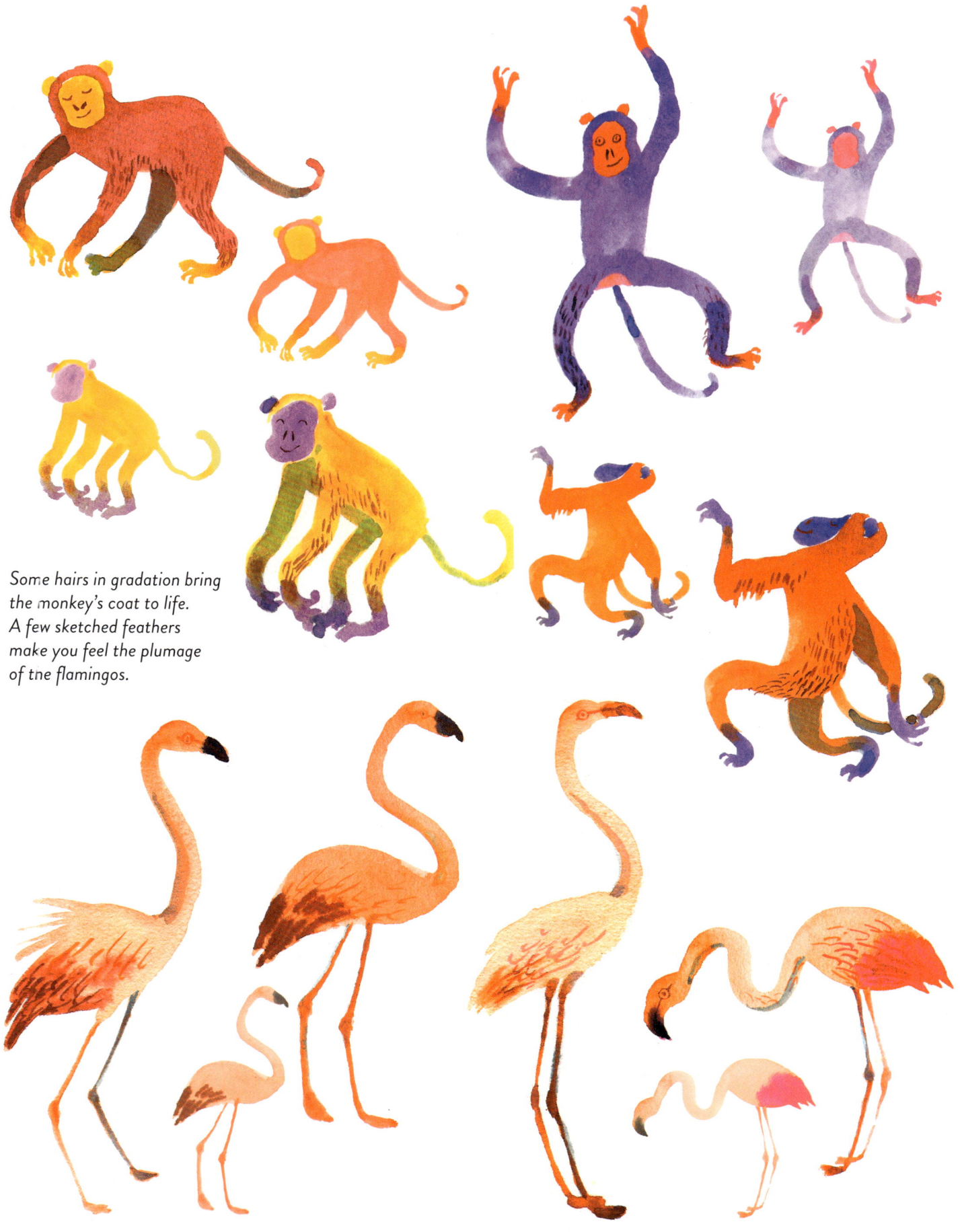

Some hairs in gradation bring
the monkey's coat to life.
A few sketched feathers
make you feel the plumage
of the flamingos.

Week 43
—
Animating with Patterns

It's not about finishing, and the same is true for patterns. To breathe life into the coats of cats, start but do not finish.

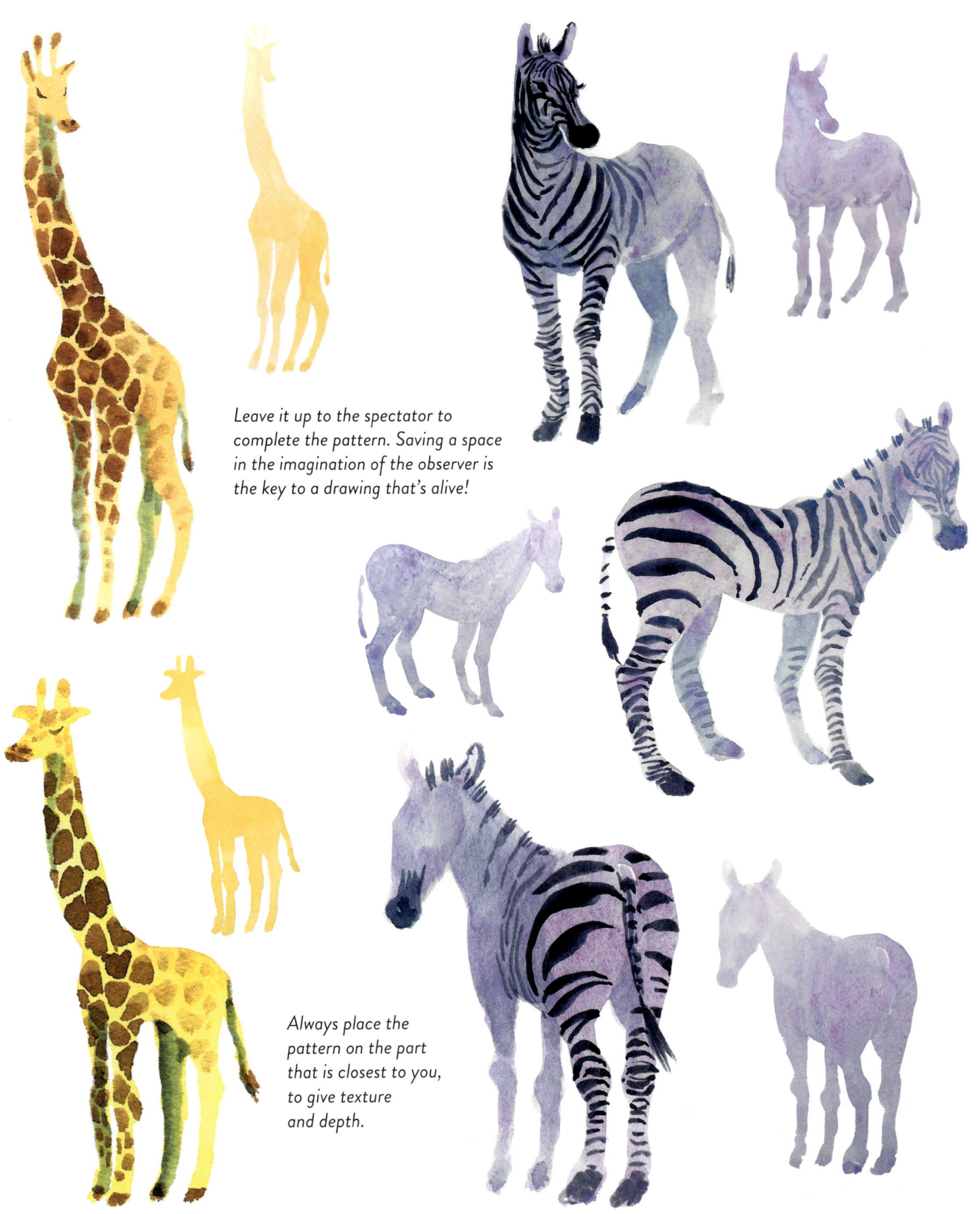

Leave it up to the spectator to complete the pattern. Saving a space in the imagination of the observer is the key to a drawing that's alive!

Always place the pattern on the part that is closest to you, to give texture and depth.

For More Practice

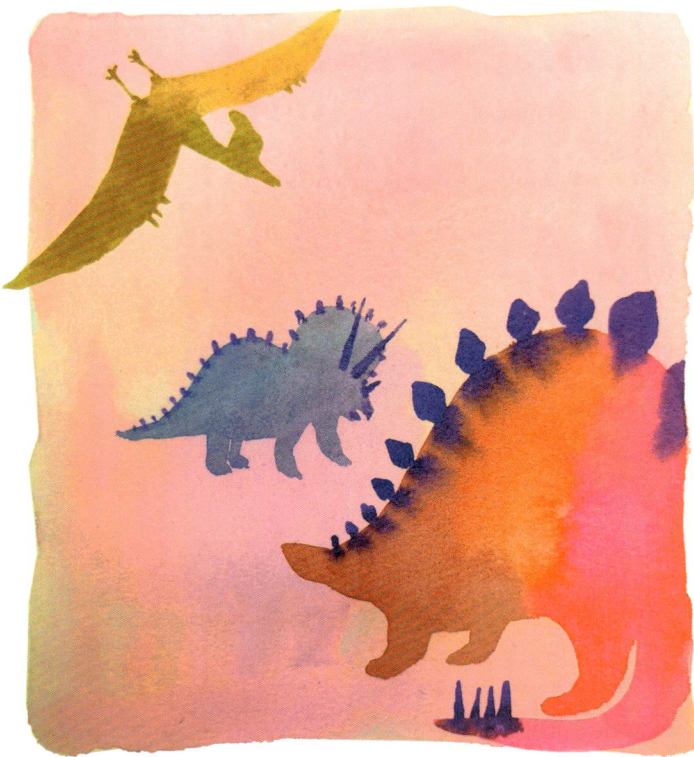

After leaving some space for the spectator's imagination, the next step is a walk into the middle of Jurassic Park, which starts with a pale pink wash.

Place a stegosaurus, a pterodactyl, and a triceratops, each with paint mixtures that blend together.

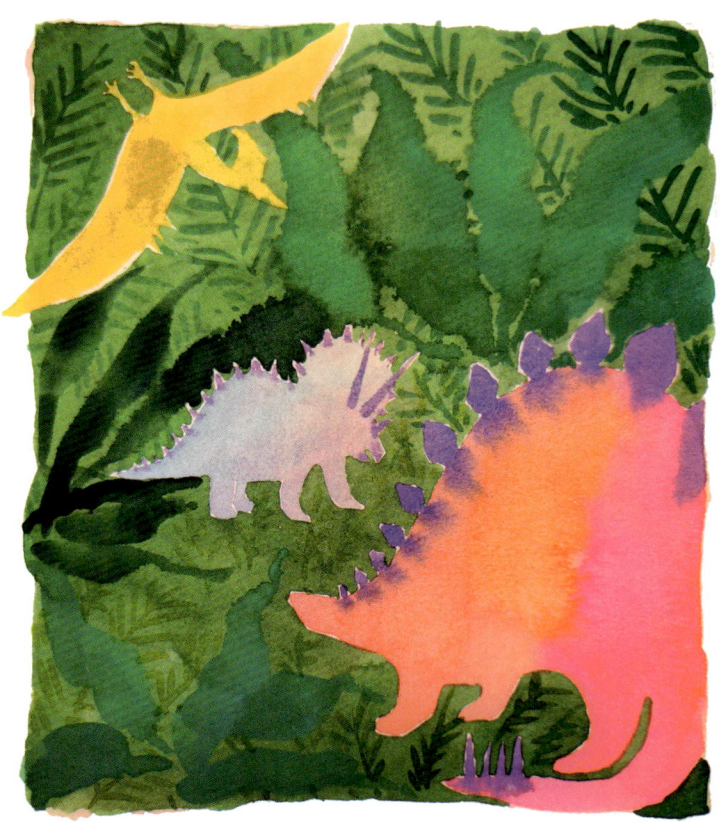

Apply a green wash that covers the original pink wash but preserves the dinosaurs. Without waiting for the green paint mix to dry, paint the vegetation in the background with a soft brush. When the green background is dry, draw the plants in the foreground, so that they will be more distinct and "pass" to the front.

Shade the dinosaurs, as well as the plants in the foreground. Bring the surfaces to life by stingily sketching in scales and feathers.

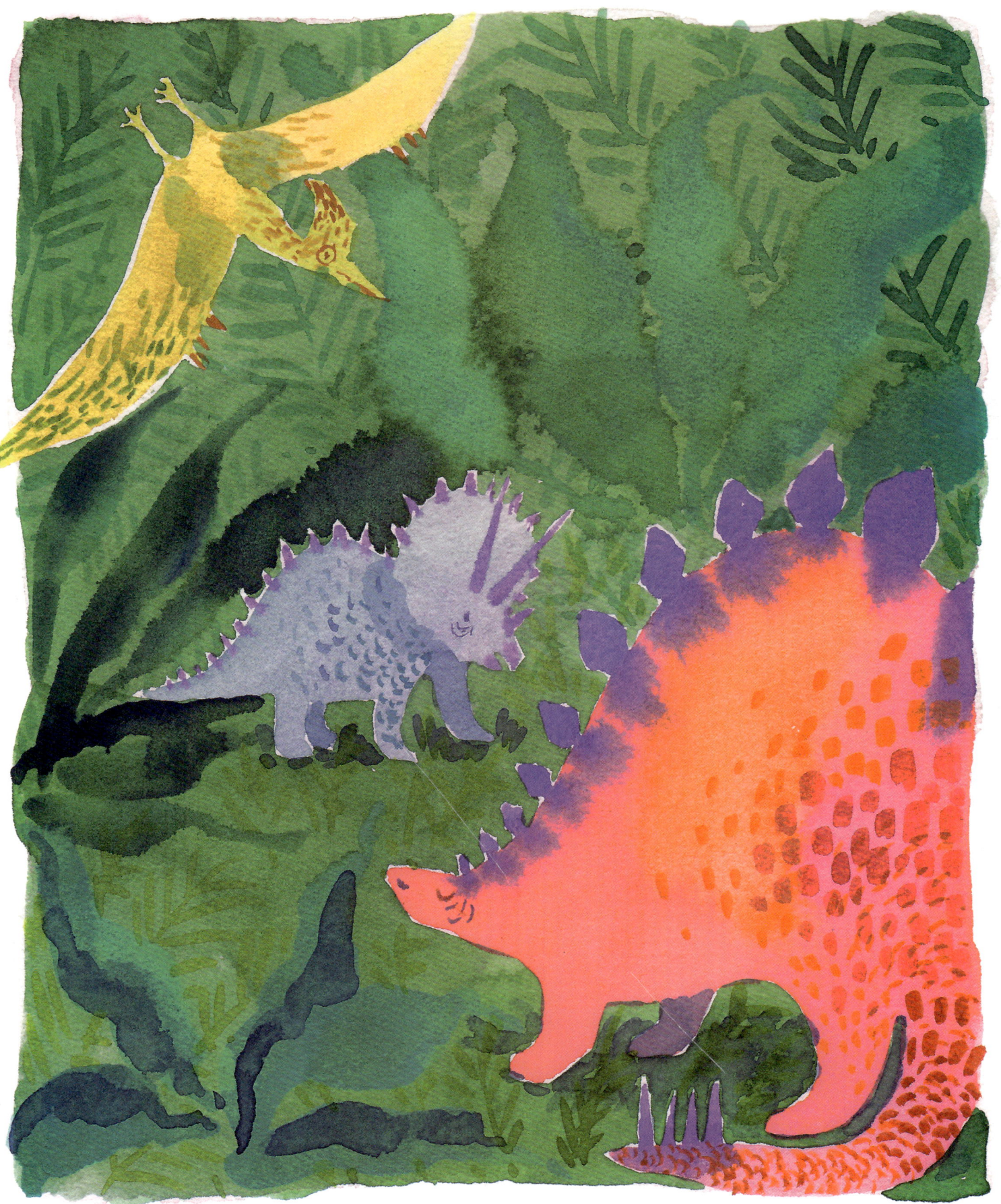

Week 44
Masses and Textures

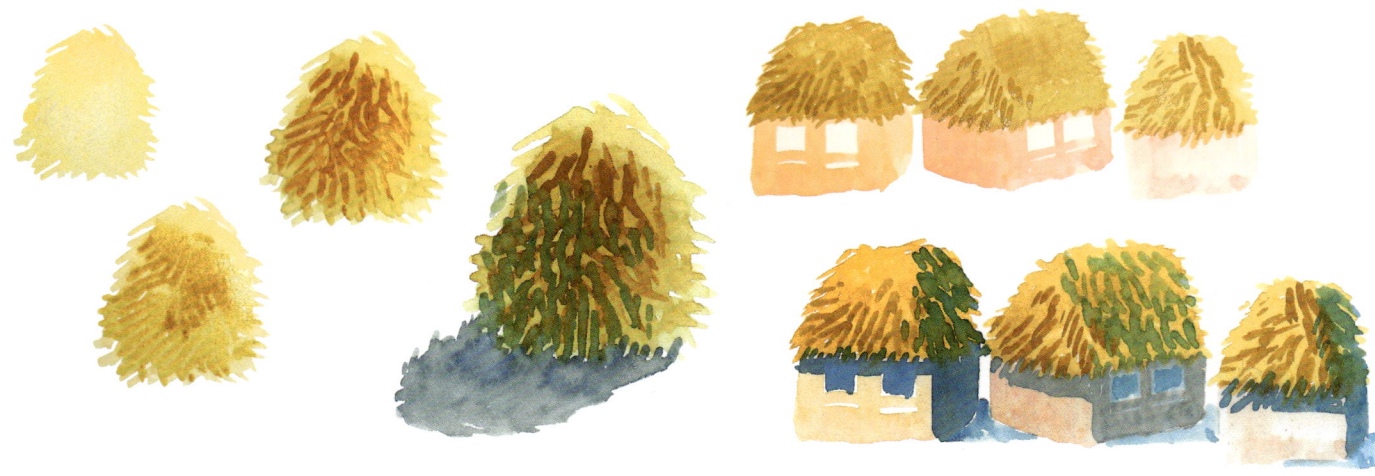

As with the animals in Week 42, in order to draw a texture, draw the mass with its general rhythm. Add details for only a few elements.

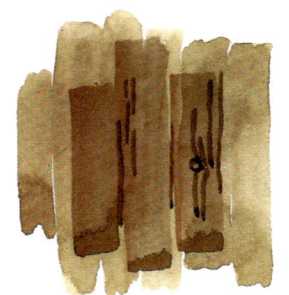  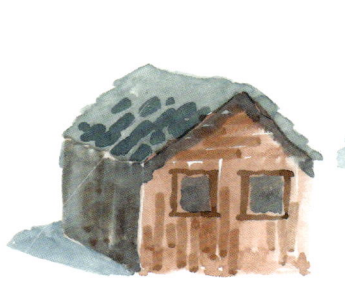 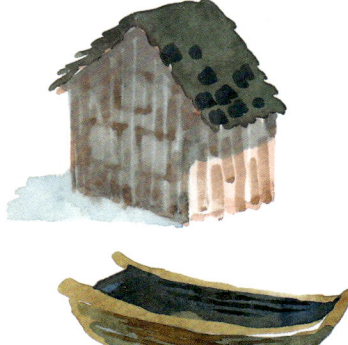

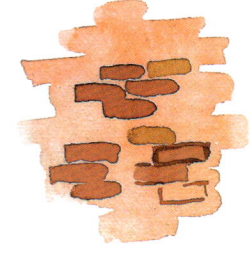 To represent a brick wall, a bale of hay, a lawn, wood, or any other "texture," don't draw it brick by brick, straw by straw, or blade of grass by blade of grass. Establish the general plan, and then add a few details.

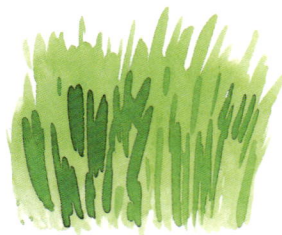 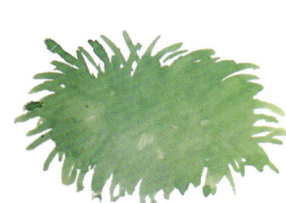 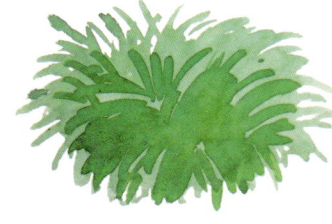 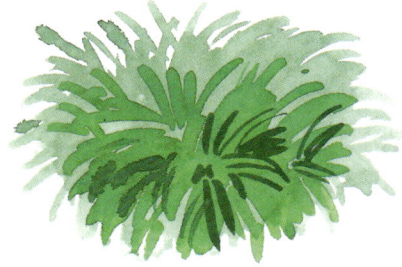

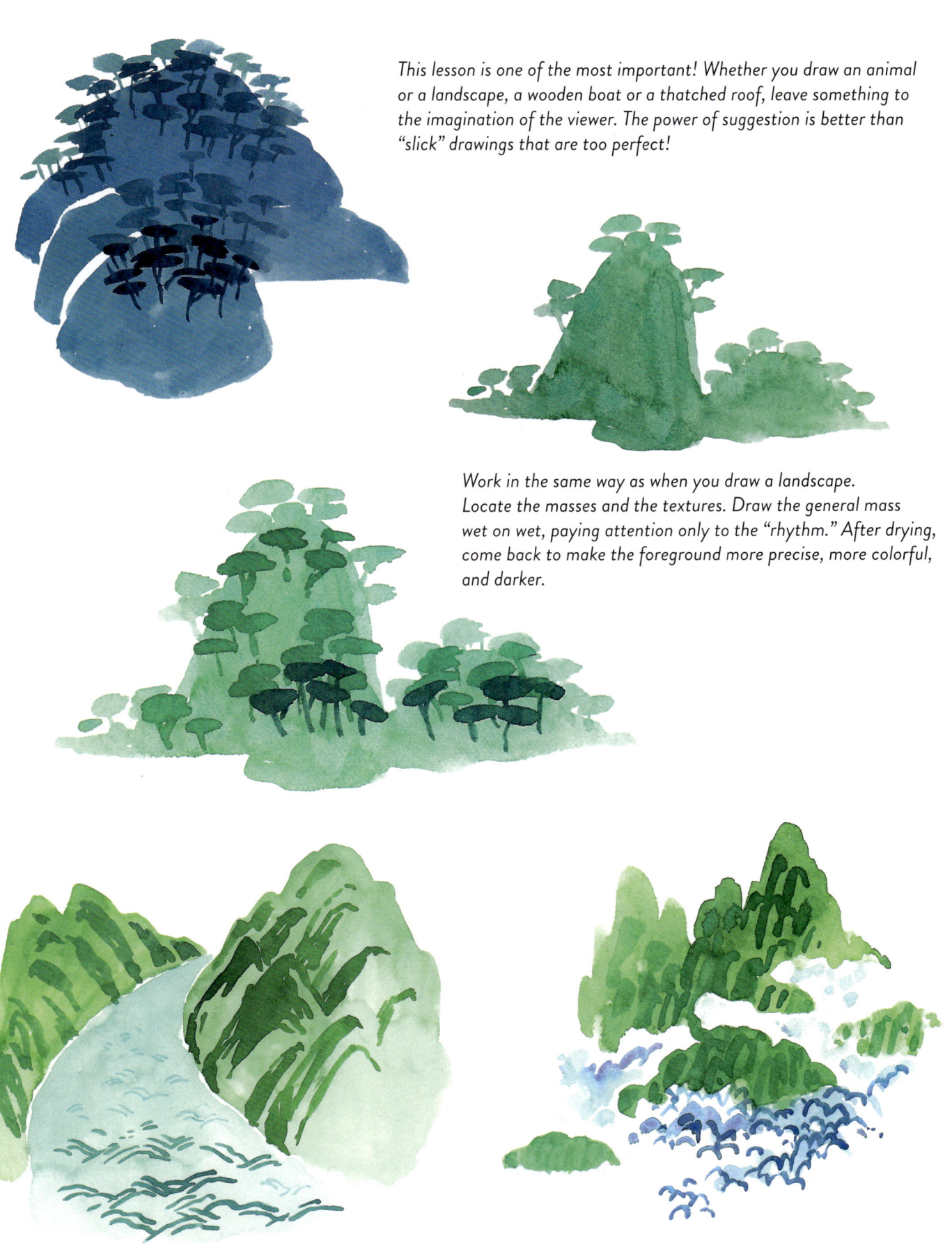

This lesson is one of the most important! Whether you draw an animal or a landscape, a wooden boat or a thatched roof, leave something to the imagination of the viewer. The power of suggestion is better than "slick" drawings that are too perfect!

Work in the same way as when you draw a landscape. Locate the masses and the textures. Draw the general mass wet on wet, paying attention only to the "rhythm." After drying, come back to make the foreground more precise, more colorful, and darker.

Week 45

Foliage, Trees, and Forests

Think of a tree or a forest as texture. Draw the mass and its general rhythm. Add a few elements as details to suggest a tree and depth.

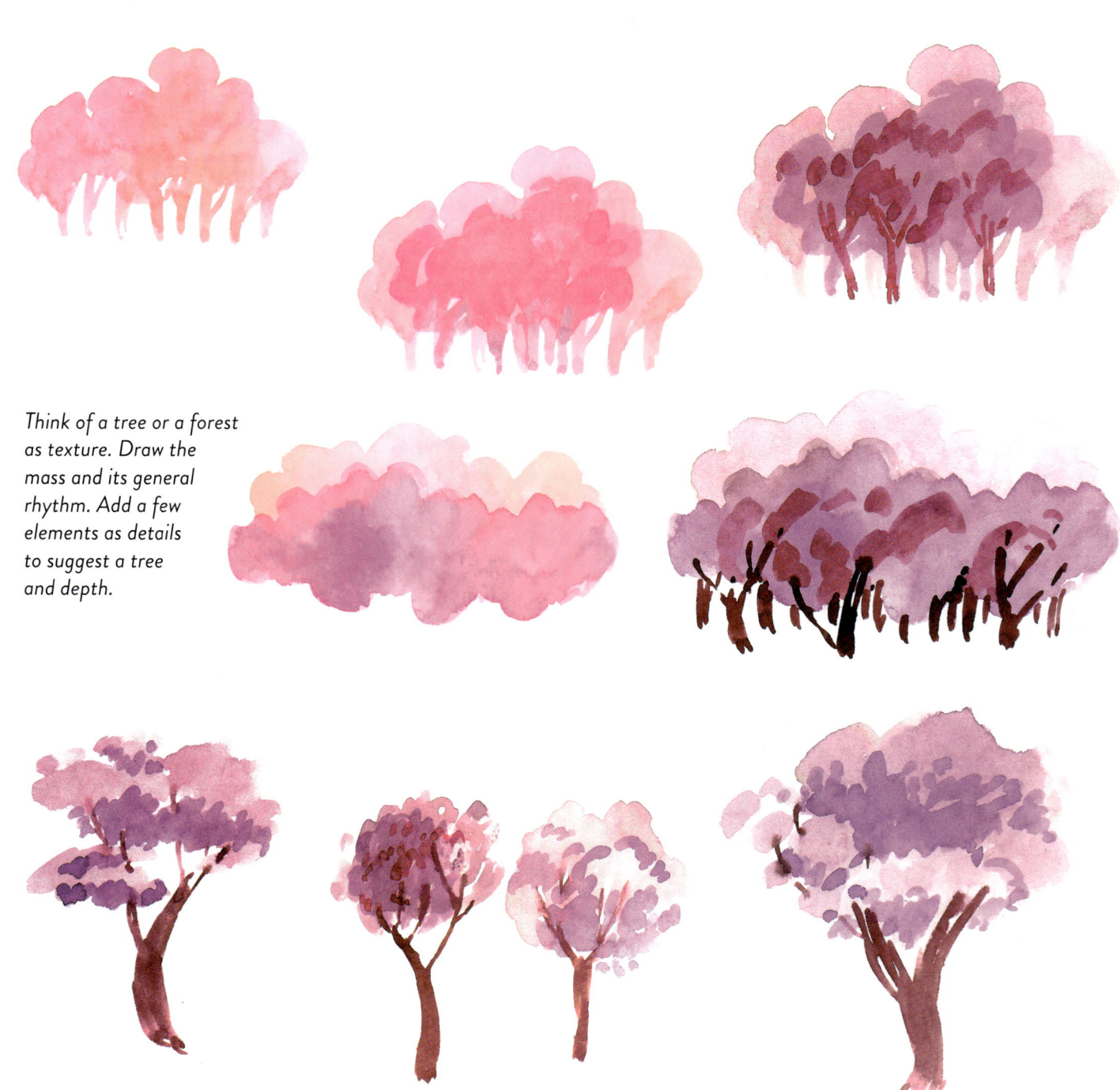

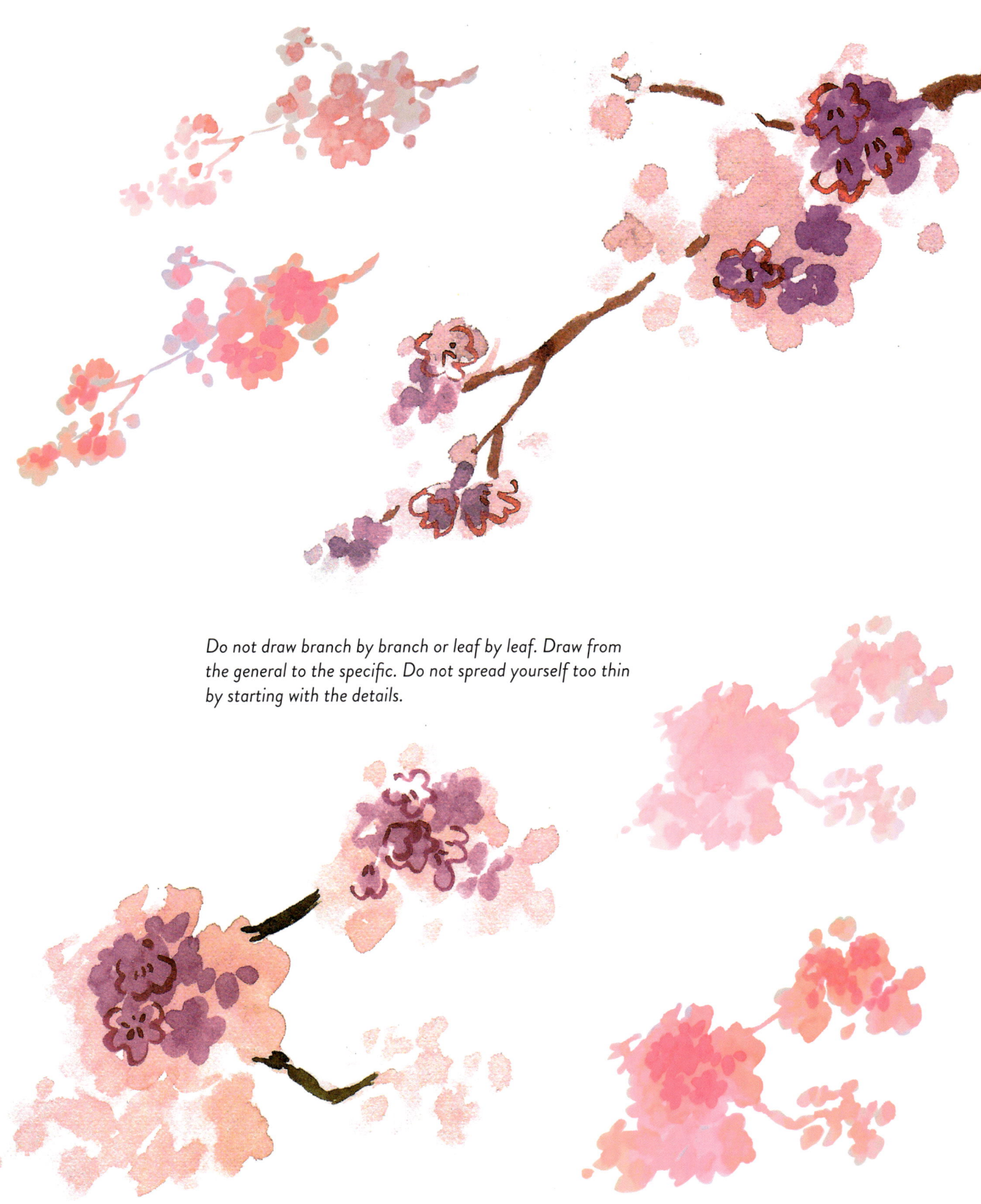

Do not draw branch by branch or leaf by leaf. Draw from the general to the specific. Do not spread yourself too thin by starting with the details.

For More Practice

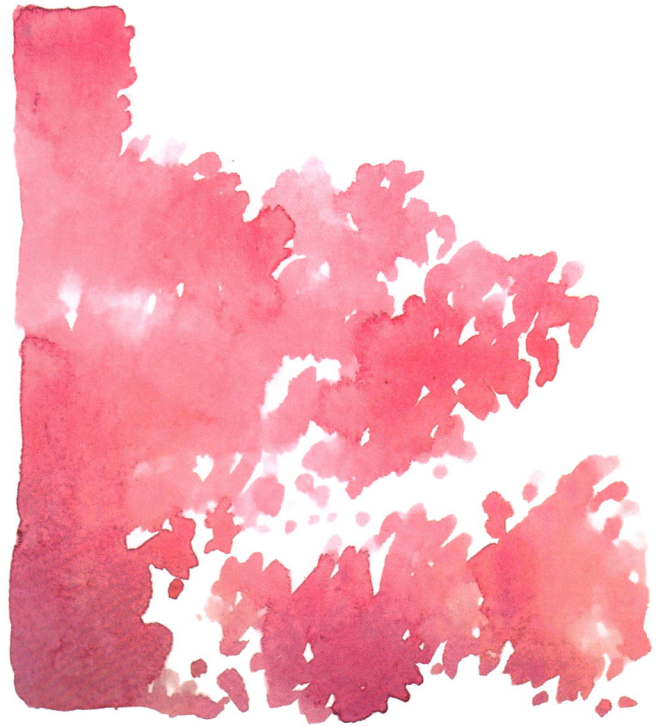

The cherry trees are blooming. Paint the rhythm of the cherry tree in a pale pink paint mix.

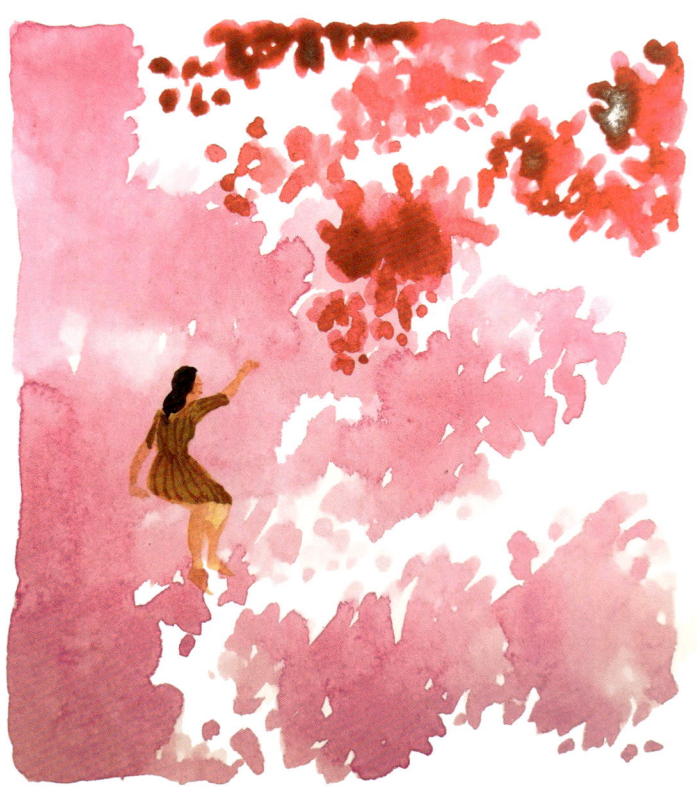

All the birds in the world come and make their nest—and a young woman is here too. Paint the foreground in a darker pink. Always paint with an alert motion that echoes the rhythm of the flowering foliage.

With some branches, just a few details, and some flowers with more precision, it works well!

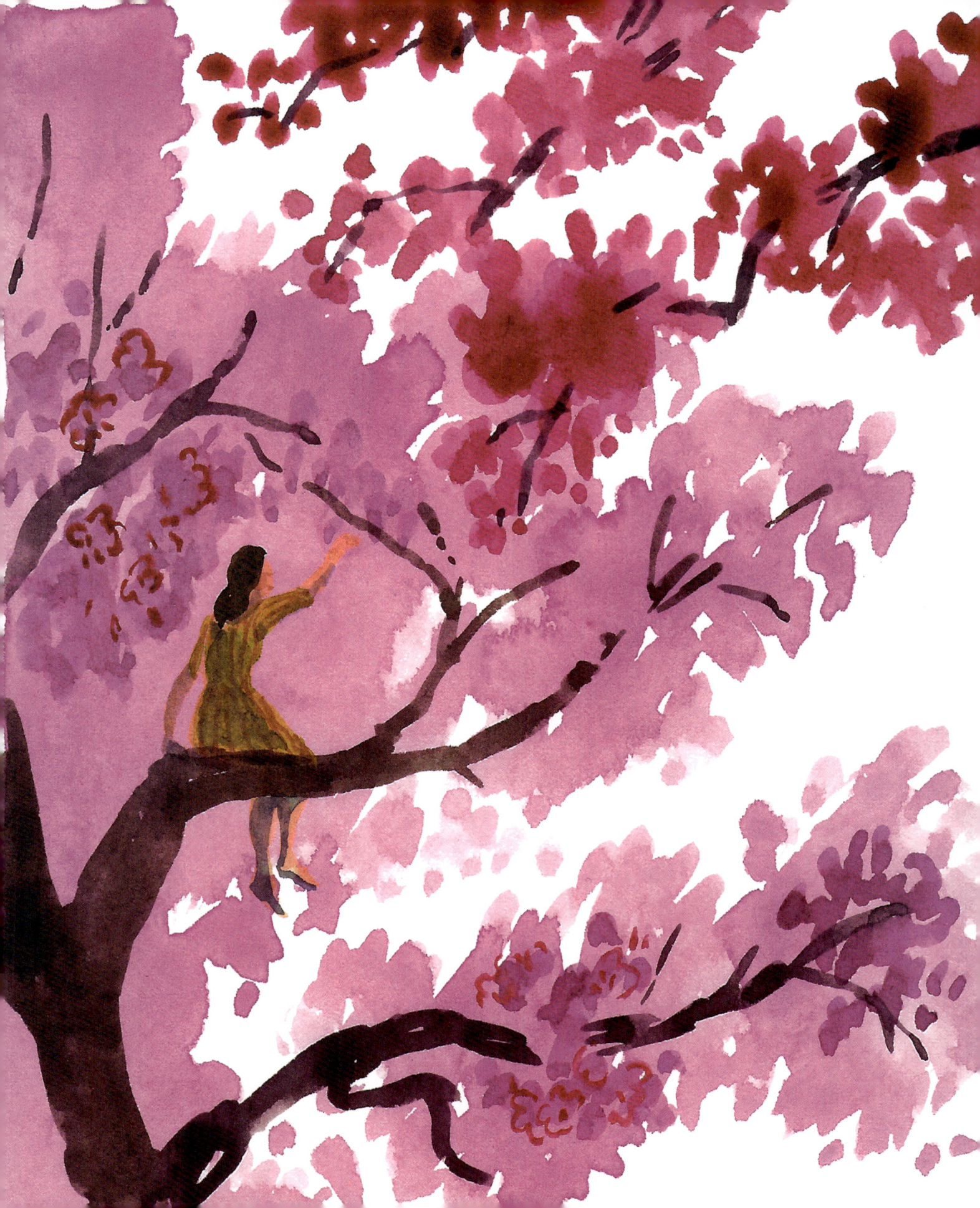

Week 46

Painting a Crowd

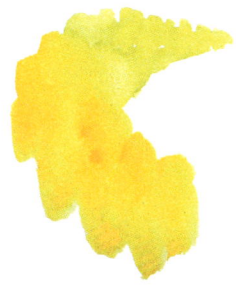

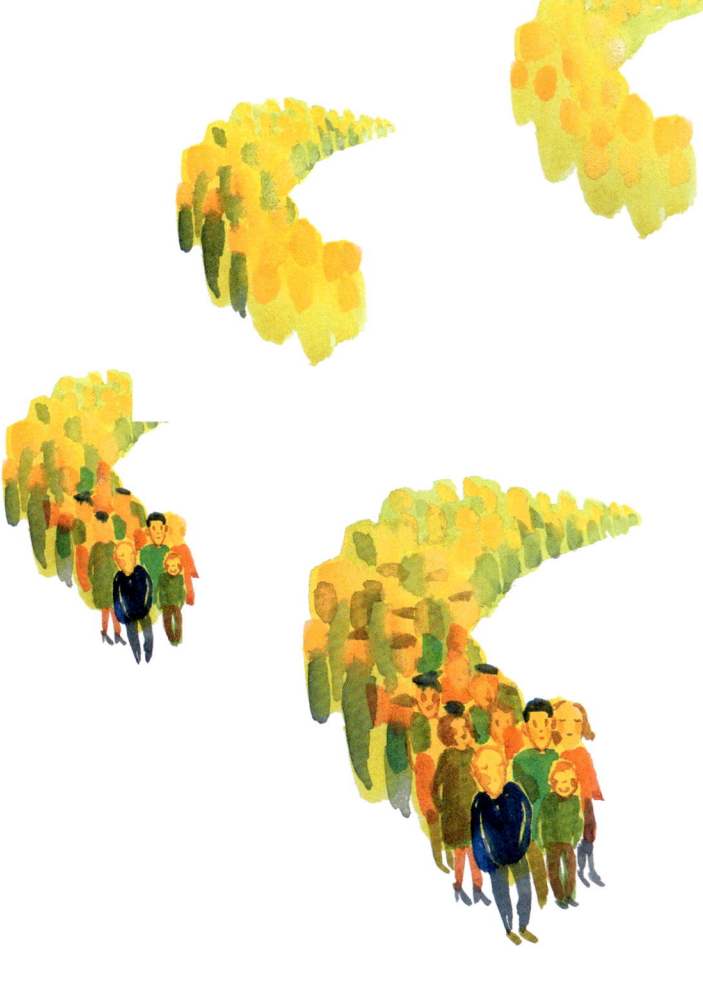

Draw a crowd as you'd draw a forest.

If you draw person by person, the effect of a crowd is not there. Draw the general mass wet on wet, paying attention only to the "rhythm." Once it's dry, add details to the foreground that are more colored and darker. Add some patterns to figures in the foreground.

Start with the mass, with its effect of unique rhythm and texture. Sculpt some details. Only a few elements are fully developed, while in the back they remain blurry, vague, and paler.

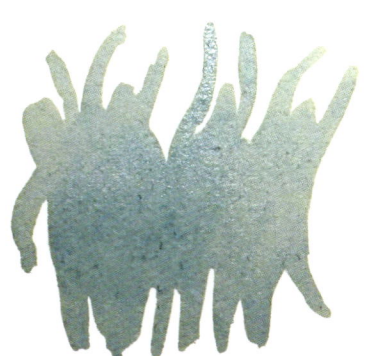

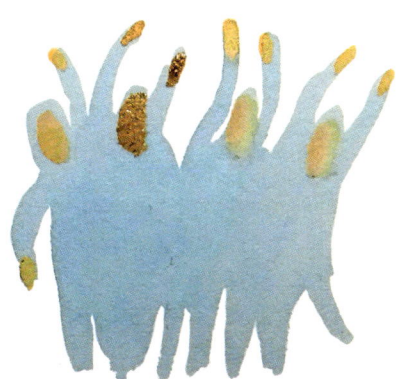

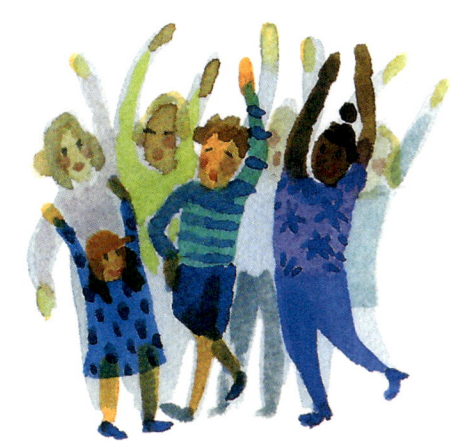

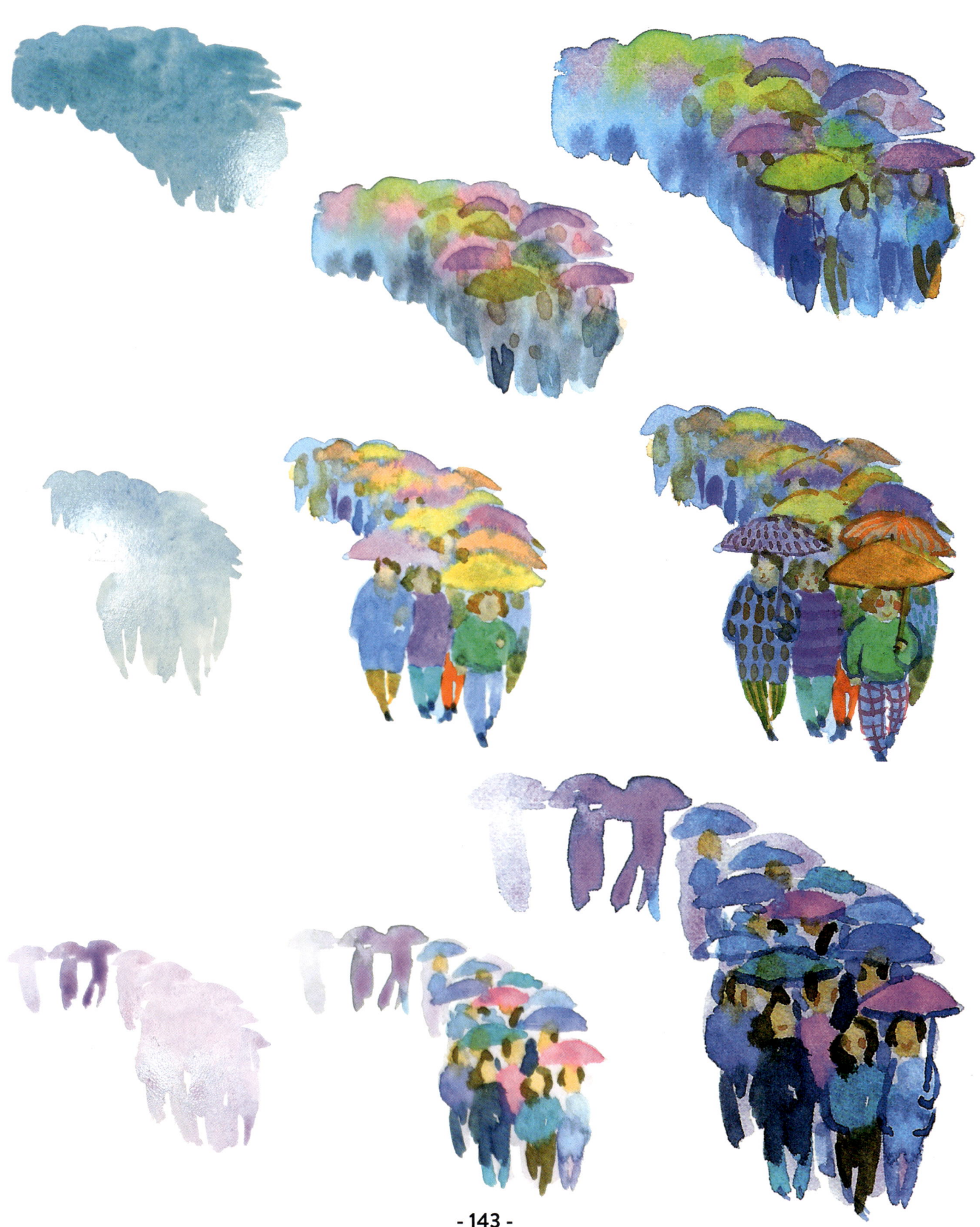

Week 47
People and Their Ways of Moving

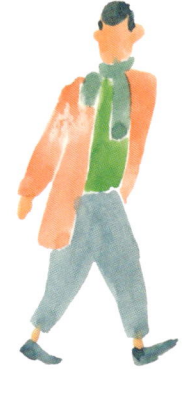
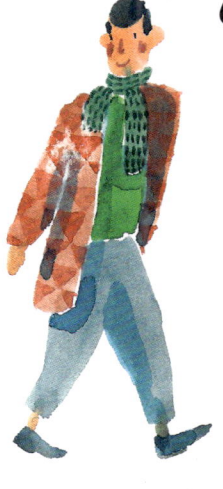

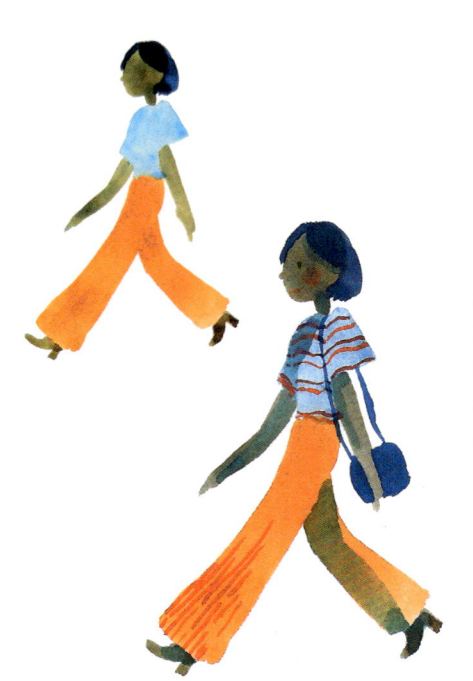

It's fun to watch people walk by and sketch their way of moving. Sketch their body and their habits in a few strokes of the brush. Draw some details, such as the patterns of their clothing. As always, do not complete them! Leave room for the imagination.

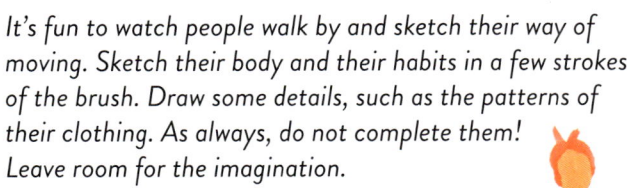

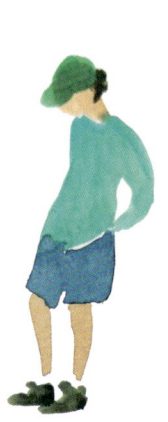
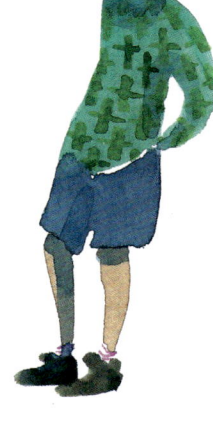
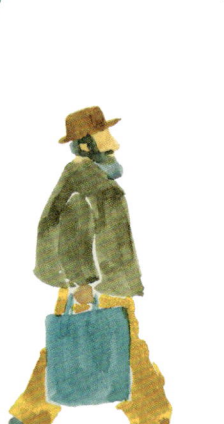
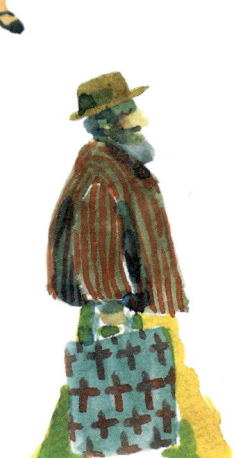

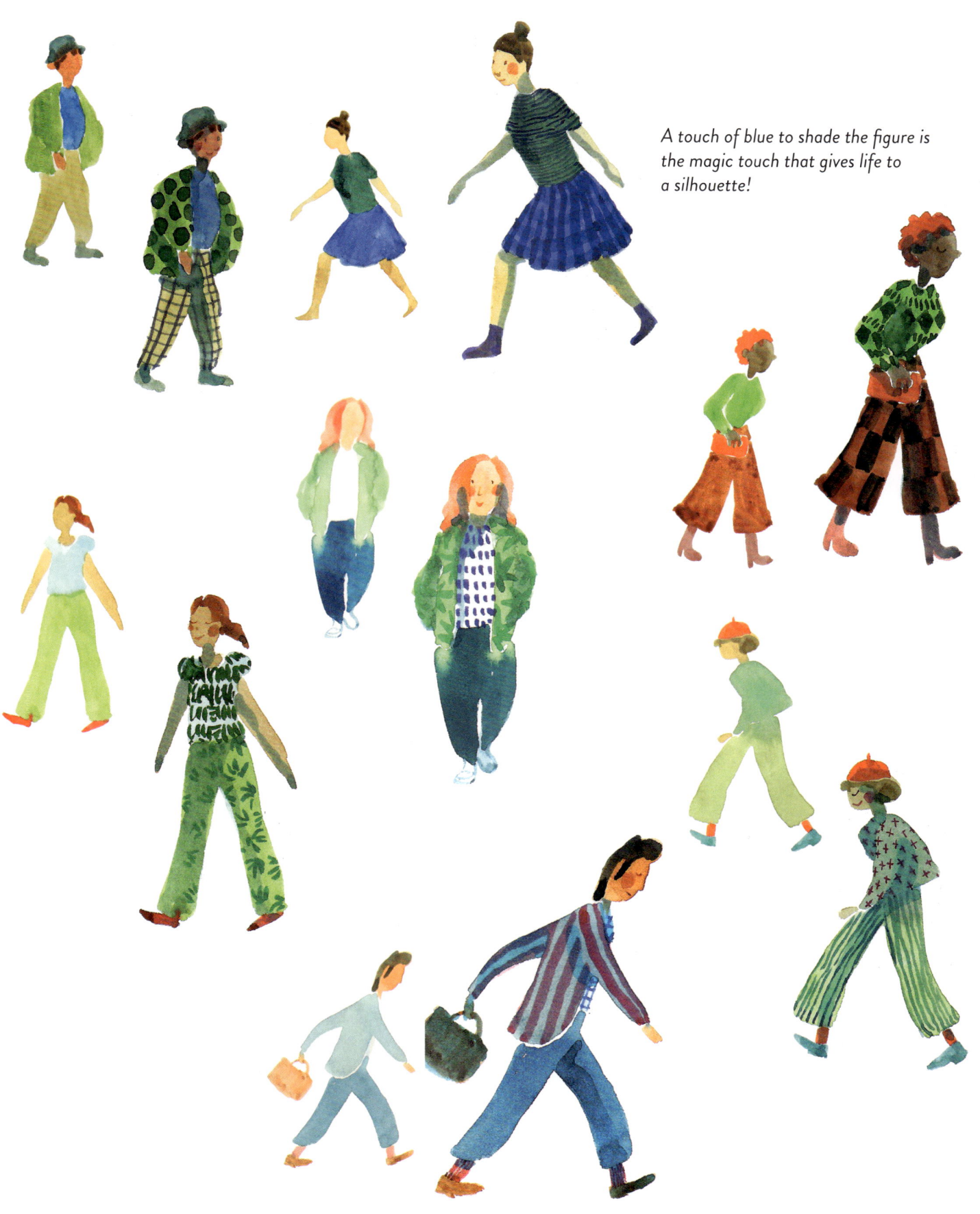

A touch of blue to shade the figure is the magic touch that gives life to a silhouette!

For More Practice

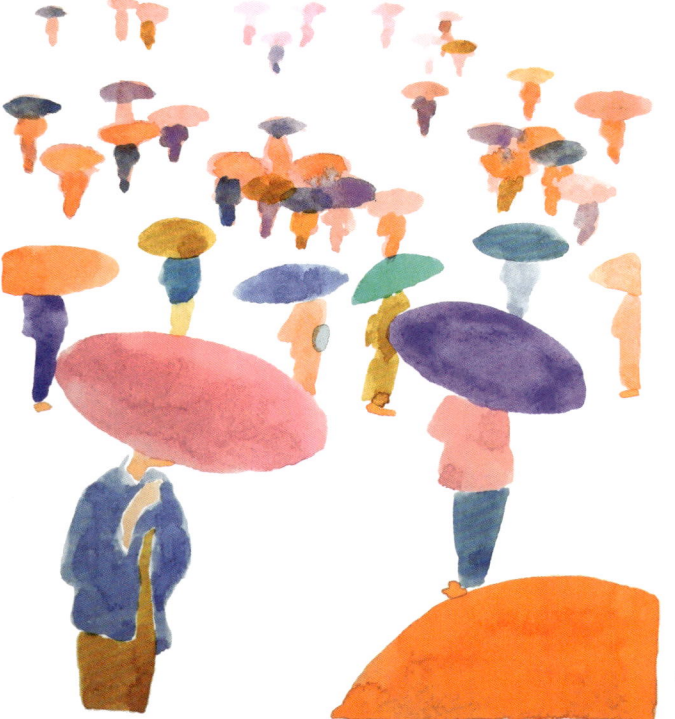

A swarm of delicate umbrellas has invaded the square.

The geishas in the distance are painted "in the mass," first in rhythmic groups. Add some touches of color while they're still wet. They appear little by little, in colored washes, from pale for the distant ones to bold for those who are close.

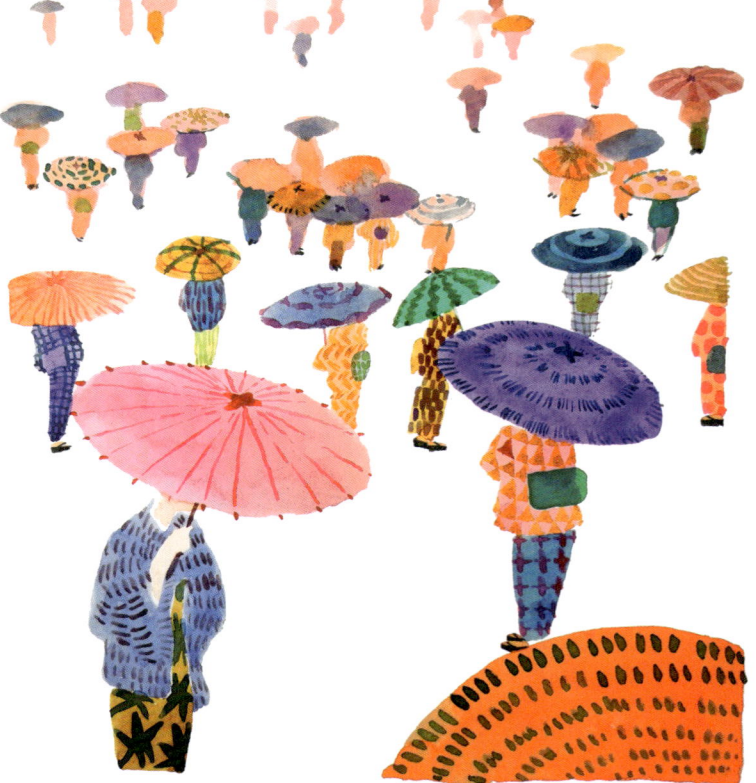

Some patterns come to life on the umbrellas and the kimonos closest to you. The blue shades everything and covers the most distant silhouettes to push them even farther away!

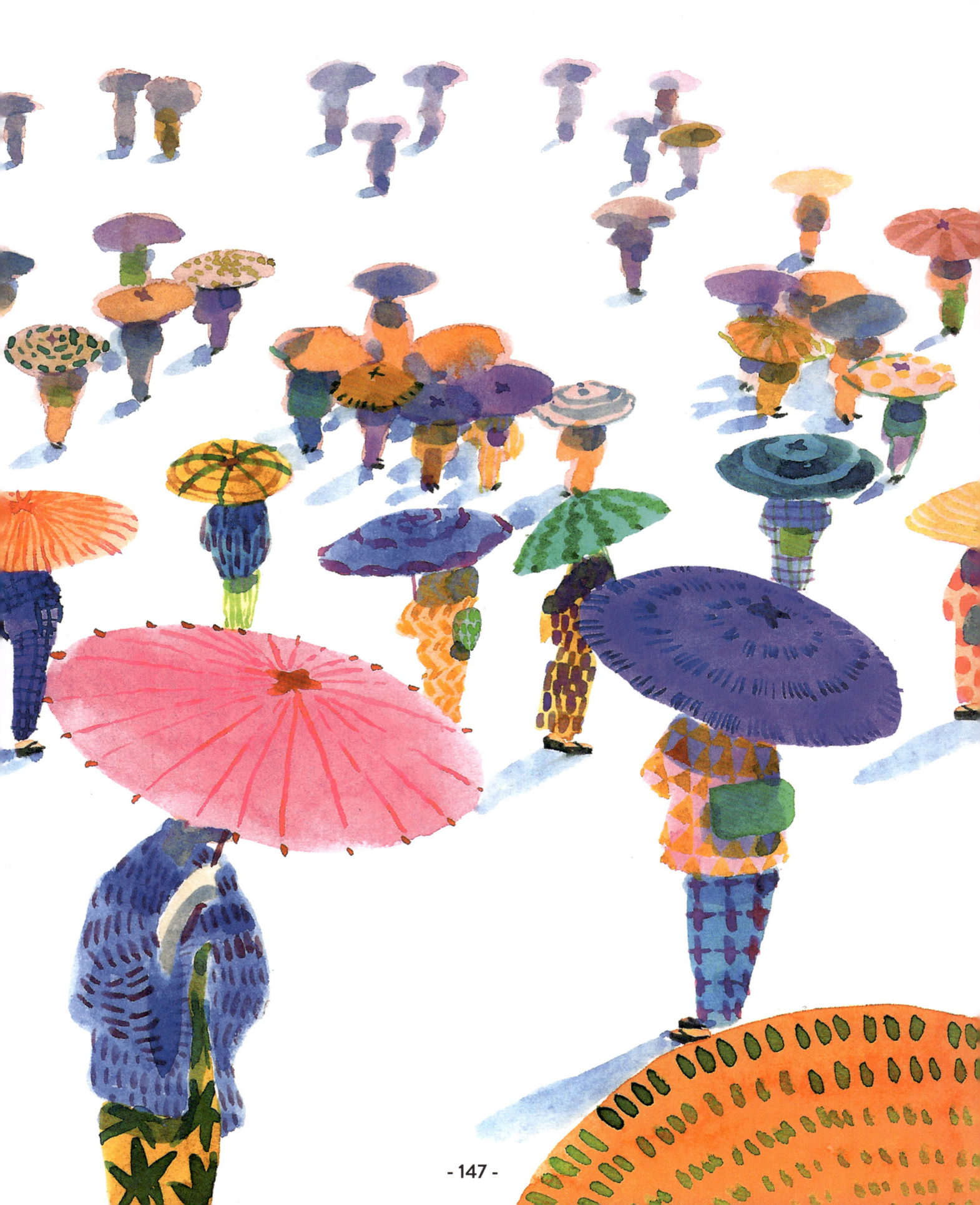

Week 48
A Little Anatomy

Let's talk about the human body. These are the basics, but of course the details vary on a case-by-case basis.

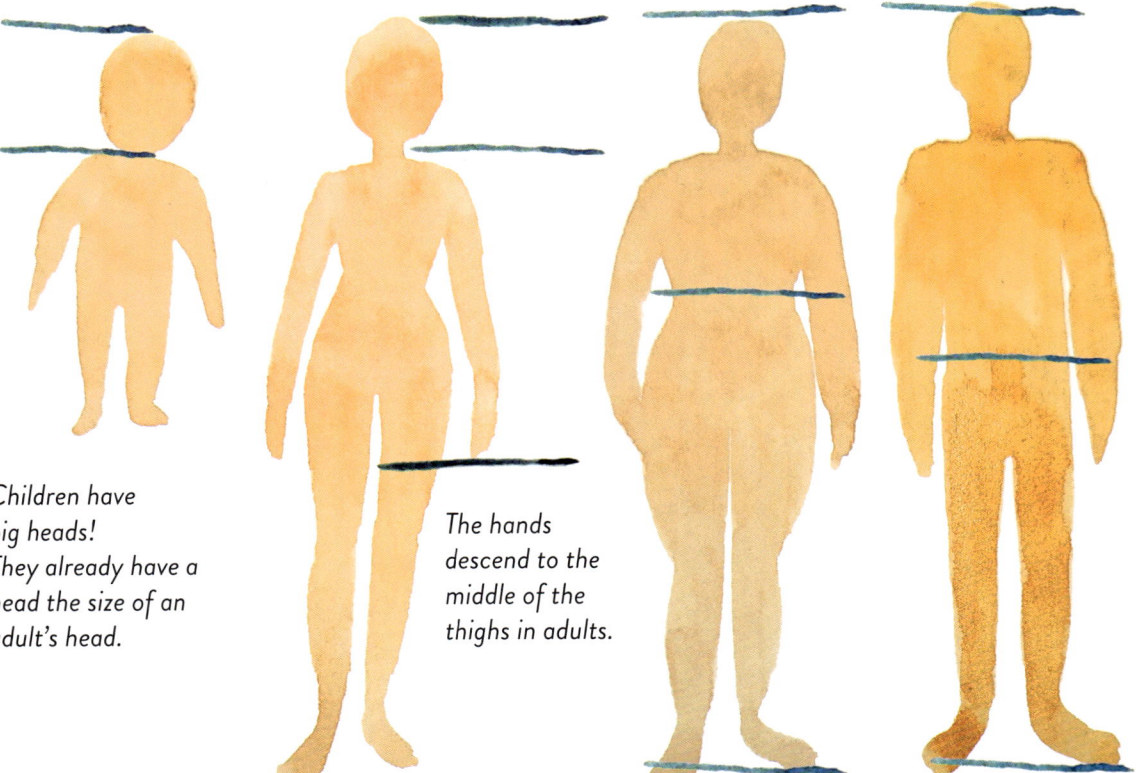

Children have big heads! They already have a head the size of an adult's head.

The hands descend to the middle of the thighs in adults.

Women have a small torso and long legs. The waist is high, positioned above the middle of the body.

Men have a waistline that isn't so clearly defined, positioned in the middle of the body.

The top of the ears is positioned at the same height as the eyes. The forehead represents one third of the face. The space between the eyes and the nose takes up a second third. The nose and the chin occupy the final third.

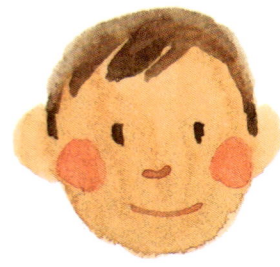
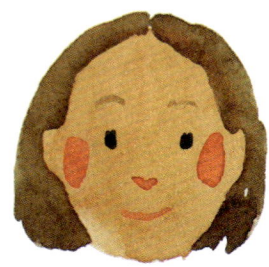
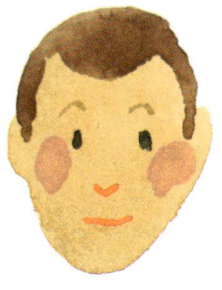
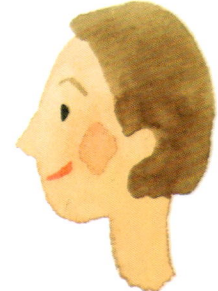

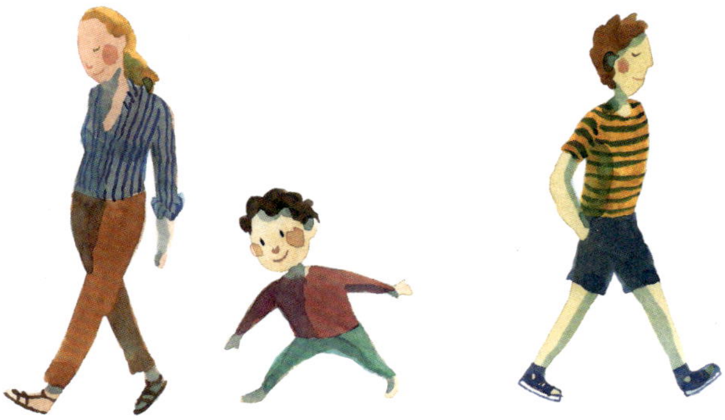

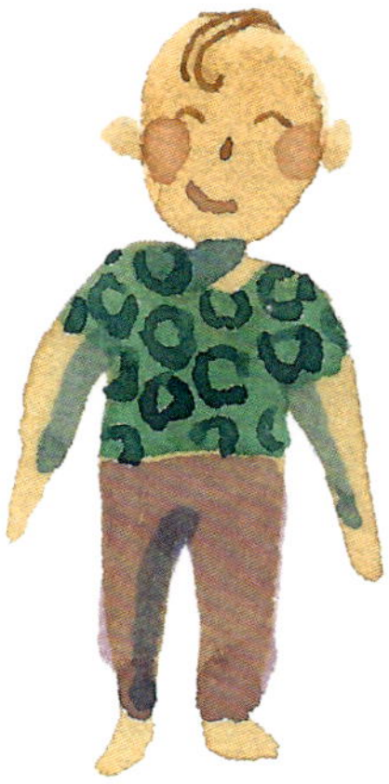

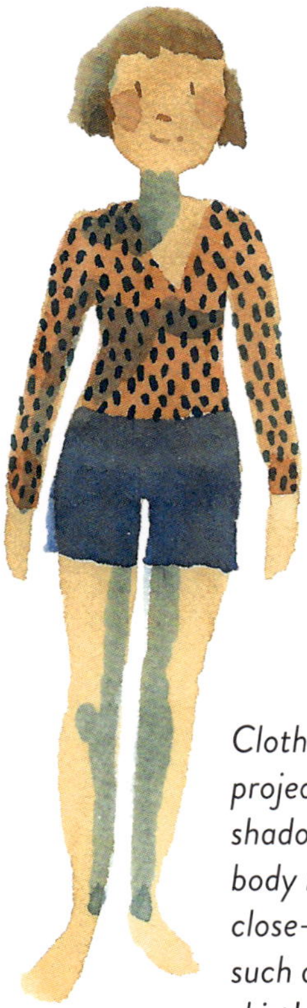

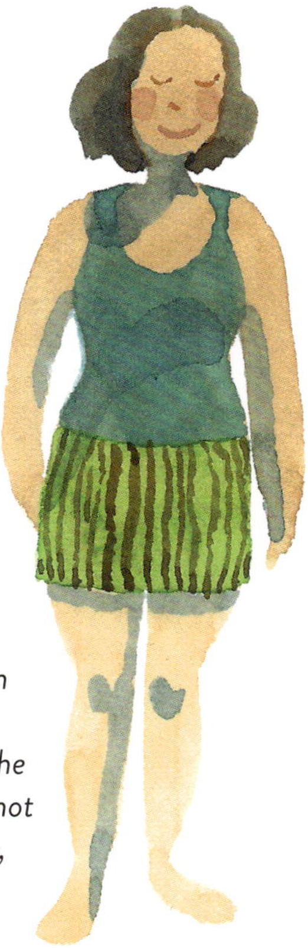

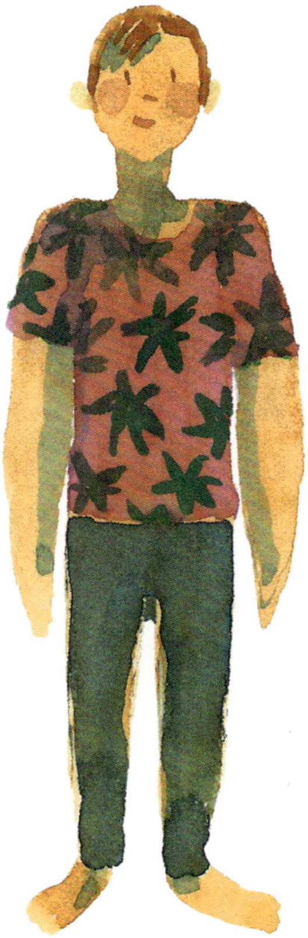

When you shade a body, if the light is classic—it comes from above—place shadows under the neck, under the breasts, and in the crook of the elbows (where blood is drawn), under the knees, and on the inside of the legs. Add shadows in the hair if it is voluminous (e.g., bangs, thick mass).

Clothing can project a shadow on the body if it is not close-fitting, such as this skirt!

For the face, if the light is classic—it comes from above—place a shadow in the hollows of the eyes, under the nose, under the cheeks (for an adult who no longer has the cheeks of a child), and on the neck under the chin.

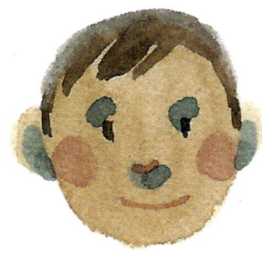
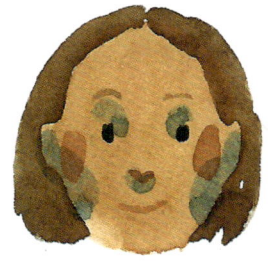
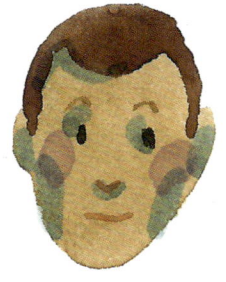
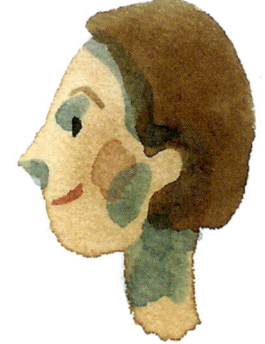

Week 49
The Lines of Force

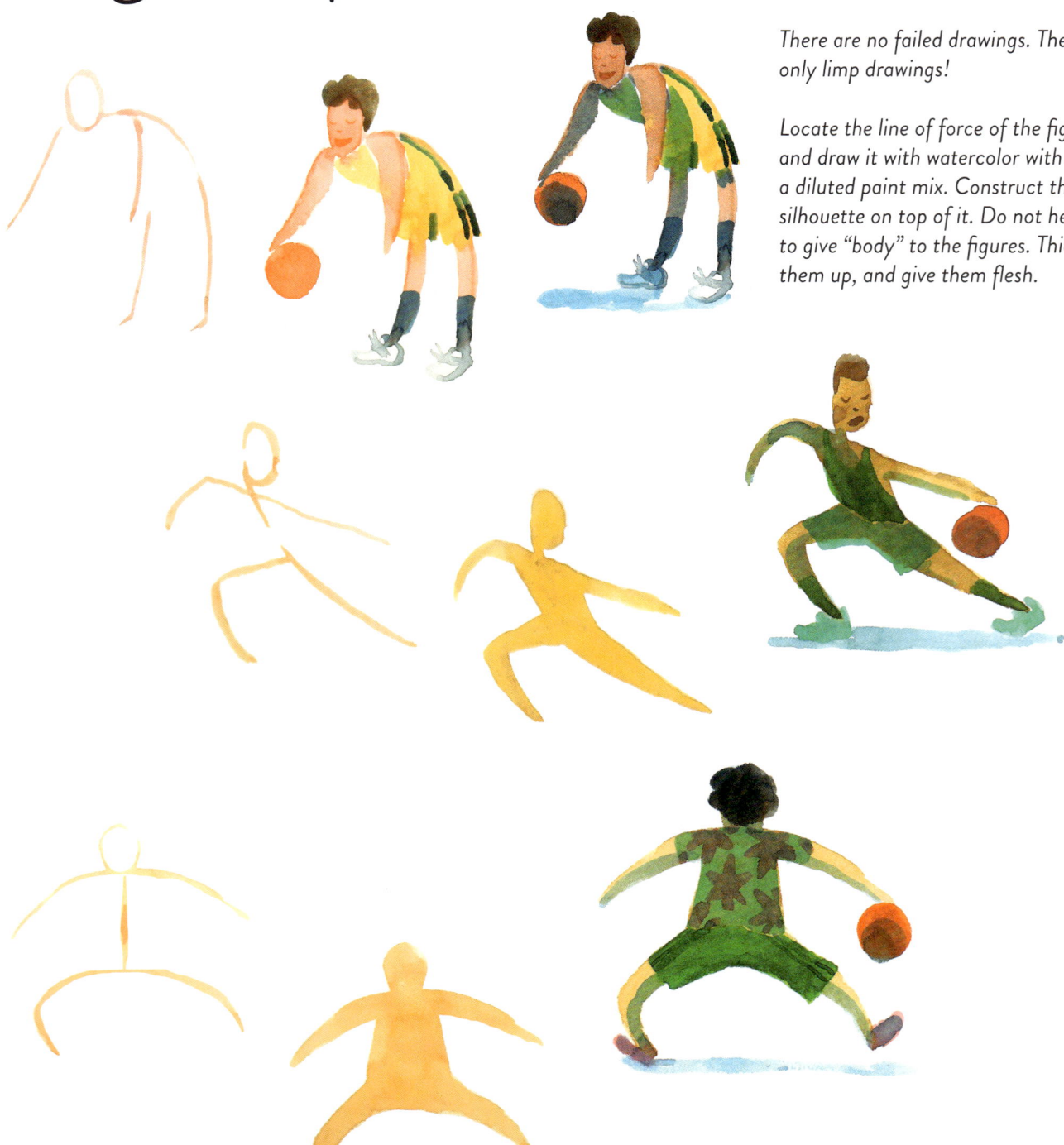

There are no failed drawings. There are only limp drawings!

Locate the line of force of the figure, and draw it with watercolor with a diluted paint mix. Construct the silhouette on top of it. Do not hesitate to give "body" to the figures. Thicken them up, and give them flesh.

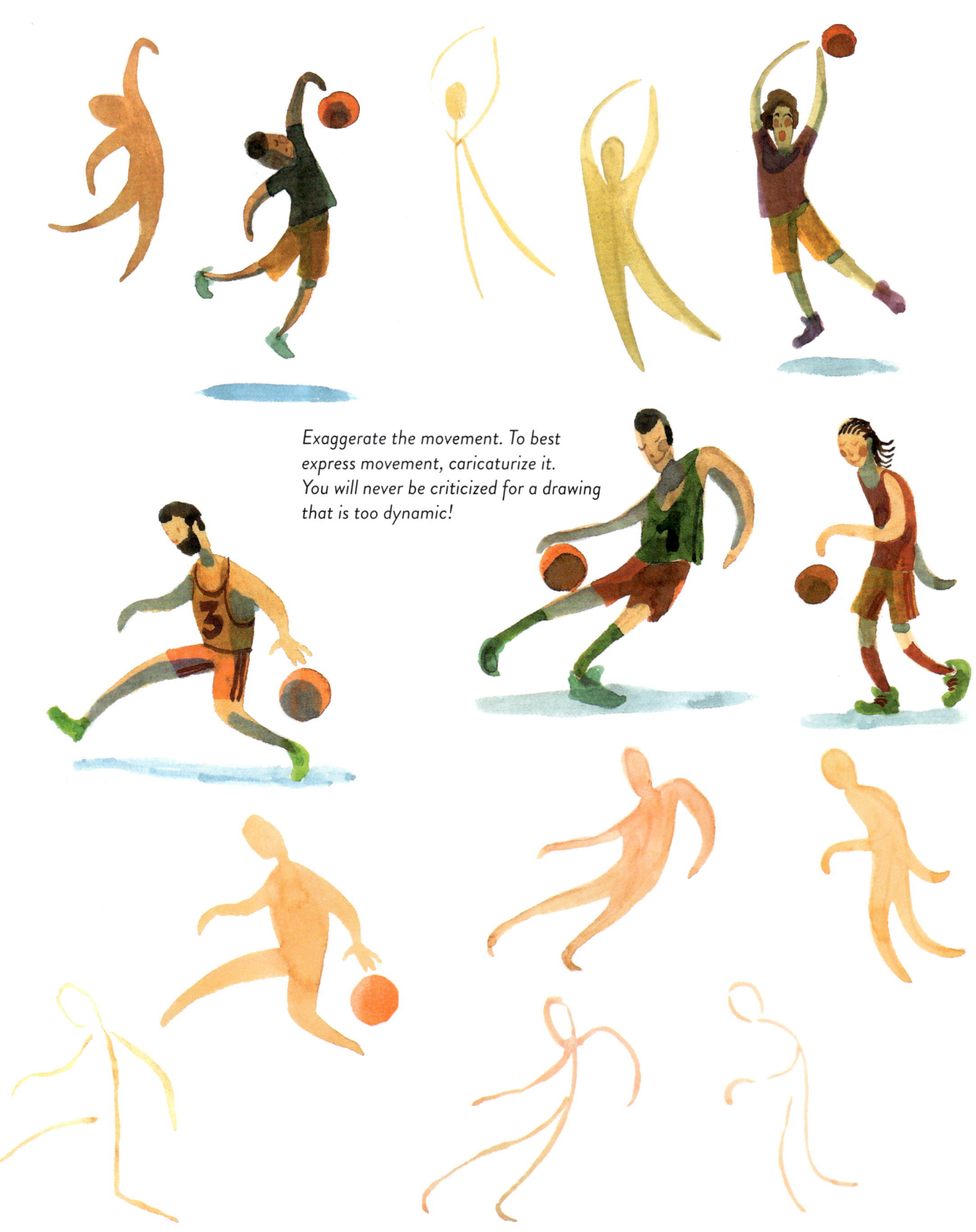

Exaggerate the movement. To best
express movement, caricaturize it.
You will never be criticized for a drawing
that is too dynamic!

Week 50
Playing with Scale

It's fun to play with scale between the figures in a very large drawing and tiny miniatures.

That gives depth and relief to the scene. It seems more alive!

If your eyes are at the same level as the eyes of the figures, all the heads are on the same line, no matter how far away they are. That is the line of the horizon.

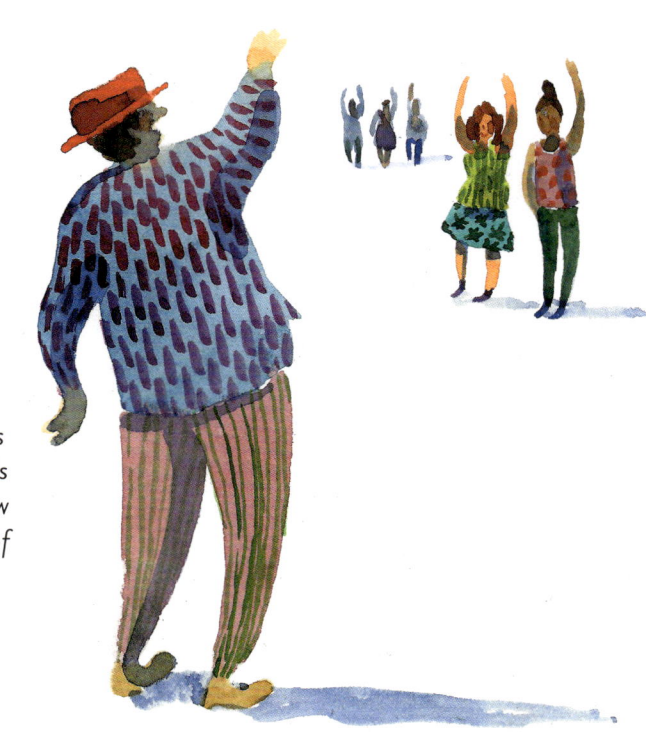

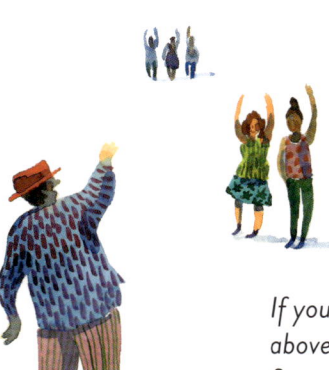

If you look at the scene from above, in a high-angle shot, the figures are arranged like this.

If you look at the scene from below, in a low-angle shot, the figures are arranged like this.

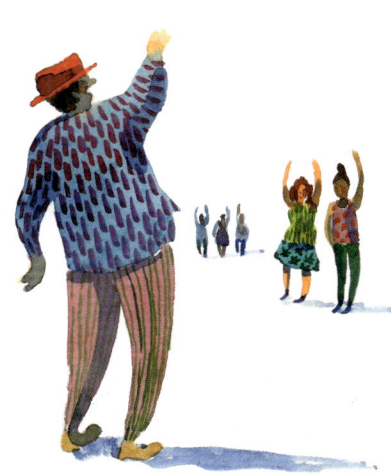

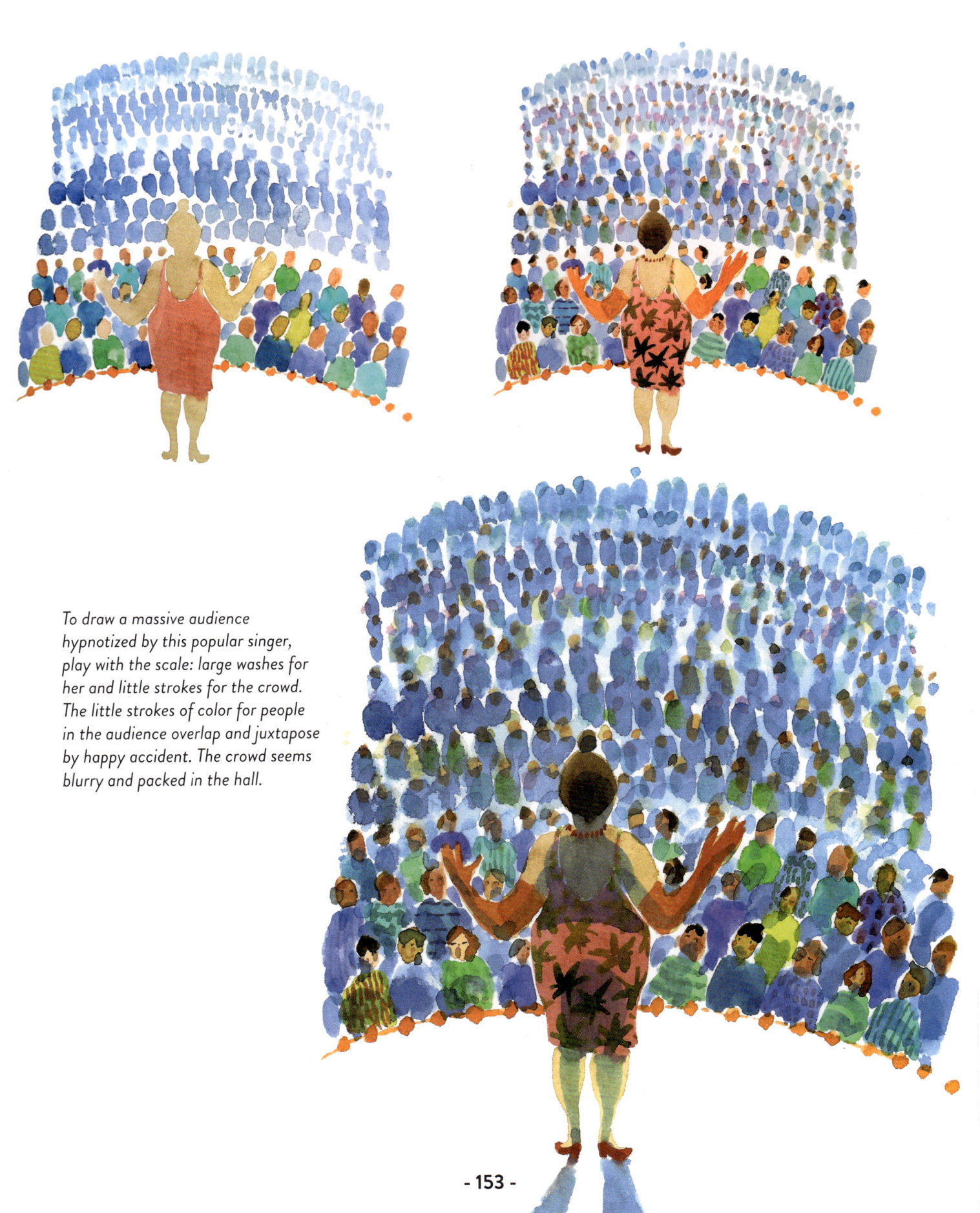

To draw a massive audience hypnotized by this popular singer, play with the scale: large washes for her and little strokes for the crowd. The little strokes of color for people in the audience overlap and juxtapose by happy accident. The crowd seems blurry and packed in the hall.

For More Practice

There is an atmosphere of madness on the basketball court—and in the huge crowd that came to cheer on the players!

Because they are so numerous, draw the spectators in a multitude of small colored strokes that overlap and juxtapose in abundance.

Draw dynamic basketball players—with lines of force—because they are under pressure in the game!

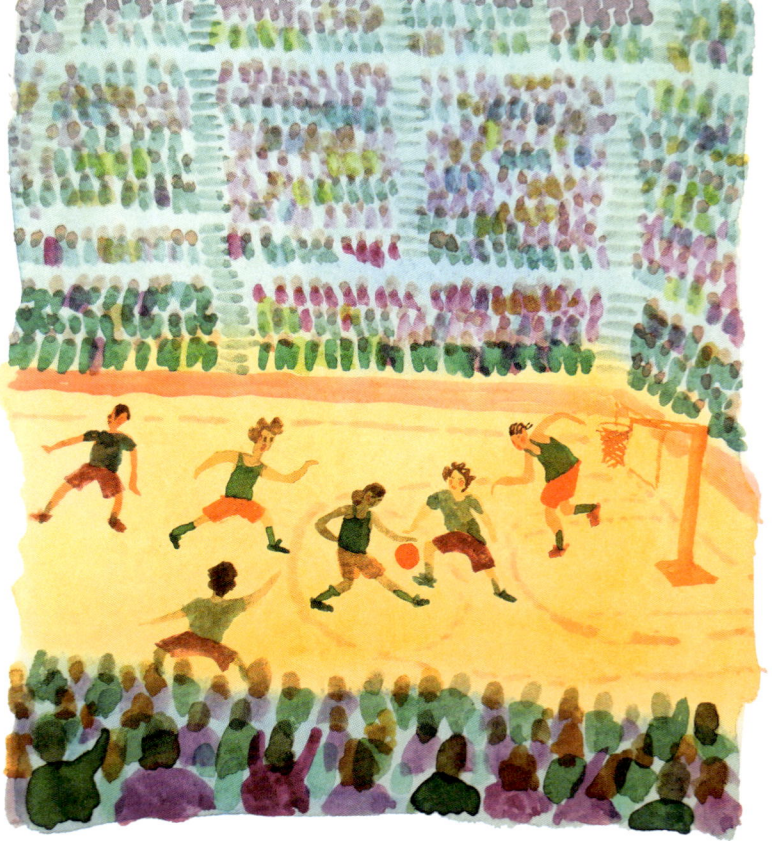

The fans in the foreground are darker and packed with patterns and bright colors, to bring them clearly to the foreground. A touch of blue shadows the bodies and the public and unifies the crowd in the distance. The game is in full swing!

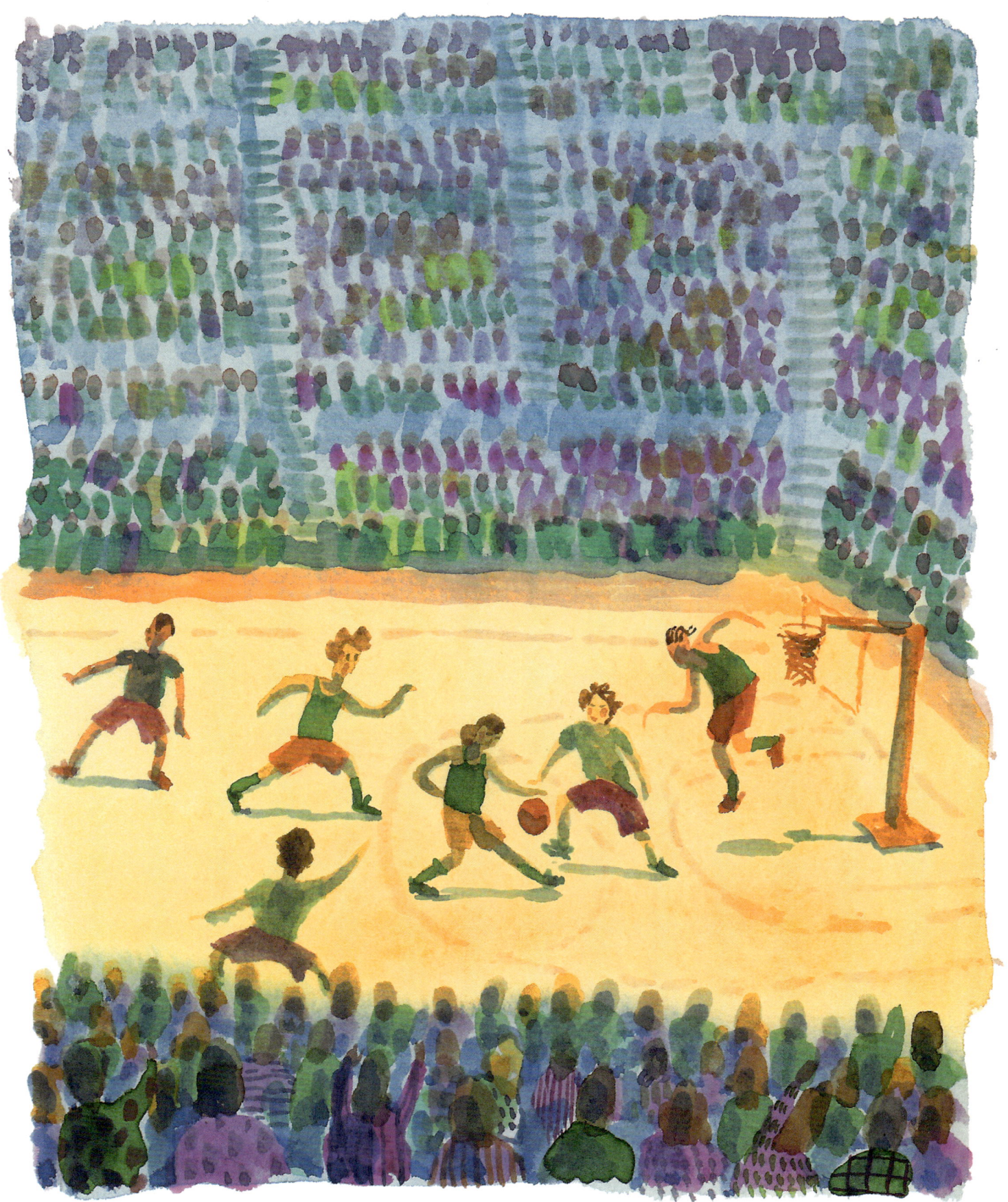

Week 51
Occupy the Space

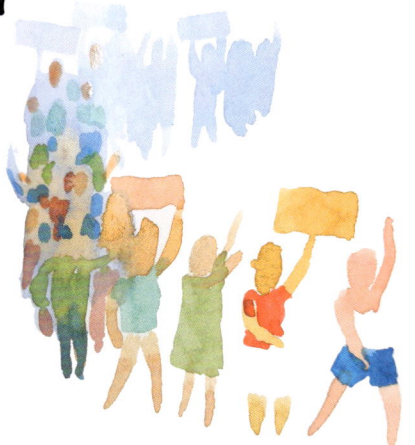

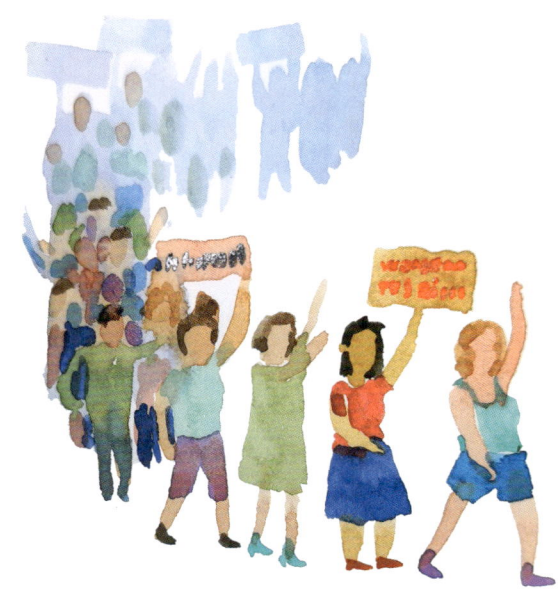

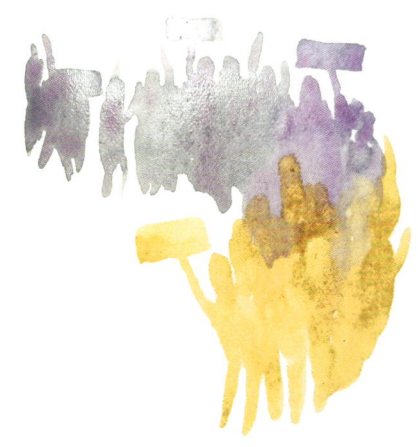

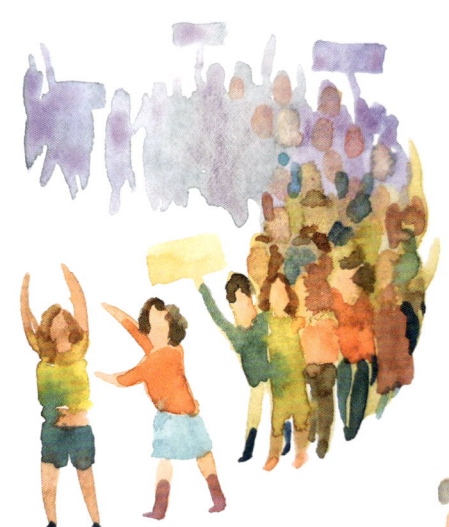

What's better than a feminist demonstration to encourage you to occupy space, take up all the space, and spread out over the sheet? This isn't about painting in a little corner and being sweet and tiny, but rather embracing the entire surface of the paper and declaring loudly the colors of the watercolor!

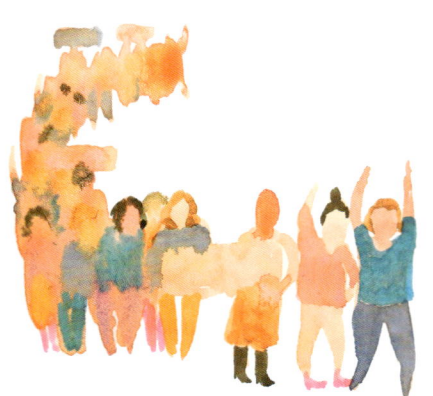

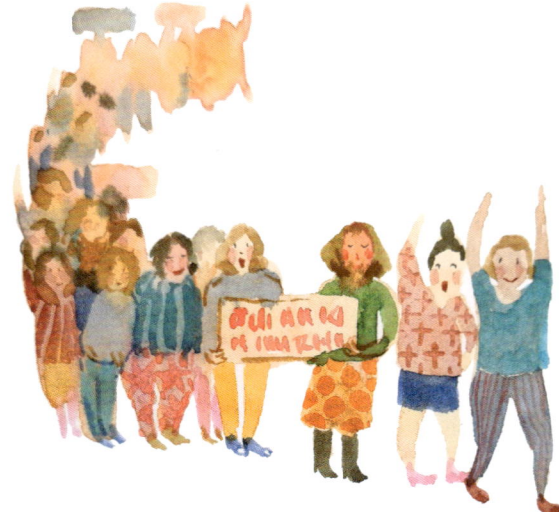

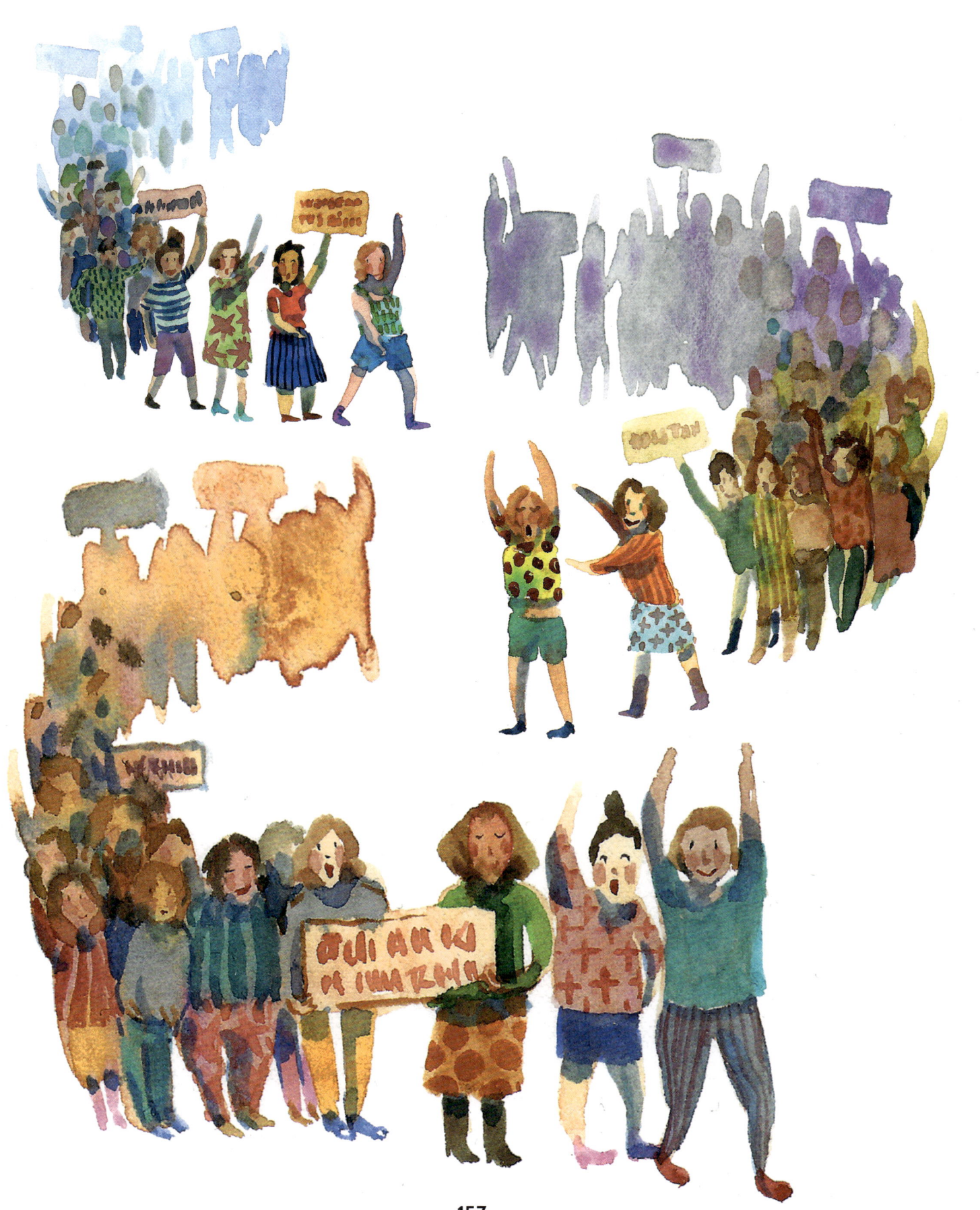

Week 52

It's Your Turn to Play!

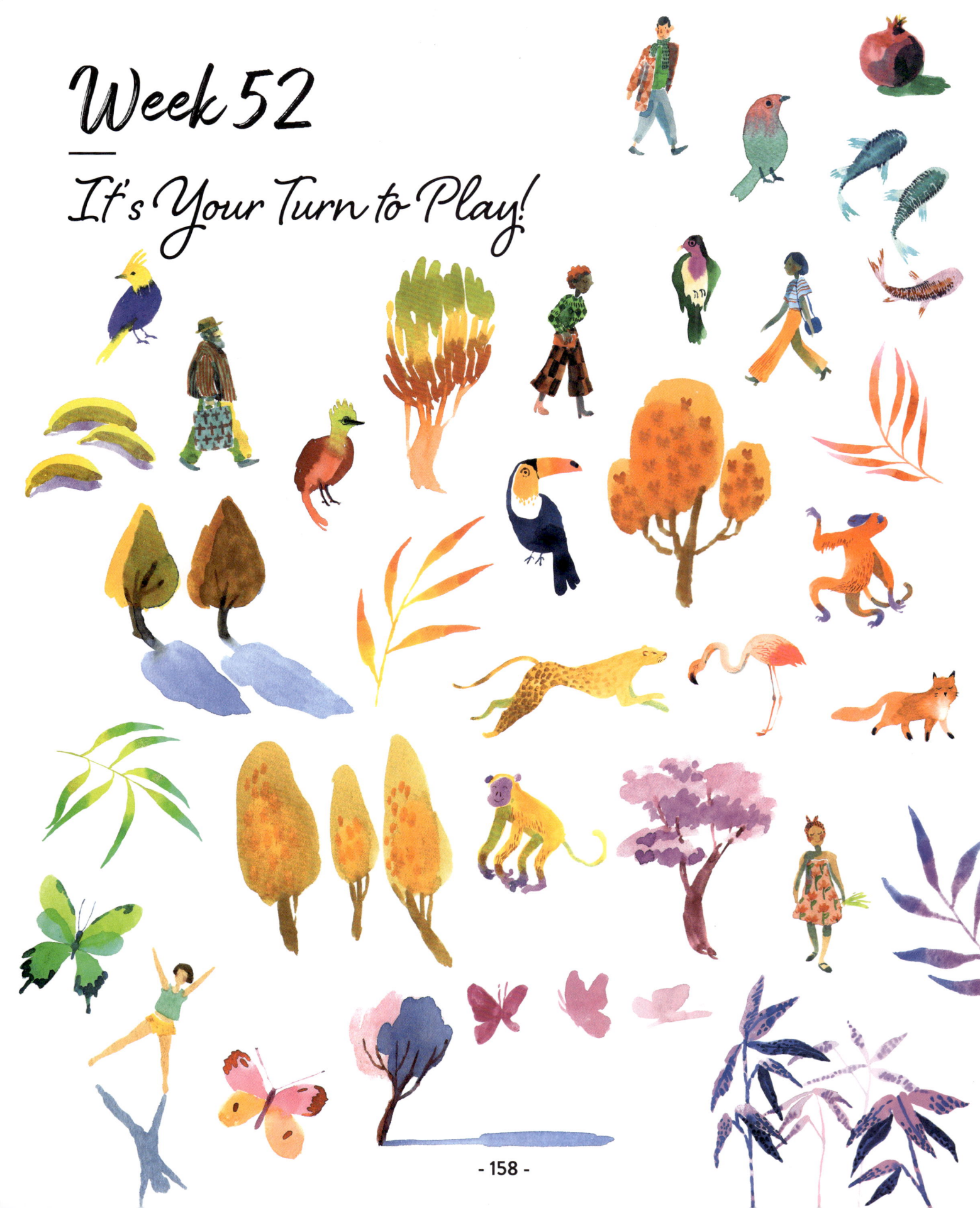

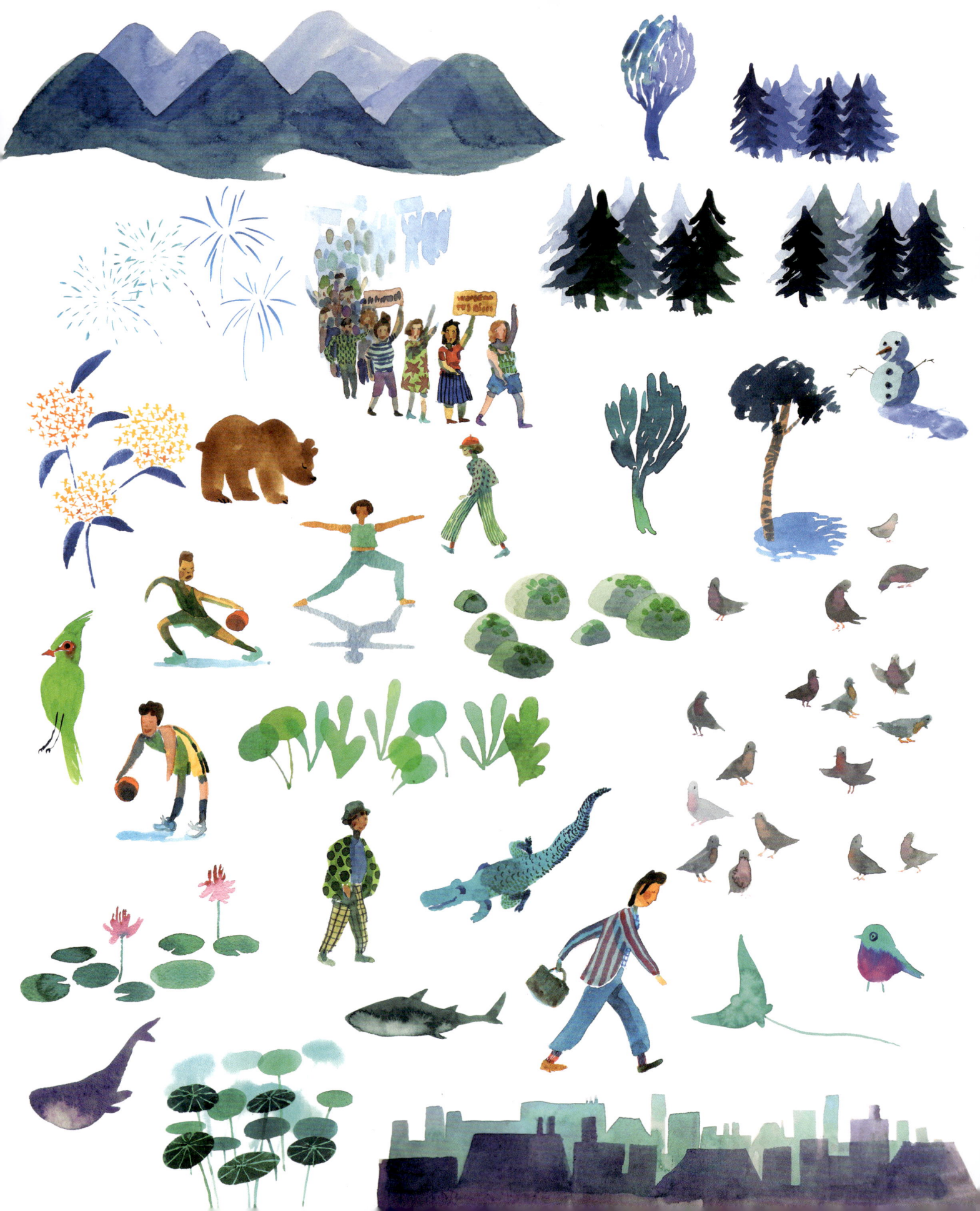

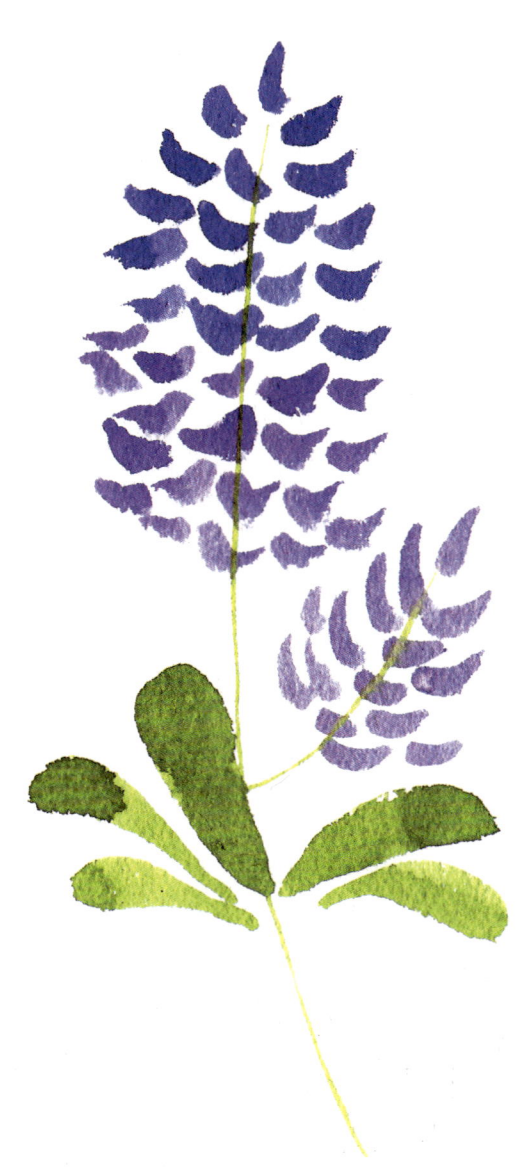